PRAISE FOR

Driving Digital: The Leader's Guide to
Business Transformation Through Technology

and Isaac Sacolick

"I have had the opportunity to know many CIOs in my career, and Isaac Sacolick is someone who hones that position to a fine edge—as is required of technology executives in this era. Isaac has written a thought-provoking book covering a wide range of the technology landscape, in a field where keeping pace with emerging change is a challenge by itself. In *Driving Digital*, he presents a roadmap for coping with disruption, staying agile, and improving decision making in a data-driven world. If you're developing innovative digital products, or getting disrupted by them, I'd grab a copy and hang on for the ride."

—FRANK FANZILLI, active board member, investor, and advisor
to technology companies and CIOs

"Isaac is a visionary IT leader who, fortunately for us, is also a great communicator. Isaac's passion for learning about transformational IT is only surpassed by his commitment to educating IT practitioners. This book is just the latest in Isaac's continuing commitment to enhancing the entire IT profession, one CIO at a time. For that I am personally grateful."

—ROB LUX, EVP and CIO, Freddie Mac

"In *Driving Digital*, Sacolick cleanly cuts through the hype and the buzzwords all too often associated with 'digital' and 'transformation.' It definitely shows that he has actually executed such transformations himself, and succeeded, multiple times. Every forward-looking technology or business leader will draw powerful insights and actionable advice from *Driving Digital*."

—ANDI MANN, Business Technology Strategist

"As I would expect from Isaac—a comprehensive and thoughtful guide to digital transformation. The importance of the role of the CTO balanced with the entire executive team's responsibility for 'digital' provides an excellent guide."

—ADRIAAN BOUTEN, CEO, Digital Prism Advisors

"Sacolick is a world class CIO who has led transformation efforts in multiple industries. If you're a CIO, CTO, Chief Digital Officer or aspire to be one, then you need to be leading your organization's business digital transformation programs. *Driving Digital* is a must-read and provides a playbook for instituting transformation through technology."

—MARC LEWIS, CEO and Partner, Leadership Capital Group

"Today's information technology leaders face a set of contradicting challenges. Recent innovations in online consumer services and Cloud-based infrastructure have driven our employees and customers to expect great user experiences and continuous innovation, and our CEOs and CFOs to expect delivery cycles in weeks and months at ultra-low cost. These shifts have put enormous pressure on CIOs and CTOs to deliver. Yet the need for strong IT governance has never been more critical, especially in a climate of increasing cyber threats and data protection requirements. In *Driving Digital*, Sacolick provides a roadmap to guide today's digital executives through these forces and towards innovation."

—JONATHAN MILLER, Chief Technology Officer, J.D. Power

"Digital transformation is here now and no business is immune! This is a great, informative, step-by-step guide that any C-Level executive, Product Manager, or Director can utilize for their own transformation efforts. There is a wealth of information gained from real-world, hands-on experience transforming world-class corporations."

—BEN HAINES, VP Global Information Systems, Yahoo

"*Driving Digital* is a CIO playbook for surviving the digital transformation and showing how we need to change ourselves."

—JASON BURNS, CIO, Sphere NY

"Isaac knows how to partner with marketing to make a data-driven campaign successful. Read *Driving Digital* to understand how to work with technology to better understand and grow your market through innovation and product management."

—LINDA BRENNAN, Vice President, Global Marketing and Communications, Phaidon

DRIVING DIGITAL

Enjoy Driving Digital!!

[signature]

@ NYSKE

ISAAC SACOLICK

DRIVING DIGITAL

THE LEADER'S GUIDE TO BUSINESS TRANSFORMATION THROUGH TECHNOLOGY

AMACOM

AMERICAN MANAGEMENT ASSOCIATION

New York • Atlanta • Brussels • Chicago • Mexico City • San Francisco
Shanghai • Tokyo • Toronto • Washington, DC

Bulk discounts available. For details visit:
www.amacombooks.org/go/specialsales
Or contact special sales:
Phone: 800-250-5308
Email: specialsls@amanet.org
View all the AMACOM titles at: www.amacombooks.org

American Management Association: www.amanet.org
This publication is designed to provide accurate and authoritative information in regard to the subject matter covered. It is sold with the understanding that the publisher is not engaged in rendering legal, accounting, or other professional service. If legal advice or other expert assistance is required, the services of a competent professional person should be sought.

Library of Congress Cataloging-in-Publication Data

Names: Sacolick, Isaac, author.
Title: Driving digital : the leader's guide to business transformation
   through technology / Isaac Sacolick.
Description: New York : AMACOM, [2017] | Includes bibliographical references
   and index.
Identifiers: LCCN 2017008707 (print) | LCCN 2017025210 (ebook) | ISBN
   9780814438619 (E-book) | ISBN 9780814438602 (hardcover)
Subjects: LCSH: Business enterprises--Technological innovations. |
   Information technology--Management. | Organizational change.
Classification: LCC HD45 (ebook) | LCC HD45 .S23 2017 (print) | DDC
   658/.05--dc23
LC record available at https://lccn.loc.gov/2017008707
© 2017 Isaac Sacolick

About AMA
American Management Association (www.amanet.org) is a world leader in talent development, advancing the skills of individuals to drive business success. Our mission is to support the goals of individuals and organizations through a complete range of products and services, including classroom and virtual seminars, webcasts, webinars, podcasts, conferences, corporate and government solutions, business books, and research. AMA's approach to improving performance combines experiential learning—learning through doing—with opportunities for ongoing professional growth at every step of one's career journey.

19 20 PC/LSCH 10 9 8 7 6 5 4 3

To my loving wife Michele
and amazing children
Ronan, Pietra, and Jasper

ACKNOWLEDGMENTS

I learned that it takes a lot more effort to write a book than articles, blog posts, speaking engagements, tweeting, and other efforts to share knowledge. I want to thank a large group of friends and colleagues that supported my efforts. Thanks to Ramón F. Baez, Linda Brennan, Jason Burns, Nicholas Carlson, Frank Fanzilli, Keith Fox, Ben Haines, Martha Heller, Brian Hollander, Anthony Juliano, Amir Khan, Imran Khan, Brian Kleinhaus, Shahzad Latif, Marc Lewis, Rob Lux, Andi Mann, Jonathan Miller, Rajiv Pant, Dan Roberts, Phil Ruppel, Julie Stafford, Bart Stanco, Timothy Burgard, and everyone at AMACOM.

I've had the privilege of working with some great teams, colleagues, and leaders over the years. Together we've developed products, improved operations, thrilled customers, and transformed businesses. Thanks to a large group, including Will Bagby, Adriaan Bouten, Sagar Bhujbal, Brendan Burns, Patrick Burns, Hitesh Chitalia, Jay Cohen, Glenn Goldberg, Greg Hart, Ian Lintault, Dean Kelly, James Kutz, Anthony Manson, Sandra McCarron, Alexa McCloughlan, Mariella Montoni, Nandakumar Mounasamy, Subrata Mukherjee, John Murphy, Roger Neal, Carter Nicholas, Chayan Niyogi, Robert Paine, Salomi Patel, Doug Sheley, PJ Sindhu, Maria Slabaugh, Rob Stoltz, David Teitler, Chris Tse, Kant Trivedi, Rich Widmann.

Thanks to an extended family of supporters: the Benzaquen, Catania, Chapman, Klein, Sacolick, and Zilbertzan families. Thanks to family members Jake, Rose, Frank, Pam, Daniel, Lisa, Langdon, Allison, Ilana, Jonathan, Matthew, and Brendan.

I couldn't have finished this book without the support of my family. A big thanks to my wife Michele and kids Ronan, Pietra, and Jasper for being such strong supporters.

CONTENTS

Introduction   xiii

The Secret Every Business Must Confront to Succeed
   with Digital Transformation   xvi

1. The Transformation Imperative   1

Beginning Transformation—Every Day Is Day One   5

What is Digital Business?   10

2. Agile Transformational Practices   17

Understanding Agile Practices   18

Agile Planning Practices   33

Aligning SDLC to Agile—What is your MVP (Minimal
   Viable Practice)?   50

Release Lifecycle   60

Transformational Improvements Through Agile   69

3. Technical Foundations for Transformation   71

Introducing the New IT Operations   71

Agile Operations Defined   73

Agile Architecture   88

IT Culture   114

4. Agile Portfolio Management   123

What Is Everyone Working On?   123

Implementing Portfolio Management   131

Financial Portfolio Practices   147

Final Thoughts on Agile Portfolio Management   154

5. Transforming to a Data-Driven Organization   155

To Become Data Driven, Start by Reviewing Our Past
   Data Sins   157

The Challenges of Enabling Big Data and Data Science   168

Transforming to a Big Data Organization   173

Transforming IT With Data Services   189

The Agile Data Organization   199

Summary of Data Governance   206

Data-Driven Culture Summary   209

6. Driving Revenue Through Digital Products   211

Strategic Planning Digital Revenue Products   211

Product Strategy in Digital Transformation   217

From Strategy to Product Planning   223

From Product Planning to Development   235

What Digital Leaders Should Do to Enable Product
   Management   250

7. Driving Digital: Smarter and Faster   251

The Cultural Underpinnings of Digital Organizations   252

Driving Digital—The Lens of Smarter-Faster   261

About Isaac Sacolick   265

Notes   267

Index   275

INTRODUCTION

I f you're a Chief Information Officer (CIO), Chief Technology Officer (CTO), Chief Digital (or Data) Officer (CDO), Chief Marketing Officer (CMO), Chief Strategy Officer, product management leader, or technology leader, then you already know that the technological landscape has changed profoundly over the last several years. There's been so much innovation that new low-asset, technology-driven, subscription "digital" businesses have successfully entered the market and are seriously competing with incumbent businesses. If you aren't facing digital competitors yet, then maybe your marketing department needs new approaches to interact with prospects digitally and requires technology, data, and skills to compete for market share. Your customers are also changing and now expect digitally immersive experiences with simple and consistent experiences across devices. Customers are expecting "life-changing" benefits when buying new products and services created by the integration of physical, personal, and social experiences.

The world is getting more competitive, and it's driving fundamental changes in how businesses operate. The entire enterprise is looking to become more data driven to better prioritize investments, target operational improvements, and identify key prospects. To stay ahead of the competition, products and services need winning customer experiences, operating processes need to be more automated and efficient, sales teams require greater mobility, and the entire organization is demanding more innovation, smarter data, and more automation from their technology.

If that wasn't enough to contend with, chances are you are partially consumed by regulatory, compliance, or security initiatives and have dealt with the paradox of meeting these requirements and threats while the organization wants simplicity, freedom to select their own technologies, or the minimization of infrastructure or operational investments.

Chances are you didn't wake up today and realize this greater need. In fact, it's likely you've been facing some of this transformation over the last 20 years. Did you build a customer-facing website in the nineties, invest in enterprise resource planning (ERP), customer relationship management (CRM), and business intelligence (BI) through the 2000s, and are now working on mobile, social, or Cloud-driven transformations? Did your teams figure out how to be more agile, virtualize servers, or enable continuous delivery? Did you partner with marketing to improve lead conversion or efficiently generate new mobile and web customer experiences? Did you put in a new data warehouse and invest in data governance? Did you enable employees to bring their own mobile devices and launch collaboration tools so that the global organization could share information and innovate on new ideas?

If you are a technology leader and didn't do some of these things, chances are you were replaced or will be soon. You will be disintermediated by spending too much effort just keeping the lights on instead of driving change or by being the business steward on risk instead of being a solution provider. Perhaps you've tried to be an instrument of change, but your business clout ran dry and you could not get the support and collaboration needed to impact the business. If you're in one of these categories, then you might be the outgoing CIO/CTO, or your CIO boss may be in that situation that puts your job at risk, or maybe the role is being boxed in by a new Chief Digital Officer, Chief Data Officer, or Chief Marketing Officer with the budget and backing to drive change and investments.

But if you are doing some of these things, or if your job or role in the organization still has time to turn around, then you'll need more strategic leadership to drive transformation and will also need to expand your department's charter. Very simply, no one cares about how well your platforms, practices, or services perform. Trust me, they don't. I've done agile, mobile, Cloud, bring your own device (BYOD), BI, CRM, content management system (CMS) and probably to lower scales than your challenges or accomplishments. They don't care about your success completing application releases, your uptime and performance of key systems, your customer satisfaction metrics on servicing requests or incidents, or your scores in the last SOC or security audit. These are all "table stakes" and what is expected of you when you work in technology.

The business cares about demonstrating strategic advantage, growing top-line revenue, executing game changing operational transformations, delighting customers, developing new customer segments, establishing new markets, developing new products, and growing through acquisitions. They care about attracting and retaining talent, growing their brand presence, and making faster, smarter decisions.

If you are a Chief Digital Officer, Chief Data Officer, CMO, or lead product management, then you either need to partner with the technology leader, or you are going to be asked to manage initiatives, teams, and skilled people that once were part of a technology organization. If you think you can be "hands off" managing these functions, then you risk falling short or even failing at your transformation objectives.

What if you are a leader that requires a lot more from technology? Maybe you are the Chief Marketing Officer looking at thousands of tools that can help with everything from lead generation to content marketing but need to have consistent KPIs from multiple systems to make sounder marketing investments. Maybe you're the Chief Data Officer struggling with how data is organized in your databases and need more simplistic tools to grow your data science capabilities. Maybe you lead Product Management or are a Chief Digital Officer and need efficient technology platforms and application development practices to help you bring new products and capabilities to market faster. Maybe you're the CEO or CFO that's feeling the pressure from new digital competitors or from the Board of Directors looking for growth from digital initiatives.

If you're one of these leaders, can you assume that technology leaders in your organization know how to transform their practices, best align with a digital business strategy, and pull it off without your collaboration? These leaders spend significant effort "learning the business" and making key investment decisions that drive growth, operational efficiencies, and competitive advantages. Can you simply write a requirements document, get a cost estimate, and hand over the project to your technology executives to execute? Are technology platforms only tools for the technologists, or do you review and utilize them as business enabling platforms? When everyone in the organization needs some form of technology investment or improvement, do you have a sense of how resources are aligned and prioritized to the areas of most strategic improvement? Is your culture ready to change, transform, experiment, and learn from failures? Do you know how to enable your business managers to make better data-driven decisions or develop new digital-first products that customers love?

The Secret Every Business Must Confront to Succeed with Digital Transformation

Now, many of you are beginning to understand the need to transform and know the difficult truth. You've figured this out over the last decade of trying to keep up with changes that have affected your industry, business, customers, and employees. Some of you have been in denial, others have embraced the changes, but you have all come to the same critical realization.

You cannot succeed without great technology, smart technologists, efficient business practices, and culture change. You can't win with legacy systems or systems that have Band-Aid data integrations. You can't expect the same year-over-year revenue serving customers the same way you've done over the last decade because customers expect superb experiences. Some of you will take matters into their own hands by procuring technologies without an integrated plan, but the world isn't cookie cutter anymore, and you can't sell differentiating product offerings without some innovative capabilities, technology to integrate business processes, or defensible intellectual property.

In short, your corporation needs you, a leader willing to take on the challenges of driving business and digital transformation. They need great technology leadership with a solutions-oriented team, outstanding platforms, and bulletproof practices. They need technologists to be maturing technology platforms, agile practices, and nimble services but assembled with more strategic purpose.

Great technology and outstanding technologists are just the beginning. Businesses need practices to grow their abilities to drive decisions and create winning products by leveraging their data assets. They need to be plugging into an ecosystem of third-party capabilities including new data sources, services enabled by APIs, crowdsourcing backed workflows, and app stores that can drive distribution. They need to better understand how emerging technologies like blockchain, IoT, and artificial intelligence will reshape their industry over the next five years and have confidence that they can incorporate new capabilities.

Businesses also need practices to learn customer needs, track new forms of competitive offerings, and evolve online and offline customer experiences. They need to develop practices to perform research to help target new markets and rank prospects. Most importantly, they need to enable the product management function to drive revenue from digitally enabled products and services.

Finally, businesses need a new form of collaboration and partnership among technologists, marketers, product managers, data scientists, and key sales executives to align on strategy, partner on execution, and drive a smarter, faster digital culture.

That's been my experience over the last few years performing digital transformation at three different organizations facing fundamental challenges. They were in different industries with different business models facing different types of digital competitors and challenges. Their industries were transforming for different reasons at different paces and inflection points. I partnered with early adopters up and down the corporate ladders, worked aggressively with supporters, and managed through different types of detractors and obstacles. There was a mix of success and failure but most importantly ongoing experimentation.

Here's what I realized. The solutions and transformational practices that I helped implement across these organizations had more similarities than differences. They were all developed "bottom up," that is, they were all implemented with tactical practices first, transformational practices second, and cultural changes ongoing. In all three cases, I started the practices in IT first, extended to business teams second, then drove business change and strategic transformations later. I had supporters, detractors, collaboration, and complete politically driven warfare. It was never, ever easy, always necessary, and occasionally rewarding.

And in my opinion, largely repeatable. While I have been sharing many of my strategies on my blog, *Social, Agile, and Transformation*,[1] this book is meant to provide a full business transformation guide covering the five most critical practices here. They include agile practices, technology operations and architecture, ideation and portfolio management, data science programs, and product management. If you are a CIO, CTO, CDO, or CMO, lead strategy, or head product management, then you'll get a firm grounding on the key business practices that I've used to enable business transformation.

I'm going to take you on a bottom-up journey that has four major steps:

1. Getting the IT team ready with *digital* practices—The technology team needs grounding in agile practices, DevOps, and the disciplines needed to enable new digital platforms.
2. Propelling investment and innovation—Enable practices that capture ideas from employees, feedback from customers, and other market research. Develop a pipeline of initiatives that can be planned efficiently, aligned to growth and efficiencies, and prioritized based on financial and strategic returns.
3. Developing the foundations for digital execution—Grow data science programs, data services, and product management practices that drive the data-driven organization to develop digital products and services.
4. Driving digital growth and culture—Gain early adopters to join the transformation program, then lead the organization to drive digital by becoming smarter and faster.

This is a book that will hopefully give you some new practices to deploy, but, more importantly, it will provide a digital lens on how applying them will aid in transformational efforts.

For more information about *Driving Digital*, please visit
http://driving-digital.com
and follow Isaac Sacolick @NYIke on Twitter.

DRIVING DIGITAL

1.

THE TRANSFORMATION IMPERATIVE

ook at your company as if it were your first day on the job. What would your first impressions be of how your business is operating? How would you learn about its products and services, key customers, and overall financial health of each business, operating unit, and product? How quickly would you absorb key business practices in sales, marketing, and operations that drive the business? Could colleagues easily tell you how products and services differentiate from your competitors and describe the key intellectual property, the "secret sauce" that enables winning and retaining customers?

What would your initial observations be if you opened the box and reviewed what customers get with key products and services? Is it a delightful, immersive experience that makes you want to continue using it? Is the service's value and benefits clearly articulated in packaging or other materials? What's been the latest customer feedback on the product, and what is the company's history in making changes or improvements to the product line? Is it an easy, intuitive product that delivers value on day one, or does it require significant documentation and training?

How well do company executives understand their competition? Do they have strategies and tactics to grab market share from them? Do they understand how their services differentiate, how they stand out by market segment, and how they compete on price and other attributes? More importantly, how broad is their lens on competition? Are they more concerned about traditional competitors, or do they have an expanded view that considers new market entrants, startups, or other product alternatives?

How is data being used for decision making? Do you mostly hear dialog and opinion when decisions are being reviewed, or are facts being presented and insights debated? When data is presented, is it handcrafted using spreadsheets and presentation tools, or is it analyzed directly from the transaction systems—ERP, CRM, or other enterprise system. Are the data and presentation easy to understand and delivered on a regular schedule, or does it look ad hoc, suggesting there may be complexities and quality issues in its construction?

What are your initial thoughts when you walk into the IT department, meet people, and see how it's operating? Are heads looking and banging away at the issue of the day afraid to look up and get asked to address a new set of concerns? Does the team show signs of battle scars from longer-term firefighting expressing a complete distrust of business leaders and criticism of their treatment? Are they complaining about the lack of funding or support to make operational improvements or keep up with the latest security threats? Are they more likely to tell you about yesterday's difficult user or rogue IT issue versus someone they helped, a business practice they improved, or a deliverable that they completed?

Is anybody in IT doing any significant application development and, more importantly, doing anything tied to improve the business's product and services? Are business executives (and ideally customers) pleased with the latest technology improvements, or are they grumbling about missed timelines, cost overruns, or quality issues? Are the tools and experiences being developed cutting edge, open, and scalable, or are they bolt-ons to interfaces that were developed decades ago?

What's the vibe in the office? Is there a buzz from people collaborating and sharing information, or are people huddled in their offices and cubicles? Do you see outdated projectors, or are touch screens always on, showing KPIs and providing access to tools and information? Is the best company information available only at your desktop, or can you collaborate efficiently on your personal mobile device? Can the people you meet articulate the corporation's mission, values, and objectives, and how they are personally contributing?

These are all fundamental questions that organizational leaders need to ask with some regularity, and the answers speak to the efficiency, intelligence, and culture of the organization. Most importantly, they are all key considerations on whether the organization is ready to compete in a digital world where having access to real-time information, delivering products that win over customers, developing a collaborative organization aligned to its mission, and instituting competitive use of technology are all fundamental requirements.

In some ways, I have been fortunate to have had that first-day experience walking into a new organization as CIO three times over the last ten years of digital enablement and transformation. At *Businessweek* magazine in 2007, my first impressions were of one team struggling to keep the content management system humming while the Editorial team was screaming for better capabilities and faster publishing, of the Sales team struggling to implement better ad-targeting capabilities, and of everyone trying different approaches to bring in new readers and subscribers.

When *Businessweek* was sold at the end of 2009, I had the opportunity to join McGraw-Hill Construction, another business of McGraw-Hill's Information and Media that sold news and data products to commercial construction businesses. As a sister business, I already had an impression of the business on my first day: Why was this business so complex? Why couldn't I easily ascertain its value proposition? What were the synergies across customer segments and product lines? Finally, why did the technology team at Construction, which had access to the same technology, practices, and resources that I had at *Businessweek*, struggle to keep their products stable, let alone competitive and certainly not innovative?

Four years later and after a series of successful business, marketing, and technology transformations, I was part of the team that successfully led McGraw-Hill's divestiture of Construction. I was off looking for another transformational opportunity and landed at a forty-year-old consulting and data provider to financial services institutions. They were like *Businessweek* and Construction and looking to transform their data sourcing and delivery capabilities but with a rich history of delivering highly valuable insights into C-level banking and other financial executives.

I'll provide more stories and insights throughout the book, but, as I said, I've now had three experiences walking in day one as CIO of a business that needed to transform. I've taken on the challenges leading different IT teams that needed to radically change their capabilities and services. I walked in as a technologist that had some success developing technology at startup companies selling software as a service (SaaS), data, and social networking products and services. So my career has taken me from the challenges of leading a startup organization through growth, complexities, and pivots to an older "analog" business looking to transform and develop digital businesses.

That background has given me a unique perspective on what incumbent businesses must do differently today to compete. Startups have many advantages without legacy practices and with the opportunity to stay small and nimble with highly driven individuals during its early years of development and growth. The experience over 15 years and four startups enabled me to wear many hats, learn several industries, work with different technologies, and have a wide-ranging list of responsibilities.

But here's the one thing I learned from all these experiences and why this is relevant to you, your current role, and whatever situation you are facing in your enterprise or in your business. Your organization needs an updated set of practices to compete in a digital environment, deliver winning customer experiences, develop digitally driven products, and leverage data for strategic insights. It's not good enough to have IT practice agile development; you need collaboration with business teams, capabilities that drive speed to market on new ideas, and estimating practices that enable the development of longer-term roadmaps. Your organization likely needs to double the number of growth initiatives and find ways to take cost and complexity out of legacy practices. You need a growing data practice to deliver more convenient and insightful products while you promote a data-driven culture. Technology platforms need to be standardized and integrated for you to develop competitive advantages with emerging technologies like artificial intelligence, blockchain, or the internet of things (IoT). These are just some of the topics covered in this book on driving digital leadership and practices.

Beginning Transformation—Every Day Is Day One

Whether today is your first day walking into your office or you've been working for the same enterprise for the last decade, I would suggest that today and every day are your day one. In your role as a transformational leader, every day is a new day to make change, transform, or do something that has a positive business impact. This is not a Tony Robbins, jump up and down and get your team motivated and excited to do more-better-faster-and-cheaper pitch. The culture of the team is very important, but what I am suggesting is that transformation happens in small baby steps that you can do or influence daily that will take you a couple steps closer to a new destination. And while you are taking these steps, you can open your eyes and ears for feedback. Walk straight, step a little to the right, or pivot completely. Your feedback can come from the people in front of you, a dashboard that you review for insights, news that you read about the competition, or a dialog that you have with customers. Every day is another day one for you to do something innovative, something that will improve a customer's experience, make a colleague's work smarter, or make the world a safer place.

The world is also changing around you. New technologies, new competitors, new mashups, new capabilities, new regulations, new security vulnerabilities, new mobile devices everyone wants, new quality issues that need to be addressed, new customers providing feedback that need consideration, new opportunities to influence employees, new marketing approaches to attract customers, and new algorithms to develop insights that can develop into whole new businesses.

Is the World Faster, Bigger, and Smarter?

Do you believe that the pace of change and your ability to influence in small doses is more significant today than it was a decade ago?

You better. Let's look at some numbers and examples:

- While the number of startups funded in 2015 declined versus 2014 by 20% to 12,371,[1] the total capital invested increased by 21% to $126 billion, according to PitchBook. The venture capitalists are getting more selective but increasing their level of investment in the startups. Some of these startups will challenge, compete, or even disrupt your business.

- 2.5 quintillion bytes of data are created daily, and 90% of the world's data has been created in the last two years alone.[2] That's a lot of data, and I'll let you translate this data explosion to your own business's velocity and acceleration of data stored. Now the question is how much of your organization's data do you properly analyze, and how does your analytics and business intelligence capabilities compare to your competitors? Per one report, 90% of an organization's data is "dark," that is, data that isn't fully analyzed for insights. At the same time, there are numerous studies showing the difficulty most organizations have staffing data science, database, and other analytic roles. Topping that is the alphabet soup of technologies that one can deploy for analysis beyond an SQL database—everything from NoSQL warehouses, to Hadoop variants, to BI solutions in the Cloud. Again, this points to more data that some organizations can leverage to strategic benefits and gain a competitive edge against those that are lagging.

- 65% of adults are now using social networking sites,[3] and 20% claim that they are online "almost constantly."[4] Pew Research Center has this broken down by age, education, and other demographics, all showing increases and activity reaching critical mass. Digital channels will continue to increase in importance in both B2B and B2C markets, but digital marketing strategies are still in experimentation stages, and the available technologies are growing. The number of marketing technology vendors almost doubled in just one year from 2014 to 2015 to 1,876 vendors[5] and another two times to 3,874 in 2016,[6] so this will be an area of competition, disruption, and experimentation for at least the next few years.

- If your company lives in the physical world of products, retail, or manufacturing, then it's hard to imagine that it won't be affected by the

IoT over the next ten years. The questions are how long do you have, how much do you invest, and will your existing product or process default to legacy if you don't make the right decisions fast enough? In retail, Beacons are expected to have influenced $4 billion in sales in 2015,[7] and 72.1 million wearable devices are expected to ship in 2015.[8] The growth in these and other IoT technologies suggests that if you are a consumer, industrial, or retail business, you'd better be reviewing how IoT may shape your business and industry over the next 10 years.

- If you are in media, publishing, entertainment, information, analytics, legal, and segments of health care, then you are already close to being a digitized business, but you may not be a fully digital business. A digitized business implies that the delivery to the customer is in a digital format as opposed to a paper or other analog format. To be digital, the end-to-end processing is done digitally, the commerce to acquire the digital product or service is digital, and then the delivery is digital. Digital disruption is now in its third decade, starting with books, magazines, and music and now in later stages where marketplaces enable services performed or made available by third parties like Uber and AirBNB. The next stage will include commerce services interchanging digital rights through blockchains. So, in 20 years, digital services have disrupted analog counterparts that have been around since the advent of the printing press 600 years ago.

- If you are in financial services and especially in banking, your world is about to go through some significant disruptive forces. In 2015, mobile banking exceeded retail bank transactions for the first time[9] and is expected to trend more and more digital. There is the emergence of blockchain technology, and many banks are testing it to replace some of the more common and complex financial transactions. Currently 25 banks are partnered with R3[10] in a consortium aiming to leverage blockchain technology in markets. But banks are also facing disruption from fintech startups implementing digital businesses in lending (LendingTree.com, Prosper.com), investing (Wealthfront.com, FutureAdvisor), and Payments (Apple, Samsung, Google, etc.).

- Another major transformation that's accelerated is the digital, democratized, and distributed workforce. Digital workforce enablement has been accomplished through a combination of mobile, collaboration, and presence tools enabling knowledge workers to be connected and productive wherever and whenever required or convenient. The White House has a bring your own device (BYOD) program,[11] collaboration tools enable business users to communicate in the context of their workflow, and Cloud-enabled desktop computing enables enterprise users to carry light devices and have access to applications and data anywhere.

- Also, let's add the poster children of digital businesses and disruption. I'm speaking about Airbnb that already has more rooms than Hilton and Marriott,[12] yet doesn't own a single hotel. Their market share of rooms in major cities is growing year over year,[13] averaging 9.9% in the top ten U.S. cities. Then there is Uber, which provides more car service transactions than the aggregate of all taxis and limousines. Uber just passed a billion rides,[14] has expanded to 58 countries (as of May 2015),[15] and now has surpassed taxis/limos for business ground transportation.[16] Businesses are facing increased competition from digital disruptors that can deliver new value and offer users conveniences that legacy businesses cannot enable as easily.

- Finally, there is a new workforce out there that can help businesses with digitally driven workflows and data processing. Artificial intelligence algorithms powered by Cloud computing systems can automate intelligent processing of complex forms of data from voice to images. If it can't be processed by machines yet, then you can hire an on-demand crowdsourced workforce through services like Amazon Turk to handle small tasks. These capabilities can be tapped into an enterprise's data using APIs to automate the data flow.

These are just examples. If you're not convinced, consult the literature at Gartner, Forrester, Altimeter and others that have all the research behind the impacts of entire industries transforming to digital business.

Still Not Convinced on the Impact of Digital Innovations?

But if none of this is convincing, consider the following remarks by Larry Fink, BlackRock's CEO, made in a letter to U.S. and European S&P 500 CEOs in early February 2016:[17]

But one reason for investors' short-term horizons is that companies have not sufficiently educated them about the ecosystems they are operating in, what their competitive threats are and how technology and other innovations are impacting their businesses

This is Larry Fink who manages $4.6 trillion of investment—not Marc Andreesen, Fred Wilson, or some other influential venture capitalist trying to drive investment in digital business and technologies. Larry is speaking to the CEOs of the largest businesses, essentially telling them to make digital and other longer-term investments to be more competitive. He recognizes that they are likely to face technology and other innovations that will challenge their businesses and that they need to be investing now to be viable in three to five years.

Why is Larry Fink going to such lengths to draw attention to the problem of short-term results versus longer-term investment? Consider that only 61 companies that were listed in the Fortune 500 in 1955 remained in this list in 2014.[18] Sixty years to topple 88% of the world's top companies, and this is with minimal impact from the digital disruption factors just outlined. What would you guess is the median duration today? How long do Fortune 500 companies have to become digital business or face massive disintermediation? This is what concerns Larry Fink and Blackrock, traditionally longer-term investors and recognizing that the world's largest companies are no longer safe bets.

A Transformation Call to Arms

If you're a leader in a Fortune 500 company or an owner of a small or medium-sized business, you can no longer take a back seat to the industry transformations that are playing out in front of you. And the game you must play is far more strategic and disruptive to your organization than merely implementing technology upgrades. Do you think just moving a data center to the Cloud, deploying mobile applications to enable key business processes, developing social marketing campaigns, or leveraging Big Data to process transaction data is a sufficient transformation?

Just a couple of years ago, Gartner told technologists that the intersection of mobile, social, Cloud, and Big Data—the "Nexus of Forces"—is what they need to focus on in transforming the business. At Gartner's 2015 Symposium,[19], they added artificial intelligence as a core need and the "Algorithmic Business"[20] and "Innovation Competency"[21] to the list of digital practices. Can technologists merely invest in the applicable technologies and develop related practices to stay competitive?

The simple answer is no. If your business is 100% on the Cloud, if all its key business processes are mobile enabled, if the Hadoop cluster already connects all the enterprise's key assets and machine learning to identify patterns, and if marketing is fully enabled to interface with prospects and customers through digital channels—if you have all that digital capability—does that mean that you've fully transitioned to a "digital business"?

As hard as these transitions are to implement for the CIO and the technology organization—and I know few CIOs that can claim successful transitions across all these dimensions—I've just described digital technology and capability transitions that are not sufficient to compete as a digital business, nor are they a true transformation. Nowhere in these transitions has the transformational leader fully addressed competitive factors, revenue growth through digital channels, hyper efficiency through automation, or digitally driven culture changes. Sorry, fellow leaders, much of the work you're doing and thinking of doing is just this generation's technology investments and practice improvements.

What Is Digital Business?

Let's look at how some expert analysts define digital business.

"Digital business is about the creation of new business designs by blurring the physical and digital world," says Jorge Lopez of Gartner.[22] One thinks about digital supply chain management, context-aware mobile experiences, and IoT using Gartner's definition.

"You must think of your company as part of a dynamic ecosystem of value that connects digital resources inside and outside the company to create value for customers," says Nigel Fenwick of Forrester.[23] While this definition also conjures images of supply chain, Nigel's more critical point is that digital business must "deliver a greater share of value to customers" to be competitive. In other words, customer experience and the value customers perceive through your channel must win a disproportionate market share versus direct and indirect alternatives.

McKinsey adds to the critical elements of digital business.[24] "Being digital requires being open to reexamining your entire way of doing business and understanding where the new frontiers of value are. For some companies, capturing new frontiers may be about developing entirely new businesses in adjacent categories; for others, it may be about identifying and going after new value pools in existing sectors." So, digital business impacts the business model and business practices and enables growth in new categories or sectors. But they add: "Digital's next element is rethinking how to use new capabilities to improve how customers are served. This is grounded in an obsession with understanding each step of a customer's purchasing journey—regardless of channel—and thinking about how digital capabilities can design and deliver the best possible experience, across all parts of the business."

Many analysts focus on and some equate digital business with customer experiences. They instruct organizations to develop customer journey maps that define the end-to-end customer experiences as they exist today, then look at the impact of digital channels and capabilities, then add the impact of new technologies to analog (physical) channels.

Putting a customer lens to help define a digital business and digital transformation is certainly a good place to start, but I would argue is not sufficient. If the taxi commission deployed a mobile application enabling me to hail a taxi anytime and anywhere, would that have prevented Uber from entering this industry in such dramatic fashion? If banks were the first to enable mobile payments, would that have stopped Apple from developing this capability? Before Airbnb, there were other large sites like HomeAway that enabled person-to-person home rentals: Why was Airbnb more successful growing their brand and reach when they weren't first to market with this model? Finally, I would argue that Craigslist offered one of the poorest user experiences when it came to market, and EBay wasn't that much better, but both platforms won over consumers against traditional newspaper platforms and over richer experiences available in competing digital platforms.

Digital Business Defined by Its Attributes

Another way to understand and differentiate digital businesses is by looking at some example capabilities and businesses that leverage them.

- Digital businesses drive recurring revenue, often through subscription business models. Think Amazon Prime versus buying goods/services directly through an e-commerce channel.
- The most successful digital businesses are asset-light. Think Uber and Airbnb, which market and sell services owned by other individuals.
- Algorithm-driven experiences can "deliver a greater share of value." Think Waze with driving routes based on traffic patterns and social cues delivered via your phone versus the Garmin GPS that we all had in our cars just a few years ago.
- Digital disruptions can radically alter cost structures and price points. Think Etsy, Amazon Handmade, Craigslist, Zillow, LinkedIn, Monster, Autotrader, Cars.com, and many other sites that decimated the newspaper classified ad business.
- Digital businesses leverage new digital tools to drive more effective and efficient sales practices. They enhance multichannel customer experiences, engage workers to capture ideas, and automate production steps to improve quality.
- For retail businesses, connecting physical and digital buying experiences that offer conveniences beyond the actual delivery of the purchased product or service will be a key differentiating factor. Think about the convenience of preordering your Starbucks, the Tide button that allows you to place an order on demand, or the Gilt experience creating interest and demand for luxury goods through scarcity. Also, think about the impact of marketplaces like StubHub connecting ticket owners with potential buyers, TaskRabbit for hiring help to do chores, and HomeAdvisor or Angie's List connecting homeowners with contractors.
- IoT sensors, integrated with Cloud data platforms like Amazon IoT, help connect the physical and digital worlds. Not only is this a new source of competitive real-time data, it is also a channel to provide additional context and intelligence to customer experiences.

These examples hopefully illustrate the need to transform businesses and analog products and services to digitally driven experiences. If you consider just these examples—and there are many others—traditional businesses will face mounting pressure when competitors leverage digital capabilities to a strategic advantage. What's more is that it is likely that multiple competitors will emerge applying digital in different innovative ways that change industry dynamics.

Can We Define Digital Transformation?

Here is the definition I offered in a recent interview with Forbes[25]:

> Digital transformation is not just about technology and its implementation. It's about looking at the business strategy through the lens of technical capabilities and how that changes how you are operating and generating revenues

Ultimately, digital transformation is about automating more of operations, generating revenue-leveraging digital capabilities, and bringing new convenience and value to customers. For existing businesses, it requires a fundamental review of everything it does today because digital disruption enables new product offerings and competition from nontraditional sources.

A transformation requires some basic understanding of where you are and where you think you want to be. Let's call the endpoint a vision of your organization's digital future. The transformation, therefore, is a journey that iterates you toward this digital future while enabling you to better define and even pivot your vision of the future.

Later chapters will cover which aspects of the current state are important to measure and include more details on how to define a vision, but for now I will keep this simple.

To kick off the definition of vision and transformation, I recommend reviewing and answering two relatively straightforward questions:

1. What would a startup do to disrupt this business model, compete digitally with your most successful products, or radically change the cost structure by fully automating key business processes? What would they do absent of legacy, physical constraints, and perhaps some regulation to compete or flank an existing model, product, or process?
2. How do you define your digital future? If this digital disruptor appeared, what would you have to become to better compete with them? What would your model, product, or process need to become, and how could you use existing assets as a competitive edge?

If you can answer these two basic questions with even some fuzziness (no one has a perfect crystal ball), then digital transformation is the path toward your digital future that you target.

Do You Have a Seat at the Table?

Defining digital business, a digital strategy, or the vision behind a digital transformation is an important exercise to take on in order to ensure a shared vision among executives. They must reflect on what's driving digital opportunities, the impact of new competitors, and the aggregate risks to legacy businesses. A transformation charter needs to be defined, and there are various approaches to bringing executives together to align, define, and document a strategic vision.

But the question I ask is whether you have a seat at the table when strategic planning efforts focus on digital strategy and transformation. In fact, if digital is not on the agenda for strategic planning, do you have sufficient clout and executive relationships to make sure it's added to the agenda? Have you demonstrated success to be given ownership of the digital agenda? How will organizations rely or redefine their leadership team to evolve digital capabilities? Will the CIO, the CMO, the Strategic Officer, or the new Chief Digital Officer be on the committee, and who will be leading it?

The path to get a seat at the table, to own digital programs, or to be the steward of the digital strategy is to illustrate that you and your team can define, mature, and master digital practices. Digital remains a new and emerging skill at most enterprises, so when you can lead by example, then that will pave the way for others to listen, consult, and ultimately partner on the transformation.

That's been my experience across three different organizations that took on digital strategies and transformation programs very differently. The rest of this book spells out these practices so that you can embark on your journey.

I am going to start with the fundamental practices of a digitally driven IT organization. You can't transform and establish digital capabilities without your technology organization operating differently with new practices, skills, and platforms. You can't have a seat at the strategic table if your organization views IT as a poor performing service desk, a champion of risk management practices, or stewards of clunky, outdated technologies. You won't hold an executive's attention if the IT team's perspective on meeting business need is centered around service levels, software releases, or compliance programs. Frustrated business leaders will find external business partners, look to outsource, or commission rogue technologies if they think the IT team can't understand customer needs and execute a digital agenda.

The first place to start is to develop the organizational model and practices that enable the executing of a digital agenda driven by customer and market feedback. You need the IT organization to learn agile practices and develop an agile culture.

2.

AGILE
TRANSFORMATIONAL
PRACTICES

hapter One showed how transforming to a digital business is critical for your corporation, your role, and probably your career. You've even done some strategic work to think through what your digital future might be, and, if there are already internal discussions about digital transformation, hopefully you've earned enough credibility to get a seat at the table.

This chapter and the following ones are to help transform the IT organization of old to one that's ready to handle new digital responsibilities and change the organization at a significantly faster pace than what it has performed in the past. I will share secrets to aligning with business need and developing differentiating capabilities that drive business growth and cost efficiencies.

My methodologies have several disciplines that ultimately roll up to a strategic set of digital and technology practices, but I will present them one practice at a time. Once we review them, I will roll them together so that you will see how they all drive digital and reinforce smart-fast execution, strategic thinking, culture change, and development of new business capabilities.

Understanding Agile Practices

Many leaders already have a good understanding of agile. Some have scrum or kanban running with multiple teams. But even when I meet transformational leaders that have some agile practices running in their organization, many have not experienced an agile culture or leveraged agile in transformation efforts.

This chapter will cover the key concepts and practices that agile leaders need to understand. I will outline some key tenets of agile governance, then go into agile planning and estimation. The chapter continues with an introduction to foundational technology practices and ends with a definition of release schedules.

Why Agile?

Let's say you know there is a business opportunity and demand for a new application. You want to get momentum to define a project and be a partner to determine whether there is a strong business case to implement it. The first thing to do is articulate a vision—what you're trying to accomplish (definition of business need and opportunity) and why (what benefits, both financial and performance driven). For this example, let's simplify your options to getting this initiative started given that it's just an idea without a complete vision.

OPTION 1—LET'S CALL THIS THE CLASSIC APPROACH

You go back to the sponsors, assign a business analyst, listen to what is required, and work on requirements and a project plan. It takes a couple of months to have all the meetings with stakeholders to gather requirements, document, and review.

At the end of the process, you ask your engineering team to estimate a solution, but under business pressure to respond, you allow them only a couple of weeks to complete it. The engineers do the best they can at outlining a technical approach and laying out a whole list of assumptions. The technologists feel pressure to provide an inexpensive solution, but they would prefer to use this opportunity to phase out a legacy system.

Your business stakeholders receive a document outlining a solution and assumptions, and some show up to the business review. But their level of understanding of the details is limited given their expertise. At the end of the day, they skip all this detail and look at the bottom-line cost and duration to execute. The engineers have recommended a minimal solution that can be implemented in six months, but the sponsors haven't read the details and assume they are getting everything they want in a reasonable time frame.

The team is commissioned to work, and all is good until you are two months into the project and things are starting to go south. The project is taking longer than expected, and the team is falling behind. At the same time, market conditions are changing, and the sponsors are asking for new things added to the scope. Your team adjusts, but by month three they are further behind and you must extend the timeline. By month four, there are more changes, and the team is getting frustrated having to modify things already developed while sponsors are getting nervous on whether the project will complete at all to their expectations.

This seesaw of changing requirements and implementation complexities carries on unless the team and sponsors decide to work collaboratively toward a common milestone. In many cases, this doesn't happen.

This project methodology where requirements are defined before implementation, known as waterfall is a less successful methodology in an environment where sponsors are challenged to define requirements fully, where changing market requirements require reevaluating implementations, and where the urgency to deliver products faster requires engineering teams to make compromises in their solutions.

OPTION 2—LET'S CALL THIS AGILE

Now let's look at the same scenario but implemented from the ground up using agile practices. We'll start off from the same point, where there is only the identification of an opportunity or need but with no other details. Instead of throwing an analyst to work with sponsors on "requirements," imagine bringing a small team of experts together to brainstorm a vision. That vision focuses on a future point with a defined statement on the opportunity, needs, and benefits. By bringing the team together, there is a shared understanding of what the opportunity is and why it's beneficial.

The agile methodology requires assigning a team to work with the product owner to identify the most business-critical aspects of the project, the technical risks, and other unknowns. The team then commits to completing deliverables in a relatively short period, usually one to three weeks. After this period, the team demos their work and then focuses on the next set of critical items for the one- to three-week period.

Obviously, I'm grossly simplifying but want to point out a couple of key differences. In waterfall, the project team must engage the business manager for a significant amount of time to define requirements. Projects are broken into milestones that have no specified rhythm of delivery (some milestones may be weeks, others months) and no requirement or expectation to demo functionality.

In agile, leadership is getting several significant advantages. Teams can start working on the most critical features and risky technical areas without overtaxing the business sponsors for upfront information. The frequency of delivery in one- to three-week "sprints" leads to better execution. Let's say your team does sprints that are two weeks in duration. In three months, they complete six iterations, giving them plenty of time to prove themselves, mature the agile process, and address risks. Agile then allows sponsors to prioritize at the beginning of each sprint, enabling a stronger business and IT alignment. The sponsor gets to prioritize based on customer feedback, and the IT team gets frequent and direct engagement from the business sponsor.

Why Agile Is a Key Transformational Practice

When you sign up to lead transformation, the implication is that you are going to review existing products, business processes, and capabilities and realign to a new vision. Transformation is a change management practice, so the organization must enable a culture, philosophy, governance, and practice to manage the change.

Unfortunately, we no longer live in a static world. We can't portray our digital business future with certainty since so many market forces are transforming in parallel. So thinking that you can manage transformation the same way we construct buildings, bridges, and rockets in the past is outdated thinking. In fact, construction projects are now leveraging elements of agile[1] and lean to enable greater flexibility.

For some organizations, just adopting basic agile practices is good enough to achieve a higher level of execution. These organizations will define their sprint and release schedule, practice standups, and use tools to document user stories. Even at larger scales, just adopting these basic practices provides value as it aligns business stakeholders and provides flexibility to adjust priorities.

But to transform organizations, you need to evolve agile beyond these basic practices into a disciplined scalable process, a practice that connects other functional areas such as marketing and operations, and organizational change to drive to an agile culture.

The rest of this chapter will provide these foundations.

Defining Agile Roles and Responsibilities

A key tenet of the agile manifesto[2] relates to self-organizing teams: "The best architectures, requirements, and designs emerge from self-organizing teams." There's a wide range of interpretation of what "self-organizing teams" means. The problem with teams that are too self-organizing is that they may lack a full understanding of the business and technology strategy, and the lack of governance may lead teams astray. However, teams that are managed tightly, don't ask questions, are slow to think out of the box, or get lost working collaboratively finding solutions with ill defined requirements may never achieve results that can drive transformation.

I have found that teams need basic roles, responsibilities, and governance to be defined in order to be successful. Unlike startups, most organizations fill their agile teams with a mix of people, some with agile experience others with minimal exposure. Some organizations rely heavily on offshore or distributed team members, and some larger projects have the complexity of requiring multiple teams. In all these scenarios, you should provide structure to be successful.

SINGLE TEAM AGILE ROLES AND RESPONSIBILITIES

Structure in agile practices starts with defining basic roles and responsibilities. Some of the constructs laid out in this section are standard for agile teams like the role of the product owner and technical lead. But beyond that, agile doesn't formalize roles within the team. I have found that teams need these responsibilities defined to achieve an optimal cadence of delivery, and the structures need to address several different challenges.

What is Scrum in 30 seconds

Agile teams operate in sprints that are usually one or two weeks in duration and are asked to commit to completing a list of user stories. Each story articulates a requirement, how it benefits the user, and a list of pass/fail acceptance criteria. Stories are typically grouped together into epics to make it easier for team members to navigate and manage the entire backlog of stories. At the end of a sprint, the team demos their completed stories, and the product owner evaluates their completeness. Issues are characterized as defects if they impact users, miss business rules, or fail acceptance criteria. Technical debt is also captured when the team acknowledges that improvements are needed in the underlying implementation.

Teams assign a size to each story and then attempt to commit to a consistent velocity of stories, measured as the aggregate of the sizes, every sprint. They use daily meetings, called standups, to communicate status and raise any blocks that might impede their ability to complete stories. At the end of a sprint, teams usually call a retrospective meeting to discuss process improvements. Releases to production can be done every sprint or over multiple sprints.

One issue is that the product owner and technical lead have significant responsibilities in agile practices but don't always have the skill or time to complete all of them. Product owners are asked to write stories, but they may not be skilled on writing requirements. Technical leaders can become roadblocks if they take on solving all the technical challenges in the backlog.

Another challenge is that many agile teams today are often distributed and may not be in a single location. Distributed teams can arise for different reasons. You may have a business team in one location and technical team in another. You might be working with one or more services providing development or testing team members at different locations. For smaller organizations, you might have fully remote individuals working from home. Very large organizations may attempt to implement 24-hour development lifecycles by distributing teams across the globe. Whatever the structure, roles, responsibilities and practices need to be defined and adjusted to the realities of distributed teams.

The last challenge is how teams balance current sprint execution and future sprint planning. Teams that completely focus on executing the current sprint's commitments can fail to respond to business stakeholder needs to forecast longer-term timelines and roadmaps. I'll be sharing agile practices to enable planning, estimation, roadmapping, and forecasting, but for now the team structure needs to enable both in-sprint execution and future sprint planning.

So, with these challenges in mind, I have used the same team structure shown in Figure 2-1 with the following responsibilities:

- *Product owner*—Defines the vision of the product, the release and the epic. Prioritizes epics and stories. Reviews story definition and acceptance criteria. Reviews all estimation and seeks out minimal viable solutions. Reviews and signs off on completed stories. Aggregates customer and operational feedback to reevaluate priorities.
- *Business analyst (BA)*—Primary responsibility is to write stories, document requirements, and define acceptance criteria. Acts as moderator in discussions between the product owner and technical lead in reviewing implementation options and seeking minimal viable solutions. Answers questions from the development team during sprints to ensure there is a shared vision on what and how to implement. The business analyst is often the best person to lead other documentation efforts.
- *Technical lead (TL)*—Leads the delivery of the product. Partners with the product owner to define solutions. Breaks down epics to stories and partners with the business analyst contributing nonfunctional

requirements and technical acceptance criteria. Leads review of completed stories for completeness and adherence to technical standards. Leads retrospective and captures technical debt. Also responsible for getting the team to a predictable velocity and for recommending a balance of functional, technical debt, and defect-fixing stories that lead to on-time releases.

- ***Dev 1, Dev 2, QA 1***—Represent members of the development team who are responsible for reviewing stories, sizing them, committing to getting the sprint, and ensuring that all stories are "done" at the sprint's completion. If you adopt the agile manifesto to its essence, the requirement is for shippable code at the end of every sprint.

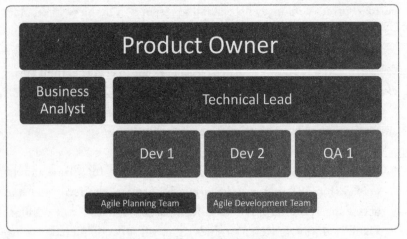

Figure 2-1. Roles on a small agile team

The *agile planning team* should spend most of its effort working on priorities, vision, and requirements for the upcoming sprints. Ideally, they are involved only in the current sprint to answer questions and to review the results. The *agile development team*, on the other hand, is primarily working on the current sprint. When they get toward the end of the sprint, they must dedicate part of their time to review the next sprint's priorities, ask questions, size stories, and commit.

This team structure and role definition also work for a distributed team where the agile planning team is collocated with the business and the agile development team is near shore or offshore, either as a captive or working with a service provider. In that situation, one of these developers should have leadership skills to lead the team through story-sizing meetings, commitment, daily standups, and retrospectives. In addition, if a service vendor is being used, it can be beneficial if the business analyst or the technical lead is from the service provider, but I wouldn't recommend both being staffed by them.

You'll notice that I've avoided using the scrum master role that is usually associated with leading agile scrum teams. I've never assigned a scrum master role in my agile organizations and prefer distributing their responsibilities across the team. If the organization is transitioning from other practices to agile and already has project managers, then it can be beneficial to assign them most of scrum master responsibilities. This is especially needed if existing business analysts and technical leads have little exposure to agile, have limited leadership skills, or have little practice working directly with product owners and business stakeholders.

However, it is very feasible to run a small agile organization without dedicated project managers. This can be realized if the business leaders and stakeholders can live with limited reporting and financial governance, which is why most startups succeed with agile without project management. In a small-team framework, the traditional responsibilities of a project manager are absorbed by the agile planning team, so for example, project reporting, communications, and financials are managed by the product owner, while resource management and risk mediation are managed by the technical lead.

LARGER TEAMS

Sometimes a program requires a larger team either because it requires multiple technical skills or the software is highly modular, and an increased velocity can be achieved by adding people. Figure 2-2 illustrates that this can be achieved but within limits. The team in that figure is the largest that I would recommend under most circumstances and the added overhead is a QA lead to ensure that testing is properly conducted. It's very important that one of the developers other than the technical lead take responsibility to oversee in-sprint activities like reviewing stories, conducting standups, completing commitments, and escalating blocks.

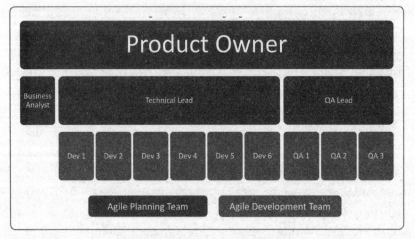

Figure 2-2. Roles on a larger agile team

DISTRIBUTED TEAMS

If you are working with a development partner, then the agile team structure can easily support this model. In these cases, I recommend that either the BA or the tech lead come from your service provider, while the other ideally should be an employee. I've done it either way, depending on what skills were available, so if I had a strong technical lead, then I would pull a BA from the service provider; other times I would request a technical lead and resource the BA internally. The latter scenario works well if you are adopting a new technology and an external service provider can provide the expertise to lead the adoption.

In a distributed team, I don't recommend having both the BA and the tech lead filled by employees or by the service provider. If they are both employees, then it can be more challenging to bridge cultures and camaraderie, with members coming from the service provider, and teams often separate into "in house" and "outsource" subteams. Even if that doesn't happen, teams must work a little harder bridging communications with the offshore team members.

Having both BA and tech lead coming from the outsourcer creates other challenges. If any of the other team members are employees, they must report to team leaders coming from the service provider, a working arrangement that isn't trivial unless other employees are overseeing the team's execution.

If the BA, tech lead, and all team members are coming from the service provider then this is essentially an outsourced team. Leaders looking to fully outsource need to consider developing service-level agreements and align on success criteria. Other considerations are documentation, knowledge transfer, and continuity if the team is being commissioned for only a fixed scope and duration of work.

The other form of distributed team is when team members are in multiple locations, time zones, and service providers. This is the most complex situation, and management needs to adopt the practice to the specifics of the situation. For certain, management will need to consider additional technologies like instant messaging, video conferencing, electronic whiteboards, and other collaboration tools to ensure that team members can collaborate efficiently. See Figure 2-3.

Team Type	BA	Tech Lead	Team Members	Best for	Challenges
In-house	FTE	FTE	Most FTE	Legacy projects or when all skills are available in house	Learning new tech, agile, or other skills
Hybrid	FTE	SP	FTE/SP	Projects with new technologies	Teaching FTEs new technologies and developing standards
Hybrid	SP	FTE	FTE/SP	Accelerate development on existing technologies	Agile process governance if BA doesn't learn the organizational practice. Learning curve on existing application
Outsource	SP	SP	SP	One-time development efforts Integration projects Prototypes Internal applications	Developing an SLA Knowledge transfer, governance Additional challenges: some team members are FTE
Mobile	FTE/ FL	FTE	FL	If specialized skills required Startups	Contracts with freelancers Additional communication challenges

FTE = employee, SP = service provider, FL = freelancer.

Figure 2-3. Filling people and skills on agile teams between employees and service providers

For a large team with a commissioned a QA lead, I have had success having this both onsite and offshore. When the team is just getting started and QA standards need to be developed, then having a QA lead working with the BA and tech lead can be beneficial. Once the technology and testing foundations are in place, having the QA lead offshore can ensure that the testing strategy is being executed properly.

MULTIPLE TEAMS

You may need multiple teams for several reasons. The most logical reason is you might have multiple products or projects with sufficient business need and rationale to dedicate separate teams to each effort. You might have geological separations where separate teams help minimize communication overhead. These are easy scenarios to carve out since there are few dependencies between teams.

You may also have products or projects that have logical separations where teams can work largely independently. It's important to craft these teams to minimize the dependencies between them but also ensure that each team can deliver business values independently and ideally through their own release schedules. One example is a team developing APIs to enterprise systems, while other teams develop applications that leverage them.

Figure 2-4 provides a generic structure to support multiple teams that introduces several new managerial and governance roles.

Figure 2-4. Multiteam agile organization

The "delivery manager" oversees the work of multiple development teams and agile backlogs. She ensures that teams adhere to both technical and agile governance practices and standards. In situations where the delivery manager is seeing the entire enterprise's programs, she will own the technical and development standards, roadmaps, and governance.

The delivery manager will likely elect a program staff that complements her skill set. At minimum, she'll need someone to oversee elements of the technology architecture with the primary role of providing reference architectures and sprint-to-sprint guidelines to each team's technical lead. In addition, depending on the expertise of the team running agile projects and the level of reporting, coordination, or collaboration required to business teams, she may employ an agile program manager and possibly an agile coach. The program manager should set agile practice standards, review implementations, and address program risks. When rolling agile out to multiple new teams, an agile coach with experience in developing agile disciplines, practices, collaboration, and culture may help accelerate the organization's adoption.

Leveraging Agile Tools

With a structure in place, the next thing you should decide on is a set of management and collaboration tools. When I started in agile, the available tools were not mature, and it wasn't a bad idea to go low tech with stickies, cards, boards, or online spreadsheets to manage a backlog and share requirements with a team. Today, you can lose two months of productivity just reviewing all the options.

For agile practices to mature, selecting a tool—even the wrong tool—is a must, and I highly recommend implementing one on day one. Why? Because whomever you select to be a part of the agile practice will pave the way for others to join and contribute. These early participants will define the practice and ideally configure the tool and workflows as the process matures. They will help shape where to collect metrics, which reports to leverage, and which disciplines to standardize on. By giving them a tool, you're enabling them to scale the agile practice as the transformation program expands in scope.

There is a prevailing wisdom that states that you should select a tool that fits the practice. In agile, I disagree. By selecting agile and ideally some related practice like scrum or kanban, you've already selected the process, and what remains is fitting it to the organization's structure, culture, and business need. My recommendation is to let the capabilities, workflows, and reports baked into the tool help shape the practice. The developers of these tools know agile and have learned many best practices from their customers that they then embed in their tools. Why reinvent the wheel?

YOU SELECTED A TOOL, NOW WHAT?

Tools can become chaotic messes unless you set some responsibilities on who owns the configurations and establish some governance on what elements to invest time into configuring. If you're working with multiple teams, you'll need some guidelines on what should be standardized across teams versus what you'll empower individual teams to configure on their own. You'll also want to take steps to make sure that teams and individuals are following the process and leveraging the tools as expected. In my experience, I've seen both issues—teams that invest too much time in their process and tool configuration and lose sight of serving the business need, while other teams lag usage to the extent that it inhibits execution. We'll explore how to handle both situations.

Once you select a tool, assigning roles and responsibilities becomes important so that team members know who drives the configuration and in what areas. But how you assign the responsibility depends on what roles you have on the team, the number of teams, the skill of the team members, the time frame for scaling the practice, and logistical considerations.

Figure 2-5 shows how I assign tool and workflow ownership.

Role	Responsibilities	Ideally Owned By
Tool configuration	Filtering, special fields, report configuration	Business analyst
Sprint configuration	Starting/stopping sprints, scheduling stories into sprints	Business analyst
Epics	Naming, definition, prioritization, epic burndown	Product owner
Story definition and lifecycle	Naming, summary, acceptance criteria, tagging to epics, labeling with required data fields, transitioning stories across stages	Business analyst
Story estimation	Estimation, sizing, technical requirements, resource assignment	Technical lead
Release management	Defining releases, monitoring the release burndown, velocity management	Technical lead
Scheduling	Assigning stories to a release and to sprints, scheduling brainstorming and estimation sessions	Business analyst
Technical debt	Creating stories representing technical debt and tagging them, ensuring technical debt is prioritized	Technical lead
Defect review	Review escalated defects, assign initial priority, lead review with team	Business analyst
Communication	Release schedules, team status, demo introduction	Product owner

Figure 2-5. Roles and responsibilities configuring an agile tool for an initiative

Product owners should spend most of their time working with customers, sales, and technologists to shape the product. They may not be too technical and may also have limited experience with agile practices. For these reasons, I think it's best to limit their role working with agile tools to areas directly tied to their primary responsibility regarding requirements and priorities.

Technical leads fall into two categories: (1) those that have some management skills and embrace disciplined agile through tools and (2) others who have less management and more technical skills. Regardless, I think the same principles apply as with product owners, and it's better to optimize the technical lead's time to working with the product owner, leading the team, and overseeing the technical implementation. Technical leads should be focused on estimating, providing technical requirements, and ensuring that the scope, feasibility, and timing of releases is realistic.

It's fair to say that I've burdened the business analyst with many responsibilities, including ones more commonly aligned to project managers or scrum masters. If you have larger distributed teams, you can split some of these responsibilities with program managers.

You should adjust these priorities if you're using service providers, depending on their skills and your level of trust with their abilities to develop core practices.

Figure 2-6 shows the governance if you are rolling out agile to multiple teams. These governance principles essentially define who owns the business rules, practices, and tool configuration.

Role	Responsibilities	Ideally Owned by
Release coordination	Scheduling, conflict resolution, change management standards, signoff on process or architecture changes	Delivery manager
Reporting and tracking	Field definition, reporting standards, velocity, productivity, and quality of team and member contributions	Program manager
Process Governance	Release, sprint, epic, story definitions meet standards. Resource allocations	Program manager
Architecture	Review technical standards, implementation responsibilities, technology selection	Architect

Figure 2-6 Roles and responsibilities in managing releases

On my blog, I've published 10 best practices in configuring your agile project management tools.[3] Once you have roles assigned and a tool selected, I would suggest reviewing these guidelines and coming up with an initial vision for the configuration. I then recommend teams to integrate practice maturity and tool definition into their agile plans. So, for example, you might start with coming up with guidelines on writing the summary line for stories in your first sprint, tagging conventions in later sprints, and reporting afterward.

Agile Planning Practices

So now with organization and team structure defined, roles and responsibilities outlined, let me provide more details on what I mean about agile planning and its key practices. My assumption is that you and the team have the basic agile process running with sprints, commitments, standups, demos, and retrospectives being practices.

To understand agile planning, let's first look at some of the fundamentals of the agile development team from the vantage point of just getting started with the practice. This is a realistic scenario as most organizations that adopt agile start with a smaller pilot team and project and leverage their wins to grow the practice.

How Agile Planning Practices Evolve

That pilot team works with the product owner to understand the vision even if it isn't formally defined. They go through a process, usually a series of meetings and discussions, to formulate an initial set of priorities. This team makes a loose commitment on the priorities, largely because they don't know their velocity but also because they haven't formalized practices to write stories or commitment. In all likelihood and unless the team has employed an agile coach, the only thing that truly resembles agile in that first sprint is the notion of a team, a set of priorities, and doing the daily standup meetings.

Flash forward, and that team adapts more practices sprint by sprint. There is an emergence of a backlog that forces the product owner to prioritize. Teams make best effort to commit and get stories done, but some complications emerge over time. The team fails on getting a story "done" or on aligning to the product owner's expectations, so at a retrospective, the team formalizes story writing standards to get a better shared understanding of requirements and acceptance criteria. In the next sprint, the team over commits and fails to complete all the stories, so they formalize commitment at the start of the sprint and begin measuring their velocity. While these are fundamental agile practices, it often takes a pilot team several sprints to realize their importance and to self-organize process improvements.

These two process maturities improve the team's execution in a sprint. When the team knows what's expected of them through acceptance criteria and has a better understanding of their velocity, the accuracy of their commitment and sprint execution (as defined by the number of stories achieving "done") improves.

FROM EXECUTION TO ESTIMATING PRACTICES

It is pretty common for product owners to begin thinking one or more sprints ahead of the active one. But therein lies a problem. The product owner knows what she wants but needs help from the team to understand cost or complexity. You might hear the product owner say, "If I know this feature is too big or complex, I might not prioritize it or might simplify what I need."

It's at that point that the product owner is ready to engage the team's leadership on a dialogue about solutions and tradeoffs. This is essentially the beginning of the product owner and technical lead working out some rudimentary estimation practices. This gives product owners a sense of cost and complexity, so they get a practice to simplify their requirements or can abandon requirements that are too costly to implement. For technical leads, sizing gives them a measured approach to manage commitment and velocity.

Two things happen while this team builds up their practice. First, executing the practice takes up more overhead. When the team started, the overhead was maybe a meeting or two to review priorities plus the 15 minutes of daily standups. Now there are commitment meetings, time spent to document stories, effort used to size stories, and practices established to monitor velocity. That investment in time diminishes what the team can use for actual development and testing, and the result creates a conflict. Should the team spend more time executing on the current sprint, or does it take on planning work for the next sprint?

The second thing that develops involves the questions and sometimes badgering from business leaders for timelines, project plans, scope "signoff," or roadmaps. Some are used to getting these from waterfall project methodologies and haven't let go of these constructs. Others grow impatient with agile and get frustrated when teams struggle to answer basic questions like, "What will you develop, and when will you deliver it?" Even when there is a product owner strongly aligned to agile principles, stakeholders will still require some forecast of what they will be getting when so that they can adequately plan business activities like marketing, training, and operational changes.

FROM BASIC ESTIMATING PRACTICES TO AGILE PLANNING

There is some reality to this need for timelines and scope because, even though the development team is agile, most likely their business teams are not so much. Marketing teams that are not agile need to plan the messaging, materials, and marketing plans associated with product upgrades. Operating teams need to determine workflow changes and consider training and documentation needs. Even when these teams culturally accept incremental releases and launching with minimally viable products, they still thirst for basic understanding of what they are getting. How can these groups endorse agile practices when the development team can't respond to the basic question of what will be released and when?

It's at this point when the product owner will likely feel external pressures to provide forward-looking projections. Telling stakeholders what will be delivered one sprint ahead is usually unsatisfactory to business leaders who want more definitive roadmaps. Now product owners usually don't have an issue articulating a feature roadmap, but understanding feasibility, defining how something will work in practice, or providing realistic dates typically goes beyond their skill set and responsibilities in an agile practice.

Let me elaborate on these two points. I remember working with a very seasoned and successful agile coach back at *Businessweek*. He taught us the basics of agile practices, set up roles, and coached the team through their first sprints. He also seeded the foundation of our agile culture.

I was hired and started a couple of sprints into the process and was happy to see where we were but was immediately asked by the project sponsors to project dates and scope. I remember the coach fighting the need to estimate or to forward-project, claiming that it "wasn't agile." He was right because the team wasn't ready to implement estimation and planning practices that lead to these forecasts. In addition, the business teams weren't ready to operate properly with forecasts. If they interpreted a projection as a fixed-time, fixed-scope deliverable, then we might be practicing agile but failing to achieve agile thinking and culture. Beyond just agile practices, it's agile thinking and culture that develop superior outcomes by adjusting priorities based on customer feedback, promoting innovation, and adjusting to practical realities.

I will tell you that the pressure never subsided. We needed agile planning practices, but they needed to be rolled out when the working team was ready to instrument and when the business teams were ready to partner with them.

The second point is a word of warning to product owners who elect to communicate scope and dates without feedback from their team and a defined practice on how these will be calculated. My history working with these product owners is that they often fail to deliver on scope and time and then will likely blame their team for the variances. The product owner's primary responsibility is to represent the customer, set the vision, and guide priorities. While some product owners are "technical enough to be dangerous," most of the ones I've worked with are nontechnical and have only a basic understanding of platforms, architecture, coding practices, and testing complexity. What looks simple on paper may turn out to be complex, and what is complex may also be simplified. Product owners generally don't have the technical skills to evaluate feasibility or develop technical solutions. In addition, they generally don't have project management skills that enable them to use data to forecast. Bottom line—many product owners generally don't have the skills to forecast. Even the ones who do run the risk of alienating their teams if members are not involved in the forecasting process.

MANAGING THE PARADOX OF AGILE EXECUTION AND PLANNING

These two needs, the need to execute on the current sprint and the need to plan and forecast future sprints, create a difficult paradox for agile teams and leaders. Focus too much on the current sprint, and you're likely to commit to getting more done at the expense of having stories written and estimates ready for future sprints. But to improve the accuracy of forecasting releases and roadmaps, time and effort need to be dedicated to understanding requirements, developing solutions, and producing estimates.

Teams that don't dedicate this time for planning can fall victim to misalignment issues with their business stakeholders. If you underinvest in forward sprint planning and resort to high-level estimates, "T-shirt sizing" as one of my teams used to call it, then there is a strong likelihood of inaccurate forecasting that will undermine the culture changes required for agile transformation. Worse, it can lead to a backlash against using agile practices.

Teams should prove they can execute on agile development first before they can take on agile planning disciplines. But reporting, communications, planning, and forecasting are needed by most organizations, and teams need to develop these practices and then balance their efforts.

The team structure proposed in Figures 2-1 and 2-2 enables assigning planning and execution responsibilities. The agile planning resources are roughly 80% focused on future sprints and 20% on the current one, while the agile development team is 80% executing on the current sprint and 20% working toward the next sprint.

HOURS OR POINTS?

Now that you have a methodology, the question is whether to estimate and size in hours or to use "story points," an artificial measure that often factors in complexity and effort.

Estimating in hours is almost always preferred by business stakeholders because they can translate it directly to cost. Unfortunately, this doesn't always work in practice for a couple of reasons. First, developers struggle estimating their effort and time, especially when multiple skills are required to complete a story or when there are varying skill sets on the team. What might be 3 hours for the technical lead may be 12 hours for a more junior developer. What might be a 5-hour story to develop may require 10 hours of testing, some of which cannot be performed until the end of the sprint. Something that was sized at 20 hours because of some technical unknowns can sometimes be implemented in far less time if the risks do not materialize. So estimating development projects in hours has a high degree of variability.

Translating hours into cost has a second issue. It may provide a measure of development cost but not the underlying support costs. For example, something that required only 2 hours of development may yield a solution that's so complex it leads to manual effort to implement or fix issues once it is deployed. Giving the business a direct translation of only the build costs without support considerations is a significant issue. It leads to quick builds and fixes with an underlying support complexity that is not formally articulated.

It is for these reasons that I never enable development teams to estimate and size in hours. I always lead them to measure in story points and ask them to come up with a rate card based on the Fibonacci sequence that measures both effort and complexity. So, for example, stories that are 1 or 3 points are low efforts and complexity, while a 21-point story has high complexity and effort. A team dialogue can help flesh out why a story has many points, and it's the complexity factor that often gets reviewed with scrutiny. Why are the requirements driving to a complex solution? Is there a way to descope the elements that are complex? Is there a different solution that leads to less complexity?

I have also seen that estimating and sizing in points also leads to reasonable accuracy. Teams size stories based on their past experiences, so if a story has a similar implementation to something they have done in the past, they will estimate and size based on this knowledge.

Business leaders can still get at cost by dividing the cost to run the program over a period of time (a sprint, or a release for example) by the team's total velocity over that period to get a cost per story point. Multiplying this by the epic's size (calculated by summing all the story points for the epic's completed stories) yields a cost for the epic. But now this cost has some expression of complexity in its measurement. There is, however, a downside. You can only use this method to calculate a cost once the stories are fit into a sprint schedule when you have an idea of what the team commits during a sprint.

Example: Calculating actual development costs.

Let's consider a simple example of calculating costs with a single team, blended cost of $40,000 per 2-week sprint, and a 4-sprint release costing $160,000. In the release, they complete three epics totaling 200 story points with epic 1 requiring 40 points, epic 2 requiring 60 points, and epic 3 100 points. Epic 1 is thus 20% of the releases productivity and costs $32,000, while epic 2 costs $48,000, and epic 3 costs $80,000. The product owner could also look at a more detailed breakout on what capabilities were the most taxing by performing a similar analysis at a story level.

Just a note that my guidance on using story points for estimating and sizing is for development teams. If you are applying agile practices to operational teams, then hourly estimates often work well and may be required. These teams usually have a breakdown of tasks and can assign hours to them based on previous experiences. Operational teams are also less likely to take on too many risky or complex tasks. Teams that have these parameters don't need to adjust for complexity as much as development teams, and their hours applied are often a crucial measurement for identifying process improvements.

Agile Estimation

If you're going to promote a data-driven organization (more on this in a later chapter), then you better show up with some data. In this case, the role of the technology organization is to review vision and requirements and to provide estimates. The estimates, in the process that I endorse, are a way for teams and the product owner to have a dialogue on the vision, brainstorm on requirements, and discuss possible solutions. Each solution offered is a scenario, and they often have tradeoffs that might be hard to understand without building and testing. Estimates offer a blunt instrument to compare solutions at least by one measure, the cost and complexity to implement.

In my experience, estimating and the resulting dialogue between the product owner and the tech leads result in more optimal solutions. First, the dialogue itself leads to a better shared understanding of the customer need, priority of the product owner, and other related nonfunctional requirements. This upfront understanding leads to less questioning later or, worse, rework because it is more likely that a shared understanding of the complete requirements gets documented.

Equally as important and likely to happen through this dialogue is getting the product owner to prioritize. I've never met a product owner who will naturally ask for a minimal viable implementation. Many do the opposite and ask for everything that must be done and should be included, in addition to what is nice to have. And why shouldn't they if all they are asked for are requirements without a dialogue on impact and options? Tell them that their requirements are 1,000 points with a team that averages 200 points every 2-week sprint and you're likely see them reconsider their requirements. What if I left this out, or minimized this, or simplified that, would it lower your estimate? That's exactly the dialogue I am seeking with the estimation process as it weeds out the nice-to-have capabilities without any development investment or stressful dialogue.

OVERCOMING ISSUES WITH ESTIMATING

Development teams will tell you that estimating is hard. They will want requirements spelled out in detailed stories before estimating them. They will be fearful to provide estimates and then held accountable when requirements change or when the implementation is more complex than forecasted. Some will inflate estimates to protect against these issues.

Other teams do the exact opposite and simplify. Without all the requirements spelled out and with limited time allocating to planning and estimating, they leave out architectural, quality, and other dependencies that can lead to underestimation.

A third and very practical issue is deciding how much time to invest in estimating. Teams that believe their estimates need to be super accurate tend to invest too much time in the process. In addition, these teams may overengineer their assumptions to complete the estimate.

Finally, there is the question of when and whether to engage the team on the estimation process. Are you going to engage only the leads of the team to enable a more efficient process or the full team to get their input? The latter is very important to get commitment, but engaging the whole team on estimations increases the expense to develop them.

ESTIMATING OBJECTIVES

These considerations are factored into this agile estimation process. Agile teams can't overinvest their time in the process but still need to provide some accuracy to the estimates provided. The process needs to provide feedback to the product owner on cost and complexity, so that one objective is that not all the stories estimated by the team will be prioritized by the product owner for implementation. This is a good thing and a behavior we are seeking because we want the product owner to lower the priority of stories that provide marginal value but are high in implementation complexity or cost. This balancing of value versus complexity and adjusting priorities or scope is the first objective of estimating.

How many stories will be estimated but not commissioned for development because they are too complex? How many other stories will see radically simplified requirements? The answers vary with the type of project, the nature of the product owner, and the team's technical strengths executing on the underlying technology platforms. In my experience, the number of stories left on the table or that change radically is significant. Knowing this, the question is how to make estimating extremely efficient when as many as 70% of stories will never get implemented once they are estimated? Does the team need to capture all the stories' details to estimate?

The answer is no, if you can create a culture and a process of estimating with incomplete information. The reality is that developers never have perfect requirements, complete knowledge of legacy or integration considerations, or full mastery of the underlying technologies. They are always taking on a certain level of risk when they commit to stories even when they have optimal requirements and knowledge.

So the question is can the development team provide a basis for lightweight estimates that can be used by the product owner to prioritize and descope? My experience is that the answer is yes, provided the team has some history of working together and sufficient mastery of the underlying technologies. These estimates can be used for deciding on scope and priority, developing a first-pass schedule and for getting an early understanding of a release plan. On the other hand, these early estimates can't be used for commitment or measuring velocity because that requires the added requirements and acceptance criteria.

For the rest of this chapter, I will refer to these as "estimates," and they are often computed on a first-pass breakdown of an epic or feature into "story stubs." These stubs are often the headline or summary of the story but lack complete detail or acceptance criteria. They are sufficient to help the team break down the business requirement and provide an estimate based on their previous experiences.

Epics or features?

Many organizations with large backlogs or multiple product teams will consider using epics to represent product themes that require multiple releases to complete. They then break down these epics to smaller features that can be implemented or upgraded within a single release. For simplicity, the estimation process described here is based on breaking epics directly into stories that are estimated. If you already break epics down into features, then use this process to break down and estimate one or more stories for each feature.

I said team, but to make this process hyper efficient, it is beneficial if the team delegates the estimating responsibility to the technical lead. Chances are the technical lead is the only one experienced with enough knowledge of the product owner's intent and the full technology stack to be effective in providing estimates.

What if there are multiple ways to break down this epic into stubs, with each approach leading to a different solution with different tradeoffs? I call these scenarios, and if the technical lead (sometimes with some added help from key team members) can provide these scenarios, it leads to a better dialogue on scope and methodology to implement. So a second benefit of estimating is that it drives technologists to consider multiple solutions and to discuss tradeoffs.

What if the product owner sanctioned a large or complex epic for estimation? That's okay, just break it down based on what's known and understood. When an epic can only be partially broken down into stubs because there are too many technical or implementation unknowns, then the technical lead may have difficulty providing an estimate without some upfront investigation and even prototyping. Knowing there are technical risks to implement the business requirement is a third objective of the estimating process. If too much R&D is needed, then the product owner should take this as a warning that she is asking for something that has complexity and risk.

There is also a way to resolve these unknowns by commissioning story "spikes." A spike is effectively an R&D story to develop or prototype a technical solution. If the team is given the priority to implement a spike, it can be used to address the unknowns in the epic. Estimates can be delayed until the more critical spikes are completed that help address the technical unknowns or risks.

So is estimating sufficient? What happens with the other 30% of stories that are commissioned by the product owner once stubs are estimated? We're not done with this process because prioritized stubs need to have the full requirement articulated with acceptance criteria, supporting diagrams, and other standards you decide on for documenting stories. Once the story is fully written, does the early estimate still hold?

The answer most likely is no. As the story is written, requirements are stipulated that may lead to additional implementation factors and complexity. However, the additional requirements should eliminate ambiguities and may lower the estimate. Bottom line is that the estimate is no longer valid once there is a written story with fleshed-out requirements.

Once the story is fully written, reevaluate it and come up with a final "sizing." The objective now is to engage the team to review all the elements of the story and come up with its size based on their understanding of both complexity and effort. I call this sizing because it's a distinct step in the process and a different metric from the original estimate.

Comparing the story size versus estimate provides the product owner a second opportunity to evaluate priority and scope. They should question what led to higher sizes versus the estimate to see if the gap is required. Bottom line is they can make changes before the work is commissioned.

If the work is commissioned, this sizing can then be used by the team to make their commitment and measure velocity. This is because the team is fully involved in sizing, and it is developed off the fully documented story.

So, in summary, this is a two-step process:

1. Estimating on stubs to provide early guidance on cost and complexity with the goal to descope, lower the priority, or provide multiple solutions with tradeoffs
2. Sizing on fully written stories with acceptance criteria to be used as a second validation for priority and scope and then used for commitment and computing velocity

THE ESTIMATING PROCESS

Figure 2-7 shows the process I advocate.

Figure 2-7 Agile estimation on story stubs followed by sizing on fully written stories

- Teams, departments, or organizations should define metrics and a process to derive or demonstrate business value. The product owner is expected to prioritize the high-level epic backlog based on the business value. Many organizations just force-rank these epics and look to develop business value measures only if needed.
- On seeing a new epic prioritized, the technical lead should break prioritized epics into story stubs. For "simple" epics, this usually isn't a difficult task for experienced teams, but for more complicated ones, it may:
  - ▸ Require sessions with the product owner to get some more details.
  - ▸ Require breaking down the epic into smaller ones, some that might be easier to break down and be more important.
  - ▸ Require some R&D (spikes) to help flesh out an approach.
  - ▸ Fall out of scope for what the team (or teams) can perform— either by size, skill, or complexity. For larger organizations, the delivery manager needs to consider how best to either reassign or get other help for a solution.
- Assuming the epic now has story stubs, the technical lead should assign estimates.
- Delivery leaders will often review story stub estimates. Is the epic fully broken down? Are there architecture considerations? Should technical debt be addressed with the epic?

- The product owner should then review and has several options:
  - ▸ Accept the estimate and move the stubs to the backlog.
  - ▸ Lower the priority of the epic or remove it from the backlog.
  - ▸ Discuss the estimate to see whether assumptions were wrong or whether the epic's definition can be simplified and yield a lower estimate. If this path is taken, the newly defined epic should be prioritized again on the epic backlog for a second estimate.

THE ONE-WEEK AGILE PLANNING SPRINT

So how do you implement this process in practice? There's a lot of "it depends" in that answer—the number of teams involved in the program, the complexity of the project at hand, and the technical skills required to complete an epic. In simple terms, larger projects with more team members and more complex assignments are going to require a lot more time and coordination to estimate and size versus smaller projects with few teams and technical skills.

Let me introduce two other constructs. First, the concept of voting, which can be used to sort out conflicting priorities when there are multiple stakeholders with different needs. The second is the architecture review meeting, which is used to ensure that solutions are complete and have included all the technical and quality considerations.

Figure 2-8[4] diagrams estimating at its simplest level as a single one-week agile planning sprint.

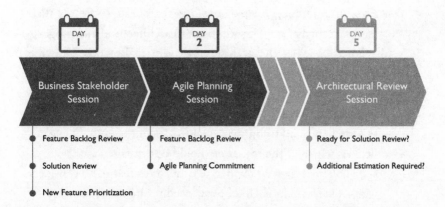

Figure 2-8. One-week agile planning sprint used to stub, estimate, write, and size stories

- *Day One, Business stakeholder session*—At a meeting of stakeholders (including product owners and senior technologists), three agendas are scheduled:
  1. Epic backlog review—The product owner reviews status on the top features in the agile planning backlog.
  2. Solution review—All epics that were estimated or sized over the last agile planning sprint are reviewed with stakeholders. These are given go/no-go votes and in/out of scope decisions on specific feature details. Estimated epics that were given a "go" will go into priority for story writing and sizing, while fully sized epics receiving a "go" are ready to be prioritized for commitment.
  3. New epic prioritization—The sponsor of a new epic presents the definition and its business value. At the end of this meeting, new epics are voted on and are prioritized in the epic backlog.

- *Day Two, Agile planning session*—The technology/program management team reviews the epic backlog for new ones and progress on epics where there is planning underway. Team leaders (often tech leads, business analysts, and QA leads—but that depends on your organization) commit to epic estimation, sizing, and story writing.

- *Days Three–Four, Team leaders work on planning*—For epics in agile planning, team leaders develop multiple scenarios (options) to fulfill the requirements. At least one scenario should represent a "minimal feature set."

- *Day Five, Architectural review session*—Team leaders present their story stubs, estimates, and assumptions to architectural and program leads. For each epic, the architecture team makes the following decisions:
  - Ready for solution review— The review is used to decide whether stubs and estimates developed fully represent the requirements and technical dependencies of the epic. The team decides which of the scenarios should be presented at the stakeholder session and which to drop. This team also considers what epic elements should be reviewed for in/out of scope.
  - Additional estimation required—The team can force an epic for a second round of planning if the story stubs don't represent an

end-to-end implementation, if the estimates are challenged and need to be reviewed in more detail, if dependencies on other teams need to be considered, or if additional scenarios need to be developed.

In this process, I'm stretching the definition of "sprint" and deliberately selecting a fast one-week cadence. This is because an epic's planning might not achieve "done" (as in estimation complete) at the end of a week either because its complexity requires more planning or because it does not pass the architecture review. This is by design; complex features that require multiple planning sprints provide feedback to the stakeholder that their ask is complex or challenging. It also forces quick estimates and solutions since some epics will be deprioritized or have reduced scope once estimates and sizes are considered.

AGILE AT *BUSINESSWEEK*

The process outlined in Figure 2-8 is very close to what we instituted when I was CIO at *Businessweek*. The steering committee met Mondays. New features were first vetted by the product management team, then presented to the committee for review. We had different stakeholders representing digital strategy, editorial, ad sales, technology, and marketing that would vote on the feature based on its business merits. I voted for technology. The final votes were aggregated into a score that would help prioritize features going into estimation.

At the same meeting, any features that were fully estimated and approved by the architecture group. The solution would be reviewed by the technology leads along with other scenarios that were considered. The voting committee reviewed the solution and would either sanction the feature for further development, ask for refinements, or suggest removing the feature from consideration.

The product and technology groups met Tuesday and worked backward. They would start with any features that had already been estimated and approved for development and review the status of story sizing. It's important that these epics get reviewed at top priority to ensure that the business analysts and technical leads were focused first on getting stories written and sized before going on to review any new epics that required estimation.

Once done, a review of epics already in the estimation process aggregated with any new epics voted on by the committee. These would be reviewed in voting rank order, so a new epic could trump planning activities for epics that had some work completed in a previous planning sprint.

Keep in mind that while the agile planning sprint is one week, the commitment isn't the same as in agile development where the team is expected to complete stories, pass all acceptance criteria, and have shippable code at its end. In agile planning, the team commits to working on estimating, sizing, or documenting the requirements of the epic, but there isn't a commitment to have it fully completed by the end of the week. The list of epics also includes ones that were planned but that the architecture review committee did not approve or requested additional technical considerations for. The product owner, along with the delivery manager, sets the tone for balancing effort between estimating, sizing, and story writing activities.

At the end of the week, the architecture review committee reviewed the estimated and sized epics. They would have authority to challenge and request more scenarios, determine that a scenario was not fully thought through and missing implementation details, or challenge the technical lead on the estimates. Ultimately, their job was either to pass an estimate and recommend a scenario or to reject the estimate and request additional work. Accepted estimates were then prepared to be reviewed at the following Monday's business stakeholder session.

The process worked exceptionally well. We had three independent programs running with this level of review happening across them every week. It led to the redesign of *Businessweek*'s homepage, the conversion of a legacy content management system (CMS), and the development of new social, mobile, and data products.

ALIGNING AGILE WITH ARCHITECTURE

I'll close this section on agile with a review of how agile teams that leverage planning practices can still align with longer-term architecture plans or product roadmaps.

Figure 2-9 shows the agile planning cycle we just reviewed for a single epic that is broken down to two scenarios. One scenario is approved by both the architecture and steering groups for story writing and ultimately for development.

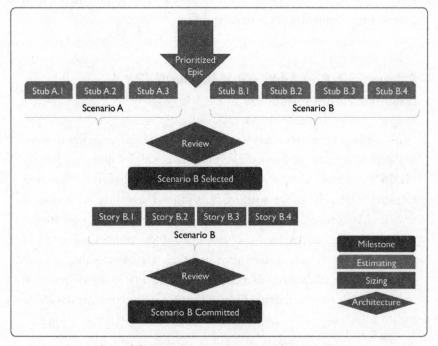

Figure 2-9. Instituting scenarios and architecture reviews
in the agile planning process

Why is one scenario selected over the other? This comes down to how well the team articulates the tradeoffs from one approach to another. In the workflow, the architectural differences are reviewed that might show that one scenario introduces additional technical debt, has reliance on a legacy system that will be deprecated, or has additional performance considerations.

But the product owner can make similar reviews for roadmap considerations. Is one solution better aligned to customer need, the product roadmap, or other strategic consideration? This too can aid in selecting an optimal scenario.

It's the balance of agile development that is focused on short-term execution and agile planning that provides a framework to plan releases and roadmaps that makes agile practices transformational. It gives leaders the ability to change course on a short-term basis based on customer feedback or to better steer the ship based on strategic direction. It naturally forces a dialogue and alignment between stakeholders, decision makers, and executing teams. It also creates a transparency that enables process improvement and talent review.

Aligning SDLC to Agile—What Is Your MVP (Minimal Viable Practice)?

While agile practices will help you organize a team and align to a process, it's only when the process includes software development lifecycle (SDLC) practices that it can ensure successful delivery of "working software" at the end of every sprint. I have found that three key technical practices lead to high-quality software that are also prerequisites to aligning delivery and operational teams (DevOps, which I will cover in the next chapter). These technical practices are establishing version control on all application artifacts, aligning a quality assurance practice, and managing technical debt. The next three sections provide details.

Version Control

I learn most about version control when evaluating an organization's technology practices during due diligence in a merger or acquisition. I'll start by asking whether the team is using version control, and I always get the same answer, "Yes." But after further questions, I learn the reality that there are multiple version control tools and repositories, that not all artifacts are checked into the repositories, that software releases are packaged independent of the repositories, and that there is very little automation connecting builds, tests, and deployments.

It's ridiculous. Developing applications and software needs to be done with basic tools and frameworks. Have you seen a construction crew building a multilevel without scaffolding and other safety constructs? Developing software without basic version control practices adds significant risk that can make it difficult for teams to collaborate, respond to production issues, or work through complex technology upgrades.

Many more organizations today develop proprietary software but are not software businesses and don't know how to implement version control properly. Technology teams in these organizations may be given little time to take steps to set up version control and other development practices. In addition, much of today's development is happening across a multitude of technologies deployed to both data center and Cloud environments. It might be easy to check Java code into Git or SVN, but the tools in your BI or CMS tool may not make it easy to check into the same repository. It is also likely that Cloud and SaaS tools may have completely independent versioning tools.

Yet I can't escape the disciplines that made me a strong developer, team, leader, and Chief Technology Officer. Code was checked in daily with comments. Releases were tagged in version control. Builds were automated and archived. Branches were possible and executed on every time an upgrade was scheduled. Code reviews were triggered when developers checked in code. Code was also tagged to the story, so that testers can click and see exactly what code was modified. When automated unit testing became available, these tests were triggered with every build. Deployments were scripted, and automated pushes to staging environments made the latest version available for internal testing and configuring.

This may sound like science fiction to business and development teams that struggle to keep up with demanding priorities. And, yes, some of this isn't easy to implement without some investment in time and skill, but I would strongly suggest that there be an MVP for these practices to ensure that teams don't create risky development environments that might materially impact a multiyear transformational program.

Here are some basic practices every development team should be able to implement without too much skill or time commitment:

- Your repository should have all the code and configuration. It needs to have everything that's changing with the release. That means database scripts to implement and back out changes, workbook files from BI tools, testing scripts, release notes and other documentation, configuration files, build scripts, and so on. Everything one needs to build, test, and deploy the software should be in the repository.

- All developers need their own accounts to the repositories and should be checking their code in daily with comments on what was changed.
- All releases to production should be packaged from assets in your version control repository—no exceptions, even if the build is done manually.
- All releases need to be versioned. Come up with a simple governance on how version numbers are assigned. Learn how to "tag'" assets in the version control system with the release number and archive the full package of the release in a separate folder.
- Back up your code repository frequently and have a backup (DR) system. You can't afford to have the whole development team out of commission if there is a failure.
- Learn how to connect your development tools (code editor, agile backlog) to your repository. At minimum, find efficiencies in using this integration.

Quality Assurance and Testing

If you're practicing agile development without QA team members, a reasonably defined testing process, and sufficient criteria to help define "done," then at some point your development process will go off the cliff of complexity. The size of your development team, the number of technologies used in the development stack, and the business criticality of the applications are all quality criticality indicators. They shape how much runway IT has before quality factors drive material business risk that can easily overwhelm the development and operations teams. At some point, the development team is going to make application changes where having defined test plans helps avoid issues that might impact users, customers, data quality, security, or performance.

WHY A QA PRACTICE IS CRITICAL TO LONG-TERM SUCCESS

Let's look at some basic concepts that point to why QA is so critical to businesses that rely on technology.

As applications are developed with more features and capabilities, more functions need testing. Every agile sprint increases the testing landscape, and if the discipline to define test cases and establish regression tests isn't developed in parallel, the backlog to create test scripts becomes too hard and long to execute on afterward. If a development team is adding functions and then breaking others, it's likely because regression testing isn't in place to catch these issues.

Applications are more complex involving multitier architectures, multiple databases, transactions spanning multiple APIs, and computing performed on multizone Cloud environments. If you aren't building unit performance tests along the way, then identifying a bottleneck can be a lengthy, painful process when it emerges.

The application may pass all functionality tests, but the data and calculations can be wrong. Many applications today are data driven, enabling their users to make better data-driven decisions. Functional testing isn't sufficient because if the data is wrong, the entire value to the end user is compromised. But, without a defined test strategy, it is hard to test data, validate calculations, understand boundary conditions, and ensure that aggregations or statistic calculations are valid.

A failed application security test may also be costly to fix. Worse is a security failure in production that could have been avoided with security practices entrenched in the development practice. If you're not testing for security issues, then it's unlikely the development team is applying basic security design principles into developed applications.

Finally, today's user experiences span phones, tablets, laptops, IoT devices with different browsers and plugins. Ensuring that user interfaces are functioning and that the user experience is optimized across all these modalities has never been easy; however, customers have minimal patience for mediocre or clumsy experiences.

ALIGNING THE DEVELOPMENT AND TESTING PRACTICES

Many developers don't know how to work with testers and don't have the experience on how to best enable the testers to do their job efficiently. They may finish the development work and throw the completed code over to the testers late in the sprint cycle. When testers are done, they throw any defects back over to the development team to fix. This may volley back and forth until the team hits issues completing the sprint on time.

A testing charter should document any business requirements, the overall risks of the project, and goals for testing. This document should exist for the application and be adjusted for the specifics for each release. The last step is to outline developer and testing responsibilities, as shown in Figure 2-10.

Type of QA Test	Example Goals	Implementation	Responsibilities
Functional testing	Validate API against known inputs and outputs	Requires APIs for key transactions Can be used to validate data quality	Developers wrap API with unit testing harness QA automates test against known input and outputs
User experience	Validate user experience with target devices and expected workflows	Test with priority devices and browsers Simulate common user flows	Product owners, designers, and developers define UX and UI standards QA defines key user experiences to develop tests
Automation	Reduce time to execute regression tests by automating existing functional and user experience tests.	Integrate testing into software build and deployment scripts Validate the full application whenever developers check in new code	Developers select continuous integration and deployment (CI/CD) tools and integrate with testing scripts QA ensures new tests are automated and are integrated into software builds
Security	Ensure application complies to security standards on PII, data security and application vulnerabilities	Leverage and automate security tests Audit with security experts	Developers implements to defined security standards QA run security tests and report findings
Performance and load testing	Test response time and performance under load at API and UI levels	Validate response time for key transactions Ramp up load to determine where response time increases	Developers build performance measures into API and follow coding best practices regarding performance QA executes load tests, pinpoints slow transactions and researches root causes

Figure 2-10. QA test types, risk remediation, responsibilities between development and QA

This matrix is generic and simplified, so you should take steps to align details to your business requirements. Take steps to clearly differentiate development and QA responsibilities and ensure that the team acknowledge their mutual dependencies.

Next, review the sprint schedule and see how to best align the full team's efforts. For example, in a 2-week sprint, I recommend developers complete coding by day seven and leave the final three days for collaborative testing, fixing, and improvements. This changes commitment and team velocity because the team now must consider the effort and time required to develop in fewer days and account for testing. Using the last couple of days of the sprint as a lockdown period also enables the team to look a sprint ahead to evaluate acceptance criteria and size stories appropriately.

Ask teams to have a dialog on which stories they can finish earlier in the sprint cycle. When teams complete a portion of the stories earlier, it allows testing to start earlier and enables the team to have more reliable sprints.

My history working with teams is that, once there are alignment on objectives, practice definitions, and alignment on roles and responsibilities, then they are more likely to collaborate. This applies to the advanced and novice teams that both need to adopt their approaches when working together toward a common goal.

WHY DO MANY ORGANIZATIONS UNDERINVEST IN QA?

With so many things that can go wrong, why do many enterprises and the CIOs that lead them underinvest in QA? The workflow may be broken. The data may be wrong. The user interface may look broken on an Android phone. The performance may be degrading over time. There may be a security hole just waiting for someone to exploit it. There is likely loss of revenue if there is an outage.

There are a couple of fundamental reasons. First, in an effort to keep development costs low, executives mistakenly believe that a team can be more productive by adding programmers rather than testers. This is a flawed assumption because most developers make poor testers. Yes, they should be implementing unit tests to ensure they are not releasing defective code. But when you factor in the other testing responsibilities related to security, regression, automation, performance, browser, and device, most developers don't have the skill, the time, or the interest to execute these disciplines.

When you rely on developers to do the full end-to-end testing, I find that the resulting practice evolves into one of two situations. If your development team isn't skilled with the practices and tools to automate testing, then testing quality suffers, and it simply doesn't happen with any regularity or consistency. The result is compounded over time depending on the gaps of what you should be testing and your ability to execute. What happens next is that developers spend more of their effort fixing things, and executives get angered over the lack of quality. It can lead to a vicious cycle of blame and mistrust.

I've also seen the other extreme where developers make significant investment to develop unit tests, automate them, and promote a zero-defect culture. Even if you have developers that exhibit this mindset, they may not have mastery of all the underlying technologies used to test security, performance, and devices. They are unlikely to have a deep understanding of how to evaluate risk and translate them to a quality assurance program that aims to mitigate risks.

But even in the best of scenarios where your development team has all the practice knowledge and skills to execute on QA program, you should ask yourself and the team whether this is the best use of their time. Is it better for the developers to spend a sizable portion of their day solving the testing challenges, or would you rather see them interacting with the product owner, developing solutions, and driving business results? Should testing be a core competency of your developers, or should you be surrounding them with these skills to enable them to be more productive in areas where they have unique skills to move the business?

So, problem number one is to make sure that executives and developers recognize the need for testing and that it is a separate, distinctive skill set from solutioning and developing the application.

The second fundamental reason businesses underinvest in QA is that they confuse QA with user acceptance testing (UAT). The belief is that the developers build the application and that they should bring in business users to validate, provide feedback, and ultimately sign off on the changes. Why invest in QA when business users are being asked to test anyway?

Testing Discipline	Example QA Testing Questions	Example UAT Questions
Functional testing	Test boundary conditions Automate with different responses Validate error handling	Do I see expected results for simple and more complex use cases?
User experience	Compliant on UX/UI standards Automation of user flows to validate outputs Performance	Is the application simple enough to use for the most critical user flows? Is the application intuitive, and are directions and messages clear?
Data integrity	Manual and automated testing against predefined inputs and outputs	Are there sanity checks against specific searches, filters, and other data considerations?
Performance	Automated testing of specific flows to ensure performance against a defined volume of users	Can I get my work done efficiently?
Security	Validate against known vulnerabilities Test conditions for defined security groups	Do the right people have access to the right capabilities and data?

Figure 2-11. Difference between QA and UAT by testing disciplines

Figure 2-11 illustrates the differences in some of the responsibilities between QA and UAT. You can see that there is a sharp contrast in responsibility and perspective. UAT should be designed to provide feedback on the product or the application from the user's perspective. It aims to answer questions like, "Did we build the right thing?" or "Did we get a requirement wrong?" or "Are users using the application differently than anticipated?" or, possibly, "Are we considering the wrong data sets when evaluating the data accuracy, quality, or visual relevance?"

If you rely on UAT without QA and business users or, worse, customers are doing the testing, then you're likely to run into a couple of issues. First, business users aren't skilled at testing. They don't know how to break things or how to automate tests that can consider many variable conditions through a workflow. You are also likely to run into business user fatigue. Ask them to test once or twice, and you'll likely get their participation, but requiring them to test repeatedly while you make fixes and improvements will frustrate them. You can't expect them to test things with rigor through multiple iterations.

This is where QA comes in. QA must assure the product against a known set of tests. They should be skilled at evaluating risk and looking at methods and tools to mitigate them through testing. The testing is often broken down to different types of testing that require different skills and tools. They need to be able to work with the development team to design tests for stories acceptance criteria, then to automate these into regression tests that ideally run with every build and release. They are there to make sure you are not passing on something "broken" to the business users for their evaluation.

So your second issue compounds the first one. First, executives need to understand and value the role of quality assurance and testing. Second, they should recognize that it's a different set of skills versus development and that surrounding them with good testers will make them more productive. Finally, they should understand the significant limitations involved with having end users test.

If you're getting push back from executives on the investment needed for testing, my advice is to take a step back and educate them on some of these principles. Part of being a transformational leader is recognizing when leaders or members in the organization don't fully understand or embrace a key tenet of driving digital, and this must be addressed. Once explained, it's important to follow up with metrics or KPIs that demonstrate the contribution and effectiveness of the program.

Managing Technical Debt

If you haven't heard this term before, then I would suggest doing some research to get all the details. Technical debt is a form of accounting for bad design, bad code, or technical areas of improvement. It's a technical to-do created by technical team members to announce that they might have cut corners to get a story done or recognize there is a better way to implement something that might be required in the future.

As a transformational leader, you want to encourage teams to acknowledge technical debt. First, it implies that the team doesn't have to design something perfectly on day one and should execute best judgment on targeting a minimal and viable implementation. Second, it means that they have a process to itemize things that need to be fixed, some sooner than later. Once itemized and ideally prioritized, it gives you the opportunity to prioritize remediation or to analyze for cause and solution to technical debt.

But here's the problem. In agile, the priorities of the team are set by the product owner. What if the product owner doesn't care about technical debt? What if she only cares about working on the next feature or improvement and doesn't encourage the team to itemize technical debt or prioritize the improvements? How do you get the product owner to prioritize work on technical debt? How do you get business stakeholders to be interested in seeing performance improvements, security testing, error logging, automated data processing, code commenting, class refactoring, automated testing, platform upgrading, and in addressing other technical debt? It's the most common question I get when discussing agile development with a team of developers that are enthusiastic about maturing their practice.

The simple answer is, without proper culture, incentives, or rules, most product owners will underinvest in fixing technical debt. There are exceptions, but in leading agile transformations, I can tell you that the pressure on product owners is simply too great, and they will almost always drop priorities on technical debt to fulfill stakeholder needs.

The simple way to get technical debt prioritized is for the transformational leader to step in and establish governance requiring a significant percentage of effort applied to this need. I usually set this at 30%, but it can be as high as 40% for complex architectures, legacy applications with significant risk, or mission-critical applications. It can be a lot lower for simple applications.

My rationale is that software companies typically charge 20–30% of license costs to provide support and maintenance. That's for software organizations selling their software, and the typical organization or enterprise isn't going to be as efficient, hence the 30–40% benchmark.

PRIORITIZING TECHNICAL DEBT

Here's the process I endorse:

1. Technical leads and their teams are responsible for itemizing technical debt stories on the backlog at the end of every sprint.
2. Delivery managers or architects are responsible for prioritizing the technical debt and should articulate their rationale for the prioritization.
3. Here's where there's room for a lot of collaboration. The product owner can get some of her needs accomplished within the scope of technical debt if she can articulate business needs as part of technical debt stories. The technical lead can also get more technical debt addressed if it is bundled in properly selected, functionality driven (nontechnical debt) stories. It can then be a win–win when the product owner and technical lead partner on what, when, and how to address technical debt.
4. The product owner and technical lead abide by the agreed-on governance principles to ensure the sprint-level technical debt percentage is addressed. The sprint-level technical debt target should be 5–10% lower than the total technical debt target.
5. The remaining technical debt should be dedicated to one or two technical debt releases per year to address larger system or platform upgrades.
6. Smarter teams will prioritize more technical debt at the start of a multisprint release and do less of this work near the end of the release cycle when the product owner feels more pressure to add more functionality to the release.

Release Lifecycle

Successful sprints get you from point A to point B, but it's only when you release new technology into production environments that you start demonstrating business value. Unfortunately, many organizations look at release planning as the technical communication and collaboration required to move an application into production. In agile delivery, release planning starts a lot earlier, even before the first development sprint. Release planning starts as soon as there is a conversation about the theme for the release, target delivery dates, and an agreement to start work. It's from that point on that teams need to align on scope, quality, dates, and costs and communication with stakeholders' needs to track with ongoing activities.

In this section, I'm going to focus on classic release planning, which targets releases at the end of one or more sprints. Over the last few years, some organizations have matured their business, development, and operational practices to enable a more continuous delivery cycle. That level of automation and sophistication may be appropriate for organizations that develop a lot of software and gain significant competitive advantages by releasing frequently. For other organizations, especially ones developing applications requiring end user training on workflows or others that are tightly integrated with other applications, a scheduled release plan may be more appropriate.

Stages Release Lifecycle

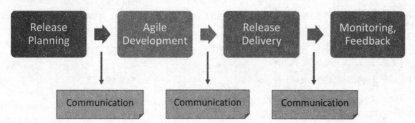

Figure 2-12. Release process illustrating major steps and communication stages

Figure 2-12 shows the release lifecycle with the following stages:

- ▶ Release planning takes place before a release is formally scheduled and the team is debating the type of release, timeline, and target scope.
- ▶ Agile development is when the bulk of the work occurs.
- ▶ Release delivery is where the release is completed and the team is taking steps to finalize testing, oversee UAT, communicate with customers, and follow change management practices.
- ▶ Monitoring, feedback begins after the first deployment to customers when the team is monitoring behavior through

metrics captured from the application or feedback collected directly from the customer for any issues.

You'll notice that at the end of every transition, formal communications are required to keep stakeholders, customers, and other members of the organization knowledgeable on status. Let's first review roles and responsibilities during these stages, as shown in Figure 2-13.

Role	Release Planning	Agile Development	Release Delivery	Monitoring, Feedback
Product owner	Proposes theme and target scope	Realigns priorities and engages UAT team	Customer communication, stakeholder signoff	Leads customer feedback review
Tech lead	Finalizes estimates Proposes number of sprints for the release	Runs agile team, tracks defects, tech debt, velocity Monitors burndown and escalates risks	Reviews final QA Documentation for operations team	Reviews application performance metrics
Business analyst	Schedules prioritized stories and estimation activities into sprints	Writes stories and reviews product Gets defects prioritized	Completes end–of–release documentation	Focuses on next release
Delivery manager	Performs Architecture reviews Reviews and endorses target scope and timeline Ensures tech debt is prioritized	Monitors programs for risk Engages Operations teams Ensures compliance on development and test standards	Ensures operations transition Reviews documentation and technical debt	Reviews performance metrics with operations, development, and product owner

Figure 2-13. Primary responsibilities in release planning

The release cycle represents a cadence of delivering new capabilities and other enhancements to end customers and users. To enable this, team leaders take on different responsibilities depending on stage. Teams are most familiar with the agile development stage where the bulk of the work is being taken on. My experience is that even mature agile teams struggle with the early and later stages, so let's do a brief review of the cycle.

Teams should be reviewing priorities every sprint, developing solutions, and estimating. Most of this work is to enable the first sprints of the release coming after the one in development, so if the team is in the agile development stage for release version 1.5, the estimating activities should be to prepare for release version 1.6. By the time the team is ready to start release planning for 1.6, the backlog should have several epics already estimated and ready for the product owner to prioritize.

My assumption is that your development sprints are two or three weeks long and that releases are one to four sprints in duration. Under these constraints, teams should have fully estimated (but not necessarily sized) releases before they start development work, and that estimating work in the current release is either for epics being scheduled for subsequent releases or are for new epics that the product owner elects to swap into the current release.

Ideally, the release planning stage should be very short. This is a formal step for the product owner to review estimates, consider customer feedback, and finalize the theme and priorities for the release. The technical lead should be doing the same for technical debt, and the team should work together to align on overall priorities. As they begin to set them, the business analyst can begin scheduling stubs, stories, and estimating activities into sprints based on the velocity of the team.

How does one develop and schedule stories into the release? Let's detail this out:

1. The delivery manager should have standards for how many sprints go into a release. Some products and teams operate on a more continuous cycle and release after every sprint, while others plan for major and minor releases of different sprint lengths. The number of sprints selected for each release depends on the nature of the product and the maturity of the team's technology practice. I've found that teams working on consumer products are asked to release frequently and ideally every sprint, while those working on business products can target monthly, quarterly, or even biannual release cycles. Teams that target more frequent releases require more automation in their testing and release steps, while those with less frequent releases can afford to have less automation.

2. Product owners and tech leaders should stick to the release types standardized by the delivery manager and first must select the type of

cycle they are targeting for the release if there are options. One of my teams flipped between major and minor release cycles to enable deploying small fixes and enhancements quickly after a major release was completed.

3. Once selected, the team now knows how many sprints they are working with in their agile development stage.

4. The other variable the team needs to agree on is their velocity—how many points of stories they are going to commit to each sprint. I like using a moving average of the actual velocity of completed stories over the last three sprints.

5. I recommend filling the release schedule with a declining percentage of the peak velocity. So, for example, if the last 3-sprint average velocity was 100 points, I would schedule 90 points of story in the first sprint of the release, 80 in the second, 70 in the third, and so on. This leaves room to add stories during the release period as unknown or new requirements materialize.

6. With that capacity set, the business analyst should schedule stories (or stubs) into sprints based on the priorities set by the product owner and any sequencing set by the technical lead with a couple of guidelines.

   a. Try to get the highest-value or high-risk (and at least medium-value) stories in earlier in the release cycle.

   b. Make sure to schedule in technical debt stories during this exercise.

7. Review with the team to finalize.

Release Cycle Antipatterns and What to Do About Them

The release cycle may sound easy, but it is hard to execute to in practice. Problems occur from at least three conditions: (1) poor execution in the current release, (2) inadequate planning for the next release, (3) the emergence of significant customer feedback that disrupts targeted priorities. Let's review these scenarios as they can be impediments to executing a transformational agenda.

For this section, let's assume the team just finished release 1.0 and is getting ready to start work on release 1.1.

POOR EXECUTION

Poor execution implies that the team released a product with defects and the product owner needs "quick" fixes before going on to what was scheduled for release 1.1. The result is that instead of the team starting work on release 1.1, they are forced to put out one or more patch releases like release 1.0.1, 1.0.2, and so on. The obvious impact is a delay to the schedule of releases plus whatever dissatisfaction the issues create with customers.

Larger development teams can manage the risk in this situation by carving out small support teams to handle patch releases and other support issues. If version control is used properly, these teams can branch the code, work on the fixes, and go through a release cycle with minimal disruption to the development team, which can go onto release 1.1.

Managing this risk in smaller teams is a lot harder. In fact, I've seen many product owners try to get the patches in while keeping release 1.1 on schedule. The best these teams can do is, if they know they are likely to have to release patches, they can build it into their schedule and delay the start of release 1.1 to accommodate.

Neither of these options addresses the root cause, so it's important to have release retrospectives to help teams discuss, identify issues, and seek out solutions.

Poor execution can come from many factors such as ill defined customer expectations, inadequate testing, or pressure to meet tough deadlines that can lead to pushing a release that has quality issues. When the team and product owner meet in a retrospective to discuss these issues, they should document them along with recommendations. They should then sit down with leadership teams starting with the delivery to discuss which remediation is endorsed. Process improvements don't come for free, so if business leaders recognize there are material issues in defective releases they will often be receptive to fixing them.

INADEQUATE PLANNING

A second issue occurs when the team is so focused on release 1.0 that they don't spend adequate time prioritizing, stubbing, and estimating for release 1.1. The result is that when they get release 1.0 to production, they are obliged to invest the time to do this planning and effectively delay the start of development on release 1.1. The problem here is that most of the development team is not involved in this planning, which is largely the responsibility of the product owner, technical lead, and business analyst. The rest of the team is left underutilized until the details of release 1.1 are sorted out.

This situation can occur for a few different reasons. The most common reason is with new teams or team members that may not fully understand the planning practices. They are too consumed working on the current release that they don't allocate time to plan their backlog for future releases. The best remediation for this issue is coaching and monitoring either by the program manager, by the delivery manager, or by a hired agile coach. They need to pull the leadership of this team aside with regular frequency to make sure they dedicate time to future planning.

Another issue is if the team underestimates the work for the current release or is having trouble with code quality or other defects coming from the development team. Both have the same impact, especially on the technical lead. Instead of having time to focus on planning, the technical lead spends efforts getting hands-on either to keep the team on track or to address technical issues created by the team.

Neither of these options is sustainable. If the technical lead is too hands-on solving challenging technical stories, then planning will suffer. If the development team is performing poorly, then having the technical lead step in will also derail planning. It's better to recognize these issues and address them directly rather than let planning fall behind. Releases that have too many technical hurdles should be descoped and simplified rather than tax the technical lead with too much hands-on activity. Development teams that are underperforming must be addressed. Again, it's the role of the delivery manager to recognize these symptoms and take the right prescriptive actions to address the issues.

The other issue occurs if the product owner falls behind. Once releases are out to market, their job becomes triply complicated because they need to manage the current release, plan the next one, and collect feedback on the releases that are already out to market. This can be overwhelming to junior product owners, and planning tends to come in third place versus these other needs.

This is a classic time management issue, and product owners need appropriate management or coaching to recognize and provide advice. Product owners need education, and sometimes some support from more senior leaders on how to balance their time and cutoff involvement on time-consuming issues.

CUSTOMER FEEDBACK PRIORITY AND VISION AMENDMENTS

Getting customer feedback must be viewed as a good thing even if the feedback is negative. At least the team knows the issues or areas of improvement and can reassess their priorities to address them.

But that's not always the case. The team may be excited to work on what was prioritized for release 1.1, and shifting priorities may create angst within the team. In addition, if multiple stakeholders are involved in the program, stakeholders that have been given priority for work in release 1.1 may voice opposition if their deliverables are delayed and if they don't agree that addressing customer feedback has higher priority.

So my first recommendation is that business teams create a defined way on how they process customer feedback. Organizations that are sales driven or are highly sensitive to customer issues are more likely to derail strategic priorities (release 1.1) to address customer feedback. Organizations that are highly customer driven can find themselves chasing feedback and almost never getting to their strategic needs. A vetting process that sorts out "improve immediately" versus "capture and decide later," along with other considerations, is needed in this situation.

The other option is to plan for it. My team at McGraw-Hill Construction did just that and scheduled "minor" releases after every major release to accommodate customer-driven improvements and other fixes. At first, it appeared less desirable because it elongated the timeline to complete a complex roadmap, but, in the end, it had many practical benefits. Improvements were made in the minor release, which was capped in duration. The allocation forced product owners to prioritize customer feedback and ensure the most important issues were addressed. It also gave teams added time to plan release 1.1 without overtaxing their time in release 1.0 on execution. But this approach does come at a cost, and the delivery manager needs to make sure senior leadership understands this strategy.

Continuous Integration and Continuous Delivery

Once you have sprints and release management practices in place, the next level of maturity is to look at releasing changes more easily and frequently. If you can release easily, then you have the option to deploy small improvements or A/B-test new ideas. Product owners often favor the option to release frequently, with the caveat that it doesn't introduce risk or slow down productivity.

Two disciplines enable more frequent, inexpensive, low-risk release cycles. The first, called *continuous integration*, is when the entire software build and test pipeline is fully automated so that new builds can be triggered by events or scheduled. Imagine developers checking in code, testers checking in new testing scripts, and a build with all the application components integrated and tested generated at the end of the day or more frequently. At minimum, this build flags the team whether it "passed" or "failed" and enables them to address issues long before release timelines become a risk.

Continuous delivery takes this process one step further and enables the deployment of new builds to computing environments. Some organizations will implement continuous delivery to staging environments so that internal subject matter experts can review changes or perform user acceptance testing on the latest build.

Other organizations will take this one step further and use continuous delivery to push production builds out with greater frequency. They can do this by moving to a single sprint release cycle, then look to shorten the duration of sprints. Teams must have significant confidence in their testing capabilities to perform production releases with this frequency. Frequent production releases work best when application changes have low impact on users, such as SaaS platforms that enable new turn-on-when-needed capabilities. On the other hand, frequently releasing changes to applications with many users performing important tasks is a lot more challenging.

While continuous integration and delivery are highly desirable, they are not optimal in every business situation. It takes a lot more skill, maturity, and expertise in new tools in the development team to implement. It also needs a strong partnership between development and operations teams to technically enable continuous delivery and for business teams to manage this rate of change.

At minimum, these DevOps practices are good targets for teams so that they develop more automation. Continuous integration should be a goal for mature development teams working on new applications but may be more challenging on legacy applications, applications that have regulatory requirements, or teams that are new to agile delivery. On the other hand, the business may be competing with new entrants that deploy new capabilities very frequently. If this becomes a competitive advantage to them, then implementing these DevOps practices should be a higher priority in the transformation program.

Transformational Improvements Through Agile

So, with this framework, you now know how to deliver transformational improvements. Let's recap:

1. Define the governance regarding team structure, roles, responsibilities, tools, sprint length, release types, and estimation guidelines.
2. Leverage agile planning to enable the development of roadmaps. Use agile practices to execute in a sprint, then use the agile planning practices to get visibility into future sprints.
3. Ensure that you are developing your technical and testing practices in parallel inasmuch as agile execution helps only to the extent that there is an underlying strong technical practice.
4. Formalize release plans to align agile teams with customers and business stakeholders.

What you've just given your team is a working process to make technological improvements based on strategic priorities and adjusted for customer feedback. It enables the team to prioritize based on value, complexity, and cost, and leverages the team's expertise to consider multiple solutions to any given challenge. It's structured in its definition of roles, responsibilities, and timelines but flexible in how it's applied to different organizational structures, geographical distributions, and other challenges.

But agile is a practice, and it by itself isn't going to make the IT team fully capable to solve transformational challenges. With a practice defined, we now need to turn toward the underlying guts of the technology itself and how the business operates.

3.

TECHNICAL FOUNDATIONS FOR TRANSFORMATION

Introducing the New IT Operations

I learned much of what I know today about systems operations from Bill, a head of network engineering that I hired at a startup about 15 years ago. We had already built separate systems for managing development and testing from production, matured source code controls, and implemented some automation around testing and deployment. What Bill taught me is that we needed to separate developers from production environments because they required a different mindset, tools, and practices to keep production environments secure, stable, and scalable.

He was right. After removing access, instrumenting some basic change control practices, and improving monitoring of our systems, we saw better stability and performance. We also saw better developer productivity largely because they were now more focused on development tasks and less on operations. There was some grumbling about procedures and some finger-pointing when things went wrong, but as the CTO I accepted most of it since the teams behaved well most of the time, and there were measurable improvements in both "Dev" and "Ops."

This step of separating duties between operations and development is what many startups must execute for them to scale. But when I joined The McGraw-Hill Companies as CIO at *Businessweek*, I needed to transition in the opposite direction. Everything was operational or support, and there was very little actual development going on.

It's easy to see how this happens. A business team develops a case for a new capability, and an investment is made to instrument it. A new CRM, CMS, or other platform is installed, and a team goes in to configure it for business purposes. The project funds the installation and development from its initial installation through several improvements and upgrades, but at some point, there is business leader fatigue to continue investing in the practice and platform. They cut staffing and oversight to this platform, and in the best of situations, they leave a skeleton group around to provide support.

And what is support? Well, most enterprises will have a service desk responding to incidents and requests. This team handles the intake and is usually pretty good at responding when there is a system's issue or need. Maybe a user needs access or a system is unresponsive. In small operational teams, they may also handle a few recurring engineering tasks such as patching, performing application upgrades, monitoring backups, testing disaster recovery, and ensuring that system resources such as network, storage, and system are meeting business needs. But as soon as there is an issue with the underlying applications, addressing it is often beyond the skills of the service desk professionals, and a developer or specialist is needed to resolve it. These responsibilities are what many organizations call support. But that's not all that application support teams typically handle.

When enterprise systems are rolled out, care is taken to service the infrastructure and the underlying business processes. This often leaves many administrative areas as "support tasks," which require a human to intervene and follow steps in order to complete them. Examples include processing data feeds, adding or removing users, or modifying data when there is something new or there is a change. This not only happens with enterprise systems but is even more likely to happen with homegrown applications. In the best of situations, these administrative tasks are handled by tools and workflows, but sadly many systems are deployed without these provisions, and administration requires technical skills to script a procedure, go on a production system to kick off a job, or access the database to modify data.

So, when you step into any organization that has a mix of enterprise and proprietary applications, you see common patterns of how they are managed. Most of the IT team is in support mode. In the best of situations, they have few incidents and requests coming in and have sufficient technical skills to do some development and basic improvements to the underlying applications. In cases where that hasn't happened, these applications fall behind in basic lifecycle management and are either near or past their end of life. When that happens, there is complete paralysis among the IT staff to make changes or perform upgrades.

That's how applications and systems truly degrade to legacy status. Between a lack of resources and skills, lost knowledge, and poorly documented testing practices, the entire organization develops a rational fear of performing upgrades. When an upgrade is finally commissioned for a legacy system, there's a reasonable chance that it will disrupt business users and create a complete lack of confidence in investing in new technologies or partnering on improving business processes.

Now here's the key question: How are you supposed to execute a transformational effort when all your IT staff is barely supporting the existing applications?

Agile Operations Defined

Let's look at the two preceding scenarios and see how we can bring them together. In the first scenario, we have a startup whose business is starting to scale and needs to grow and separate out operational responsibilities. The goal is to make sure the applications are performing well, that infrastructure can scale and developers can be freed up to focus on the customer and product enhancements.

The second scenario evolved over time, and virtually all the staff is on the operational side to the extent that very little customer-driven or strategic improvements are occurring. In this scenario, development responsibilities need to be separated out from support related tasks.

These two scenarios, one likely happening in small startups and the other in larger, more established organizations, have a common organizational solution. Figure 3-1 represents a target end state organization and responsibilities.

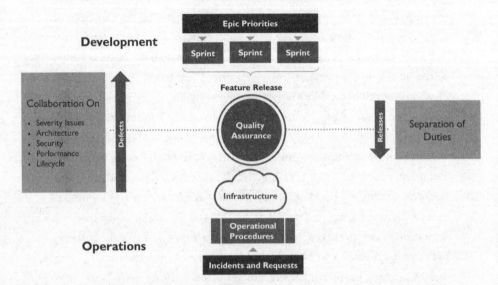

Figure 3-1. Defining DevOps practices maximizing agility and operational responsiveness

Development teams take a prioritized list of epics as their primary input and are responsible for delivering customer and strategic improvements through agile sprints and releases. With respect to operations, their goal is to hand over releases that adhere to technical standards, deploy easily, introduce few operational issues, and include updates to any operational procedure.

Operations teams are procedural and are driven by incidents and requests escalated by users, by recurring and standardized operational processes, or by operational projects that get prioritized. Their goal with respect to development teams is to free them of operational issues. When there are issues that require fixes to the applications, they escalate these to the development team as defects.

Quality assurance responsibilities and tasks enable this separation of duties. Releases need to be certified that they meet business requirements and technical standards. When defects are raised, QA's job is to triage them, determine severity, and ideally suggest a course of remediation to development teams, who then need a workflow to add them to the development backlog.

There are times when these teams must collaborate. Collaboration is often required if there is a severity issue affecting customers. Many IT departments will convene a "war room" to bring individuals with the right knowledge and skills to triage and resolve the issue. Another time is when changes are needed that require steps and skills by both teams like architecture changes or higher-risk infrastructure upgrades.

This structure can be contracted and expanded in two dimensions. Larger enterprises are more likely to have this separation in place already, and the strategic challenge is getting funding, resources, and practices to establish development teams that can perform ongoing improvements. But even the smallest of startups can have these practices. Even when there is a single CTO in a new startup, separating development activities from operational responsibilities enables scaling the operation when the business grows.

While I am showing multisprint releases, this separation is still required for teams that have the tools, skills, and practices defined to perform continuous delivery. In those situations, the testing, deployment, and operational practices are automated to an extreme that it enables development to push very frequent releases with very low operational impacts.

Let's look at the organizational responsibilities in more detail.

Development Teams Must Align with Business Priorities

The development team should operate as the technology extension of the business. This means that they must be looking to provide expertise in enterprise applications and specifically on how business users can be more productive, drive data-driven decisions, connect with customers, or make supply chains more efficient. It means that they should be spending their time learning user needs, researching solutions, or building and enhancing applications. Ideally, developers ought to be spending 70–80% of their time working with users on new capabilities and ideally only 20–30% on "support."

I'm using "support" as a catchphrase for time spent on anything that is not development toward building or improving applications. It can be chasing an operational incident or diagnosing a defect. It can also be upgrading versions of anything from an enterprise application to a JavaScript library used in an application.

It can also be anything technical to make the development team more efficient. It can be investing time in configuring version control, automating builds, or scripting deployments. It can be time spent researching technology tools. All this time, while very critical to an efficiently running development program, is time balanced against direct efforts to improve the business.

More than just how developers spend their time, the impact of responding to noncritical operational issues is a major distraction from their development activities. Picture developers with their heads down, headphones on, intensely banging away at multiple screens being distracted several times while coding a critical algorithm to answer user requests escalated from the operations team. It not only disrupts the concentration required to engineer efficient, defect-free code; it also affects their psyche. Developers that anticipate these distractions have no choice but to lower their agile commitments to have bandwidth to respond to operational needs and manage through the distractions. In extreme situations where the distractions are significant, it can degrade the working environment to the extent that top developers may seek to leave the organization.

While development teams optimize for speed and agility, they may compromise stability and quality. Sometimes this happens because of business pressure to release upgrades quickly, or because QA is underfunded and can't adequately test everything, or possibly because they are new to a technology and can't anticipate exactly how it will perform in a production environment. It may also happen if there isn't sufficient infrastructure to perform different types of testing or if the data available in testing environments does not sufficiently match the disparity, velocity, or volume of data in the production setting. However this happens, it is the operations team that often feels the pain points of remediating what the development team released, and their goal is to minimize the impact to end users.

Operations Align with Stability and Reliability

While development is optimizing for speed and may compromise reliability, operations teams have the opposite charter and look to ensure the performance and reliability of the environment as their top priority. Their practices, such as incident management and change management, align with this charter and aim to protect the business from disruption. Disruption can be outages that affect customers and business operations but also include incidents that hamper organization productivity.

The by-product of protecting the organization is often rigidity. Examples include infrequent time windows for change management or lengthy lead times to deploy new infrastructure. Operations teams may also have a very limited, IT-centric view of service levels when they define uptime at a system or even application performance level rather that a business success metric.

Why do operations teams become so rigid with their practices, and what's the impetus to get them to become more agile? The rigidity starts with the nature of their work of protecting the enterprise, which requires them to develop standard operating procedures. They have change management practices, but their culture evolves to be less flexible because of the number of times they have been burned over the years managing bad deployments and defective applications.

It's not just the pace of business and application development that has changed, it's also the technologies. Instead of managing racks, servers, networks, storage arrays, and appliances, many organizations are moving more workloads to Cloud environments. Instead of maturing information technology infrastructure library (ITIL) practices and learning how to diagnose infrastructure, operations teams must manage vendors, keep up with growing security needs, and support more flexibility around computing devices. In addition to providing more business and data services related to the enterprise applications, there are now more customer-facing applications with even higher demands of reliability.

So, operations departments still have the same charter of protecting the enterprise but are now facing the need to do so faster, with new technologies, with more personalization, to greater business impact, against a wider variety of security threats, within the requirements of greater regulatory controls, and at lower cost.

What Is DevOps?

DevOps is about the culture, collaborative practices, and automation that aligns development and operations teams so that they have a single mindset on improving customer experiences, responding faster to business needs, and ensuring that innovation is balanced with security and operational needs. For development teams, that usually means standardizing platforms, following an agile development process, and participating in operationally driven initiatives. For operations teams, it means targeting better stability, reducing costs, and improving responsiveness.

"DevOps" is a recent industry term used to describe the organizational structure, practices, and culture needed to enable the services businesses require inasmuch as the importance of reliable and improving technology in the organization and to customers is a competitive necessity. Most experts in the industry agree on many of the core DevOps practices that center around infrastructure configuration standards, automation, testing, and monitoring. Everyone agrees that DevOps requires cultural and mindset changes in IT. But not everyone agrees on the organizational structure and how responsibilities are assigned between development and operational teams.

Some stress a merging of development and operational people and responsibilities so that one DevOps team carries both responsibilities. This does have some cultural advantages as both developers and engineers are now forced to respond as a team to both operational and business needs. Some argue that this structure is more efficient especially in smaller shops that can't easily dedicate resources to focus on development or operations independently. Many also argue that when you standardize on Cloud infrastructure and automate everything, there is less of a need for having separate people with different skills and responsibilities.

While this may be possible, it's a difficult hill to climb for organizations carrying legacy systems and without super skilled engineers that can enable all the standards and automation. Even when that's possible, I still believe that most organizations that are driving digital need to separate first, achieve their digital business agendas, and then perhaps look to merge when there is a maturity of IT practices. It's from this perspective that I will define DevOps and how transformational organizations need to implement it.

HOW DEVOPS EVOLVED

You can understand how DevOps evolved by looking at what happens when an organization big or small begins to execute an agile development practice.

An agile development team is humming along, maturing its practice, putting out regularly scheduled application releases, improving quality, and making business users happy. Then, something happens. Maybe the infrastructure needs an upgrade or needs to scale. Maybe there is a difficult to diagnose performance issue. Or maybe the business and development teams are looking to deploy a new enterprise application to support a new capability.

Operating teams are confronted with a wave of change that they historically haven't been accustomed to supporting. They go back to classic operational procedures that were designed to manage data centers with heterogeneous computing environments. They attempt to apply them to the new requirements of supporting frequent agile-driven application releases, enterprise applications that now run in the Cloud, or sophisticated transactions that involve API connections to multiple environments.

Confronted with these new challenges, two behaviors emerge. First, many in operations hold to their procedures that have worked for them in the past and try to force these new demanding channels of activity into existing practices. It often doesn't work because existing practices were never designed for the speed of change or for the flexibility of different computing environments and workload. The net effect is that their resistance slows down development teams and the business as they adjust their operational practices and skills.

The other thing that happens is that some on the development team attempt to take over some of the operational responsibilities. This is facilitated by the availability of Cloud infrastructure that can be purchased by a credit card and a few clicks. Even after that, the developer may have the better skill sets to fully operationalize this environment since most of it can be configured with web tools and scripting. Need to configure load balancers? It's a few clicks. Need to automate the elasticity of the front-end web servers? No problem, just develop scripts with the appropriate business rules and connect to the Cloud service provider's APIs. If the operations team can't get the developers what they need and when they need it, skilled developers can sometimes challenge them by taking on these responsibilities.

When these scenarios occur, the question is whether the operations teams are ready to partner with development teams on the timing, complexity, or scale of the task at hand. *When there is a mismatch in culture, values, methodology, timing, skills, or operational practices, a classic Dev vs. Ops clash arises.* Finger-pointing, bottlenecks, anger, or isolation may form between the development and operational teams.

It's not just business or development driven needs and issues that can drive this rift. Perhaps developers are pushing changes and breaking operational procedures. Maybe there is a mismatch between an application and some required systems upgrade that's holding back operations from maintaining an environment. Or maybe development isn't as good as they think they are in releasing defect-free, secure, high-reliability applications that perform well, and operations is left holding the bag responding to outages.

DevOps aims to reduce this conflict. It attempts to educate developers on operational responsibilities and operations teams on how to serve business needs smarter and faster. When there is a shared understanding and a better alignment on priorities and process between the development and operations team, a more customer-centric DevOps culture emerges.

The basic technical concept in DevOps is that, as you automate more of the interactions with the infrastructure from building, testing, deploying, and monitoring, you can remove many operational defects and better align development and operations processes. From a practice point of view, the big questions involve what tools and to what degree to invest developing any single DevOps practice area.

WHO IMPLEMENTS DEVOPS?

When I've discussed DevOps with colleagues, other CIOs, and DevOps practitioners, the big divide is who "owns" DevOps. Does the DevOps starting spark come from developers encroaching into operational responsibilities? Is it operations engineers who standardize configurations and push developers to align their development and release practices? Or is it better to reorganize into a single DevOps team that collectively owns this practice and its maturity?

I'm not sure if there is a consensus best practice on this question, but it certainly is one of the more heated topics around DevOps. While all will acknowledge that DevOps requires a culture change, there is some debate on who should take ownership and how to align the IT organization to achieve business and operational benefits.

DevOps practices are designed to make development more reliable and operations more agile and nimble and effectively help each organization with its weakness. For development, practices such as automating test cases, scripting application deployments, and standardizing application builds all aim to improve the quality and reliability of handoffs from development into operations. For operations, standardizing system configurations, automating server changes, and scripting Cloud operations are all tools to help automate operational tasks and enable them to be more agile with infrastructure. Therein lies the transformation, more specifically a better balance between agility and stability.

DevOps practices are most often associated with the following technologies and services:

- **Configuration management** tools store infrastructure configurations in a database and help automate setup and integration. New server configuration, installing applications, adding storage are all operations that can be automated. Container services enable build, ship, and run applications on different types of environments.
- **Code deployment** tools integrated with configuration management know what environments exist, provide visuals on applications deployed, and enable automated mechanisms to deploy new application versions or back out ones if there are issues.

- **Testing tools** make it easier to develop regression tests and automate them to run during application builds or deployments.
- **Change management** operations formalize procedures for versioning and backing out changes to computing environments and applications.
- **Monitoring systems** automate data capture from many disparate systems and provide tools to diagnose root causes of complex performance or stability issues.

As organizations invest more in application development, these practices become more important in order to enable predictable and stable releases. Configuration management enables scaling the infrastructure. Code deployment automation enables easy changes and back-outs when required. Automated testing establishes quality validations to occur repeatedly and quickly. Change management formalizes controls that aid in diagnosing production issues. Monitoring helps alert staff on when an application or system isn't performing as expected.

Most of this is enabled in software tools or in scripting, especially in Cloud environments. An inevitable problem for many organizations is defining who owns these practices.

In the emergence of DevOps tools and practices, some agile development teams have taken the initiative and gone beyond their core responsibilities into system and operational domains. Some argue that because technologies like Docker and Chef and Puppet enable software-driven configuration management and scripted system deployments, it now falls under development responsibilities to program virtual environments and automate their scalability.

Recall that I target developers to spend at least 70% of their time on development efforts that directly improve business capabilities. That means they devote only 30% of their time to operational and support tasks like responding to incidents, addressing application lifecycle issues, resolving technical debt, and improving development processes. These are critically important, but keeping up with these responsibilities is a tall order and difficult to fulfill within their 30%.

Developers, especially ones being asked to drive digital, simply do not have the time to take on additional operational responsibilities. They should not be involved configuring servers or automating their configurations. If they are going to participate in a DevOps transformation, they should support their operations teams by focusing on the development practices of DevOps such as standardizing their application builds, automating testing, or strengthening their version control practices.

Agile development teams should be self-organizing, but if there is a need to take on DevOps practices, they may elect to put this work on their own backlog. A product owner that senses infrastructure or operational gaps may support them. If there is a strong cultural divide with the operations team, if there is weak governance on procuring Cloud infrastructure, or if there aren't practices to ensure that development priorities are applied to appropriate technical functions, then agile teams may cross the line and take on operational practices.

I doubt agile teams would like their product owners to start designing databases or developing technical standards (though some try to) because they lost confidence in their development teams. Development teams need to have a similar respect and collaboration with their operations teams regarding operational responsibilities.

If operations teams aren't getting it done and DevOps is a strategic priority for business transformation, then the technology leaders need to work out the details of roles, responsibilities, skills, and platforms. If the CIO accepts developers handling operational responsibilities, then it might create longer-term animosities or produce conflicts with fulfilling business priorities.

DEVOPS PRACTICES ARE ABOUT AGILE OPERATIONS

My perspective is that most of the DevOps practice areas should be owned by operational teams. The ones that are tied to application development, such as version control, testing, and automating builds, are exceptions and should be owned by the development teams especially if continuous delivery is a priority. Here's some additional rationale why operations teams should be stepping up:

- The largest benefit in Cloud environments falls with enterprises that manage thousands of server instances and petabytes of data and where standardization and automation provide significant cost advantages.

New tools like Docker, Puppet, and Chef are designed to automate configuration management to these extremes, but it is Ops that should learn the technology and take on the responsibility of configuring them.

- Agile development teams have already aligned their efforts to business-driven priorities, but their frustration is when operations or the infrastructure can't support frequent changes. Perhaps development needs to spin up new environments to test an upgrade or evaluate a new platform, and it takes too long to configure. Maybe releases need to be scheduled more frequently, but the deployment steps are too complicated. Operations should collaborate with development to define application, configuration, and other changes that will enable them to perform these activities at more demanding service levels.

- The increase in Cloud instances and applications, along with higher expected service levels from customers and stakeholders require an updated approach to monitoring applications and collecting performance data. Applications need many more monitors, real-time alerts, and longer time frame performance trending. Operations teams need to invest in their skills to respond to this greater need.

- Security is only going to get more business critical and more difficult to perform. Because operations are in the front lines protecting security, they are in a better position to drive infrastructure and configuration standards that help simplify the disparity of assets that need secure configurations and support.

- Server loads are increasingly more dynamic especially when many applications must handle variable loads driven by global, Big Data, or mobility computing needs. Operations are already versed in handling load balancers, application clusters, storage area networks, software defined networks and other technologies to dynamically scale system resources in the data center. Cloud technologies offer these and more capabilities, but the tools and methods configuring them are different. Cloud and automation tools might require more "coding" but should not be outside of operations' ability to learn.

Operations teams and engineers should seize the day and take responsibility for these improvements and transformations. When agile development teams elect to tackle these challenges, they are doing the overall business a disservice by focusing on operational needs rather than business improvement drivers.

Transforming to Agile IT Operations

A CIO should recognize when one team needs support and another team is overrunning them. If an operations team is struggling with the new DevOps practices and tools, the CIO needs to step in and pace the program accordingly. A CIO driving a DevOps transformation should look to invest in the following areas:

- ▶ Defining roles and responsibilities so Dev and Ops people under- stand who owns what practices and where collaboration is required
- ▶ Bringing in a coach who adapts to the CIO's and organization's governance to help define and transition the culture
- ▶ Recognizing and addressing skill gaps by bringing in experts, investing in training, and providing sufficient time for practicing new skills
- ▶ CIO may also consider bringing in outsourcing partners to address some of the DevOps skills or to provide manage services around Cloud infrastructure.
- ▶ Resolving the potential conflicts on platform and technology selections by engaging both development and operations and creating a selection process
- ▶ Defining reasonable scopes and goals especially on transformation initiatives and articulating a timeline

The CIO owns the DevOps transformation. Transformation requires a senior leader to sponsor the investment, prioritize the effort, drive the culture, and market the wins.

But regarding development and operations collaborating through a transformation, the CIO needs to step in and be very specific about what challenges and opportunities to address. In what areas does development need to be more stable? To what business benefit and to what extent does operations need to improve monitoring? When instituting a configuration management tool, what is operation's primary objectives, and where must development contribute? The CIO needs to lead these discussions, set priorities, and secure the collaboration required to make this transformation successful.

A DevOps transition for an existing business or enterprise is not trivial. There are several strategic challenges for large businesses going through a DevOps transition.

The first is financial. Most of IT operations today is wrapped in sunk infrastructure costs and operational practices developed over significant amounts of time. Many organizations simply can't afford the dual costs of running legacy infrastructure while developing Cloud infrastructure and new DevOps practices. In addition, there is also the shift of what were capital infrastructure investments in data centers, servers, storage, and licenses to Cloud, SaaS, and services that are usually sold through subscriptions charged to operational budgets.

The second one is talent and skills. Cloud engineering, automation, and software-driven configuration management are all new skills for IT operations that have been operating data centers of heterogeneous platforms and workloads. Simply giving them Cloud infrastructure and new tools is not sufficient to reach the automation for continuous delivery.

The third issue remains cultural. Even once you get some alignment on DevOps roles and responsibilities, platforms, and priorities, getting practice areas redefined so that it drives positive business impact remains a challenge.

Therefore, DevOps must be managed as a transformational program; otherwise it will likely fall short of expectations. It can be even worse if the CIO succeeds only in driving a partial transition in technologies, leaving too much unaddressed legacy systems and practices. The CIO also must address how business users perceive the transformation and work with the new services. For example, if business users skip the service desk and walk right up to the development team for their immediate needs, then a key objective of the transformation of freeing up development resources will fail or fall short.

My recommendation to CIO is to build this up as a transformational program slowly. Start with a few practice areas and get some success leveraging Cloud, developing automation, or advancing monitoring. Pace what is added to the programs based on achieving business-impacting success, so drive harder when you achieve it and slow down if it requires more time or investment to materialize. In these early experiments, avoid programs that require material investments, training, or organizational changes.

At some point, the cultural conflicts will emerge. You might see debates on platforms, arguments on who owns what practices, conflicts over priorities, or stress from trying to drive both agile and DevOps programs. It's at this point that the CIO needs to articulate DevOps as a transformational program and lay out a vision and charter to the staff. They need to be aligned on strategic drivers and then asked to participate in defined priorities and articulated goals.

The vision and charter should be modest because the CIO hasn't brought business leaders on board with the program. Having some defined success on early programs is exactly where the CIO needs to start but then needs to define the business details of the program, showing the benefits, priorities, investments, organizational change, roadmap, and financial impact. Failing to position this transformation for business leaders will mean that the CIO is likely to get cut off as soon as there is business impact, organizational conflict, or significant investment.

Here are some things the CIO should consider preparing to present the transformation:

- Focus on a description of benefits aligned with business drivers, especially demonstrating opportunities for business growth or other areas where regulation is going to require investment.
- Define priorities in business terms, ideally with meaningful business metrics. Minimize how these translate to technical priorities.
- Be very clear and transparent on the organizational impact especially in IT investing in skills, hiring resources, and possibly reorganizing the team. You're likely going to need help from HR and other leaders to execute this change.
- Make sure you present a realistic roadmap. It needs to be reasonably detailed for the first six months, but the full scope should be represented.

> ► Get help articulating a financial model showing current versus future state costs and transition investments. Make sure your colleagues understand that this is a model that will need to be updated as more decisions are quantified during the transformation.
> ► Be specific on how communications will be handled during the program and when the leadership team can expect updates.

With two practice transformations now defined—agile largely for development groups and DevOps largely for operational teams—let's now look at key aspects of technology, platforms, and architecture that drive digital.

Agile Architecture

Developing extendable technology platforms is what makes agile businesses nimble. For simplicity, I'm going to call a *platform* any single technology or stack of technologies designed to be leveraged in more than one product, application, or business process. Since a product or business process is somewhat fungible, what I mean is more than one application developed for more than one target user group.

It's easy to see the economics of why establishing reusable platforms fares better than adding optimal platforms for every business case. Consider all the startup costs from selecting a technology, physical installation, configuration, integration, training, and developing support processes that make up overhead above developing applications. Even if the technology is SaaS or Cloud deployed, there are still startup costs to research the technology, negotiate on price, evaluate service levels, pilot its use, and share knowledge.

What is difficult to understand or estimate is the benefit when individuals and teams develop a competence with the platform. In addition to better productivity, the team develops better expertise to guide the business on capability, feasibility, and innovation applying it in new contexts. Strong teams will develop reusable components and services that promote speed and quality of future applications.

Challenges in Selecting Technology Platforms

Finding extendable platforms has been the role of CTOs, application architects, and enterprise architects. Individual systems are considered "building blocks" of the architecture that can be assembled efficiently toward new business benefits. We like to think in idealistic conditions that platforms will work as advertised, applications and system interfaces will perform as expected, developers will be able to leverage the capabilities in standard ways, and business sponsors will leverage the capabilities and reduce their appetite for customized solutions.

But as technologists, we all know it isn't that easy. First, it's hard to get any new platform selected, installed, leveraged for a first business case, and then structured so that it can be reused in new business cases. In many situations, IT teams fumble through the initial project, sometimes because they don't fully understand the platform and how to use it properly, other times because they've been oversold by the vendor on its capabilities, and sometimes because the business sponsors push the team to customize the platform's configuration beyond its best capabilities. Likely all three happen, and by the time the project is done, there's enough spilled blood among the technologists that implemented it, the vendor, and the business sponsors that there is little appetite to apply new business cases.

A second issue is that business leaders, regardless of what IT assets already exist in the enterprise, go out and select technologies that "best" fit their needs. This is one flavor of "Rogue IT" because business leaders often do this without any support of IT, and when things go afoul, they either blame IT for the problems or push IT to manage the issues with a problematic vendor that they didn't have a voice in selecting..

In some cases, these business leaders may not be rogue and will partner with IT to select platforms. But their motivation remains to pick something that suits their business needs first, with secondary business needs a distant afterthought. The problem remains that a single "point" solution is being selected for a business need, not a business platform that is intended to be the basis of transformation. Every time a business leader selects a new solution, it's one more asset the enterprise needs to pay for and support and one less that will help propel standards.

A third problem involves the platforms themselves. The most versatile platforms are programming environments like Java, PHP, Javascript, and Microsoft .Net, which offer complete programming flexibility at the cost of instrumenting tools, maturing development practices, and selecting third-party components to help accelerate development. Your other option is to select higher-level platforms that provide an out-of-the-box solution for a specific business need and with sufficient configuration capability that it can be tailored without custom programming to business need. Examples include CRM, ERP, BPM data integration, content management, and business intelligence platforms, which all deliver customer and internal-facing workflows and reporting. The most capable platforms then offer APIs, SDKs, App Stores, and full development environments, enabling technology teams to either integrate across platforms or to engineer customized capabilities.

The problem, of course, is that virtually all technology platforms are now marketing these extendable capabilities but are not all equally capable. Are they easy to learn? Are they sufficiently flexible? Do they offer defined testing capabilities? Do the vendors provide adequate support to developers? When there is a platform upgrade, do they ensure that applications connected to their development interfaces continue to work without modification? Do they provide sufficient operational logging or diagnostic information? Are they transparent with performance and security considerations?

Bottom line is that programmatic platforms is a maturing space and not all of them perform equally. It takes a lot of learning, prototyping and investment to discover what really works, what's maturing, and what is hype.

The last step is getting the developers on board with the skills and practices to make architecture and platform practices a reality. Some developers can code but lack the engineering experience to know how to structure code for reuse. Other developers are versatile and fast but want to develop things "their way" without considering other people's code or defined architectures. Some developers are conservative and want to stick with platforms they know or ones from specific vendors; others love to shop and tinker with the latest coding tools.

What CIO and IT leaders need are developers who buy into the architecture and development practices, have the skills to develop off the selected platforms, and have sufficient business acumen to be able to recommend appropriate solutions. They need platforms that enable superstars to deliver amazing innovative solutions but that also let average developers build, enhance, and support applications. It's a difficult intersection of skills, and it takes some time to cultivate this mindset.

Selecting Agile Platforms

Given the constraints, investment, and patience it takes to establish technology platforms along with their importance to the transformation effort, it is critical that a high level of care is taken in their selection. There are several criteria and considerations technology leaders should leverage when undergoing a platform selection or review. I call these agile platforms, and they have the following properties:

- **Delivers a user experience that people love**—Reviews of digital business and technologies starts with an analysis of user experience across multiple sales channels (omnichannel) and device (multimode and especially mobile). This is for good reason because if the experience sucks, if it doesn't simplify life for end users, if the value proposition is irrelevant, if the data and experience are not ubiquitous across devices, if the user interface isn't intuitive or if it exhibits other poor usability considerations, then the platform will fail to achieve the desired transformation goals.
- **Fast and easy to learn**—It lets average developers learn and be productive with short ramp-up time. It has a combination of tools and documentation that lets the whole team start using it quickly.
- **Built on standards**—It's easier to find developers with skills in "standard" platforms and harder to find niche vendor platforms with proprietary methodologies. Also, consider that many platforms die and if you need to migrate, you will want the coding to be largely portable.
- **Has an open, extendable architecture**—This means the vendor can't enable all the desired capabilities, and sometimes the platform needs

to be extended for proprietary needs. Also, the platform doesn't live in its own ecosystem, and it probably needs to be integrated with other services, applications, and data sources. Does it have a published API that's easy to understand and leverage? Can it be developed and deployed in Cloud or virtual environments? Is there a healthy ecosystem of development partners, plugins, and other components?

- **Well-defined performance/scalability**—Because no one wants a platform that requires lots of servers for low levels of activity. "Well-defined" means that the platform's architects have documented, benchmarked, and delivered tools to help developers know the performance and scalability boundaries of the platform. It should have defined approaches to monitor capacity.

- **"Easy" to install, configure, and administer**—I'd like the operations team to own the production environments, and developers need to be hands-off them. Agile platforms need the basic tools for administrators to perform their functions easily and quickly.

- **Must support Big Data**—If it's easy to learn, then a development team should be able to prototype applications easily. But if it can't scale to handle larger volumes of data, then these prototype applications may be no more than "tinker ware," that is, nice applications that can't be deployed to end users or customers.

- **Easy diagnostics and troubleshooting**—If the development or operations team needs to call the platform's Technical Support, then that's a big red flag. Good error messages, diagnostic tools, and useful log messages are all minimal requirements.

- **Well-defined security model**—Security capabilities often need to be evaluated prior to any prototyping, so the model and capabilities need to be well-defined and easy to leverage.

- **Has embraced self-service capabilities**—"Enterprise" applications enable configuration and customization capabilities largely by providing application development and administrative tools to the IT staff. Today's SaaS platforms are better measured by how easy and how much of this configuration can be accomplished easily and correctly (without complications or quality issues) by nontechnical business users. Many self-serve applications allow users to customize look/feel, publish forms, configure dashboards and reports, enable simple workflows, or perform common data operations. The more sophisticated platforms are fully self-service and enable "citizen developers" through simple visual interfaces, low-code tools, or entire desktop applications fully designed for business self-service.

- *Has achieved critical mass of fanatical developers and users*—At minimum, users and developers should love the technology and be promoting it on social media. The vendor's conferences should have huge attendance and growing every year. Chances are if the social sentiment of a technology is strong, it's a significant endorsement that it's easy, powerful, versatile, secure, and stable. Developers and users do not socially endorse platforms too easily or have the budgets to attend conferences regularly, so when you see thousands of daily tweets, tens of thousands attending the conference, subreddits[1] that have frequent and positive feedback, then it's a sign that this is an easy to use platform that has made others successful in a wide variety of opportunities.

Why do I list these criteria as business and not technical driven? If you ask the vendors, existing customers, or third-party analysts to evaluate the size, financial strength, or customer satisfaction of the technology, then you're likely to get an incomplete and possibly biased picture of the platform's long-term viability. When you can measure a growing ecosystem of passionate supporters, then you can benchmark this endorsement against competitive options. That's one reason why leading platform providers like Google, Apple, Amazon, Salesforce, Twitter, and Facebook all work hard to cultivate large and supportive developer communities.

- *Demonstrates a strong commitment to data portability and quality*— Technologies can create, process, and deliver data, but they often don't do all three in isolation. Digital platforms should enable growth and that should drive a slew of both data and quality considerations. What usage data is the platform collecting, and how is it used to improve user experience? Does it have well used APIs and other tools to get data in and out? Does the platform provide sufficient functional, regression, and data quality testing tools? What tools, reports, and guidelines are provided to ensure that business-driven configurations do not yield performance issues? What is the performance and cost impact of using the platform with Big Data and increasing volume or velocity of data? What flexibility does the technology have to configure data security and enable auditing? This is a partial list and needs to be tailored to the type of platform and how it will be used.

- **Participates in the digital ecosystem**—It's one thing to have an API, but is the technology already out-of-the-box integrated with other technologies? Can you easily enable single sign-on with Azure Active Directory, Okta, or some competitive platform? Is it already configured in a data integration or IFTTT platform like Zapier, Informatica Cloud, SnapLogic, or similar? Can your self-service BI platform like Tableau or Qlik automatically connect to it as a data source? What app stores is the technology plugged into? I'm not talking just about mobile applications on IoS or Android; what about SalesForce, AWS, or Azure marketplaces?

Architects Must Confront New Terminology, Similar Capabilities

What's very difficult to manage—and what can make me irate as a CIO—is the selection or review of new technologies that overlap with platforms and capabilities that already exist in the enterprise without considering reusing existing platforms or calculating the future costs to consolidate technologies.

Technology media and industry analysts enable this issue by developing new and sometimes proprietary terminology for technologies that have common capabilities. For example, are you buying a CRM, a sales automation platform, a 360-degree customer experience platform, or tools for marketing automation? These tools and platforms have some overlapping capabilities that can be competitive strengths or commodity offerings, but selecting multiple tools leads to complexities.

The best way to avoid this is to develop reference models that document a technological future state that aligns with strategic priorities. Reference models are often useful to document platforms, capabilities, reference data, data flows, and enterprise workflows. Then, when someone wants a "new solution," the organization is in a better place to review existing capabilities or identify primary requirements for any new technology selections.

What Digital Platforms Are Needed?

This is a difficult question to answer holistically since it depends on industry, business need, and what platforms already exist in the enterprise. That being said, some new platforms and requirements become more important when taking on a digital transformation. I'm going to highlight these considerations here.

THE FRONT OFFICE

First and foremost, digital transformation requires rethinking and developing holistic, omnichannel customer experiences. Front office platforms are designed to deliver customer-facing capabilities, some sold as products, others as business services as part of a nontechnical product offering. They need to be flexible and robust because they need to evolve to mature interfaces that have personalized user experiences.

The exact nature of platforms used to deliver customer experiences will vary considerably depending on the nature of the application. There are content management systems, business intelligence platforms, search engines, portals, e-commerce catalogs, and other front office platforms that can be leveraged for customer-facing applications. There are development platforms and frameworks used to engineer proprietary applications.

But certain principles become critical for these platforms to support:

- *Multidevice and browser*—Any front office framework today needs to support mobile, tablet and other interfaces without adding a lot more development effort. Ideally these should be responsive to handle the device and browser specifics. In many business contexts, front office applications need to be "mobile first" and designed for users expecting to access information from mobile as often if not more often than desktop.
- *Separation of content, presentation, and logic*—Front office applications require some form of separation to enable multiple

developers to understand and extend the code base. This usually is done by separating the code that interfaces with data source, code that handles all the business rules, and code that controls the presentation and user interface. A common framework that supports this separation is a model-view-controller (MVC), and most web development languages (Java, .Net, JavaScript, PHP etc.) have several frameworks to choose from.

- **Modular to support reuse and extensibility**—Modularity should enable you to plug in third-party components and configure them or enable you to develop your own components. This option can be very powerful especially on open source platforms or ones with component stores offering businesses the option to buy and configure rather than build on your own.

If you're leveraging a front office development platform to develop these applications (as opposed to a development framework), then you'll want to use the following to develop an evaluation checklist.

THE FRONT OFFICE—APPLICATION DEVELOPMENT

- **Business tools for configuration**—A big part of the business benefits of front office platforms is the extent that they enable business users to self-support applications. This can be anything from adding users, setting entitlements, publishing content, developing data visualizations, and publishing reports. The easier, more flexible these tools are, the less you have to develop these tools on your own.
- **Extensibility**—APIs and plugin frameworks for more advanced automation and integration are needed to enable developers when customizing something is truly required.
- **Modularity**—Should enable centralizing code and configurations for reuse and enable multiple developers to work on separate modules simultaneously.
- **Self-documenting capabilities**—Once developers configure the application, the business tools used in configuration become buried in the application and hard to review when cross-training new developers or explaining to users how the system functions. Tools should extract

basic documentation such as metadata on the application's configuration, business rules, formulas, styles, and parameters.

- *Version control*—At minimum, this should enable developers to edit the application without impacting production usage. It should then support automated deployment, rollback, and assigning version numbers. Ideally, the platform should interface with version control repositories and saving all business configurations and code there.
- *Developer pool*—At some point you might need to custom-develop something, at which point the availability of talent becomes critical.
- *Availability of third-party platforms*—Front office platforms should have an ecosystem beyond just third-party modules and components. Ideally, they have a marketplace where you can identify components and a published list of approved service providers.

THE FRONT OFFICE—TESTING CAPABILITIES

- *Interface with testing frameworks*—One of the bigger issues when working with these frameworks is finding methods and tools to test the application. This is very important for tools that enable customized applications like BI and CMS systems where organizations are likely going to need to automate regression tests or conduct performance tests.
- *Test as user in role*—This is a key need, so that developers can simulate the experience of end users with different roles, entitlements, or preferences.
- *Profiling*—Tools should have built-in capabilities to help developers identify and diagnose performance issues while they are developing the application.

THE FRONT OFFICE—SYSTEM ADMIN, OPERATIONS, AND SECURITY

- *Single sign-on interfaces*—Should enable organizations to provide single sign-on for applications developed.
- *Encryption*—Should be standard for any data transmissions and storage. Ideally, vendors should provide capabilities to interface with private keys and to mask data when moved to development or test environments.

- **Caching**—Enables higher-performance delivery to end users by storing computed data, content, or visualizations in memory for a defined time.
- **Load balancing**—Ideally has options to leverage elastic Cloud capabilities.
- **Disaster recovery**—Should enable reflecting data and cutting over to backup environments.
- **Logging and diagnostic information**—These tools are needed by administrators to diagnose production issues.
- **Metrics**—On usage by end users. Not just the basics of who logged in when, but also what parts of the application they utilized. Ideally, they should offer plugin capabilities with third-party analytic platforms.
- **Auditing**—Should enable logging changes made by end users, tools to identify who changed what when, and ideally tools to roll back changes made.
- **Exporting**—Many development tools lock in developers and prevent exporting the code if they need to rebuild the application in a different environment. Toolmakers should have more confidence that even if they offered this capability, most developers won't actually use it, but it's a big selling point to IT leaders who have concerns about being locked in.

What are some examples of front office development platforms?

- Content management platforms that enable authoring, editing, and publishing content, such as WordPress, Drupal, and Joomla
- Business intelligence tools that enable developing dashboards and charts, such as Tableau and Qlik
- E-commerce platforms that enable publishing product catalogs and enable selling products
- Mobile development platforms, specially designed to develop mobile applications on multiple devices and operating systems

DATA INTEGRATION, SERVICES AND APIS

Data management platforms are responsible for aggregating data, cleansing it, aligning it with master data, storing data, making data searchable, providing transaction services, and providing export capabilities. Here's how these break down:

- **ETL and data quality** are extract, transform, and load platforms that are tools to automate data aggregation and loading into data warehouses and other repositories. They are often bundled with data quality tools that enable profiling data for quality issues, identifying duplicates, defining automation rules to cleanse data, and providing workflow to handle exception cases.
- **Master data management** tools manage databases of "golden records" of entities such as accounts, contacts, and other entities that are core to the business and used in multiple applications.
- **Data preparation** is the latest technology used for easily loading, cleansing, and in some cases analyzing data stored in data lakes and Big Data stores.
- **Data virtualization** tools are often combined with business intelligence and other reporting tools to enable defining data marts and simplifying access to data scientists or other end users.
- **Web service platforms and service-oriented architectures** enable creating reusable data access patterns and business services.
- **API platforms** provide security and other services around APIs that are exposed to internal or client use.
- **IoT and data stream processing** are designed to process ongoing streams of data in real time, whereas ETL platforms are designed largely to batch process data loads on fixed schedules.
- **Artificial intelligence and machine learning services** are new forms of capabilities that can be plugged into and provide higher-level pattern recognition and personalized services. Some are designed to process human inputs such as voice and image. Machine intelligence services are designed to process large amounts of data in order to find complex patterns and summarize and personalize output. Finally, other services are designed to mimic or automate human decision making. As most organizations will not have the technical capabilities to develop proprietary AI solutions, technology providers such as

IBM, Google, and Microsoft are opening their AI capabilities through APIs and other data services.

- **Blockchain services** are for organizations that manage digital or physical assets and provide transaction services for them. Blockchain technologies are a digital ledger to securely track both the asset and transactions across multiple parties.

BUSINESS PLATFORMS

Are traditional enterprise platforms like CRM, marketing, financial, and HR the same old thing, or are the requirements and capabilities different to support digital business?

The simple answer is that while many of the core capabilities are the same as they were a decade ago, digital creates new and accelerated needs in these platforms. Here are some examples:

- While CRM is often thought of as a sales automation platform, in the last decade it has taken on far greater importance as the leading platform to bring customer and prospect information and activities to the greater organization. The potential is to make the entire enterprise more customer driven and data driven when defining customer segments, prioritizing prospects, establishing customer engagement protocols, and matching customers to products.
- Coupled with CRM systems are marketing automation systems and tools that aid marketers in all aspects of marketing from branding, capturing social and other customer 360 feedback, prioritizing digital marketing activities, and nurturing leads to prospects. The need to compete for the digital consumer has become so important over the last five years that CMO technology budgets rival the CIO's, and the number of marketing technology products has doubled every year for the last couple of years.[2]
- While financial and ERP systems continue to support the financial capabilities of the enterprise, the capabilities and integration have extended significantly beyond accounting needs. Many digital businesses are subscription driven, a financial model that can be challenging to implement in traditional financial systems. To compete

at digital speed and intelligence, more department leaders need access to manage their budget and understand operating performance by linking financial with sales or operational metrics. To enable executives to realign business strategy, make intelligent investments, or pivot their operations, they need access to more real-time financial analytics that enable them to perform both top-down and bottom-up analytics.

- HR and employees have received a lot more capability over the last five years as payroll and benefits have become digital capabilities and talent management has become a critical business activity. In addition, enterprise collaboration platforms that enable employees to share information and develop networks have helped larger organizations improve productivity, to develop cross-functional teams to take on new projects, and to retain top talent.

OPERATIONAL PLATFORMS

Operational platforms are the specific technologies used by one or more departments to enable their operational responsibilities. They include business process management platforms that enable workflows, knowledge management tools, and communication and collaboration tools. Some may be very specific to the type of work being done, and others are more generic platforms that have been programmed or configured for a specific need. They can be industry-specific systems, as well as CAD engines in construction, electronic health record systems in health care, or manufacturing systems. Technically even the application development tools used in IT fall into this category.

There are a few platforms and classes of platforms that are often critical in digital transformation:

- Agile portfolio management, ideation, or innovation platforms aim to engage the entire organization to solicit ideas for new products, operational improvements, and other investments that drive innovation, growth, or cost efficiencies. These platforms also serve as a central tool to communicate the status of active initiatives and enable individuals to step up and get involved.

- Collaboration platforms include everything from voice, video, and conferencing to "social" collaboration tools, wikis, project meeting spaces, and document management systems. The exact tool selected is less important than getting employees to use them regularly in meaningful business collaboration that drives results.
- Crowdsourcing is a way to elicit outside help using digital tools. In digital transformation, these tools can help get access to the resources to do many repetitive data-oriented jobs such as data cleansing, monitoring, and editing.
- Citizen development may be an attribute of a platform or a platform in by itself that enables business users to self-service the development of their own applications. This empowerment enables teams to be more efficient and data driven.
- Data science tools include analytic modeling tools, data-wrangling tools, and data visualization. It is the toolkit used by data scientists for discovering insights from data.

These technologies all lie at the intersection of business and IT and are the foundations of digital business practices. I will cover more about these platforms for engaging with business in Chapters Four through Seven.

Big Data Platforms Are Strategic

While relational/SQL engines are still appropriate for many applications, architects have other options today, ranging from document stores aimed at storing semistructured metadata and content, NoSQL parallel processing engines like Hadoop, columnar database, key-value stores, and graph databases. These Big Data platforms are designed to handle massive volumes of data that have a high velocity of new and changing data or a variety of structured, semistructured, and unstructured data types.

Databases are at the heart of running digital enterprises, so selecting the appropriate databases, establishing the infrastructure, identifying talent to work on these new platforms, and demonstrating business value from the investment is a significant challenge. In essence, you are taking approximately three decades of built-up capabilities, expertise, and legacy investments in SQL databases and making a bold statement that the organization needs an additional data engine to compete digitally.

Implementing big data technologies is no small task, and IT leaders can get consumed with selection criteria and the overhead to establish the capability. It's easy to lose sight of the business needs and opportunities while investing the time to develop the infrastructure, skills, and data integration. Yet for many businesses where data is the future of the business, this is one of the more critical investments.

I will be dedicating a whole chapter to the data-driven organization, which speaks to practices to enable the organization with smarter data practices. This covers the role of data scientists, how IT should upgrade its data services, and how to enable the collaboration required to give the business a competitive edge with data. For now, let's turn to the underlying technologies that have emerged under Big Data.

BIG DATA TECH EXPLAINED

For those of you that are mystified by all the Big Data technologies, I hope this brief history of how they emerged will help you understand it better.

Twenty years ago, if you were selecting a database, you were largely choosing between one of three options; Oracle, Microsoft, or open source. Under open source, you were probably looking at either MySQL (now owned by Oracle) or PostgreSQL. The new "use case" beyond enterprise computing was using these databases as the "back end" for web applications. The challenges 20 years ago were largely about performance and high availability.

Media companies in the late 1990s had what was at the time a unique challenge in storing and searching content from short blog posts to long form content and eventually whole books. Back then, you had one of two architectural choices, either store the content as a CLOB in an RDBMS and limit your functionality to basic keyword searching or use a "search engine" that indexed the full content and offered full text search capabilities. Search engine technologies became very competitive into the 2000s until a breed of databases based on document storage presented a new technical opportunity. These document stores enabled storing and searching content out of a single repository designed to store documents and not rows and columns of data. They also enabled new search paradigms that were looking to simplify query construction by using key/value pairs or by offering more expressive searches based on XML and XQuery. These document stores are now one of the options to handle the "variety" of Big Data as these stores can store and search a variety of formats such as straight text, XML, various document formats (MS Word, PDF, etc.) and digital assets (images, videos, etc.).

Now if you were processing a lot of numerical data back in the 1990s, you had a different set of challenges. Databases were relatively slow back then and had exponentially worse performance on larger data sets. If you had a larger data set, your best option was to replicate, partition, or shard the database onto multiple servers. Then you had to find a way to load balance queries to them. It took a little bit of engineering innovation at the larger web companies to execute and demonstrate horizontal scalability at the database level and handle large volumes of data, but there were many ways to accomplish the task.

The main limitation of this approach to scalability is that it largely worked for static, slow moving, low-velocity data. Any data that changed needed to be stored in a "master" database, then replicated to the partitions before it was available for all search activity. The higher the velocity, the greater the technical challenge in keeping databases in sync with the changes.

The approach was most challenging in at least two important use cases. First, companies doing analytics with enterprise BI platforms wanted to do higher levels of computation on data sets that needed updating more frequently. Beyond just handling higher volumes and velocities of data, the computations required were often no match for BI platforms or the underlying databases. If the computation was too complex to compute in either of these technologies, engineers often elected to compute them in batch as part of the data integration pipeline. This gave engineers some more options on how to scale the computations without affecting end user performance, but it implied that users had to wait for data refreshes if batch processing took time to process.

The second place where database partitioning became challenging is when online social networks emerged and e-commerce sites required higher levels of personalization. Social networks and e-commerce sites collect and store lots of user information that needs to be leveraged in near real time to produce a personalized experience for both the end user and their "friends" in the network. The engineering challenge is significant as social databases do much more writing activity, real-time processing, and more complex queries to implement personalization.

So it's no surprise that the emergence of Big Data technologies came from Google and Yahoo inasmuch as both companies had the challenges in the early 2000s of handling both the volume and the velocity of these payloads. Hadoop and MapReduce technologies emerged as the answer, and their innovation was largely about simplifying the work required to parallel-process queries across thousands of computing nodes. This, of course, was made possible by the emergence of Cloud computing and other methods to virtualize servers. Developers could then dial up all the computing resources they needed and run queries on Hadoop without having to understand the communication, storage, and synchronization complexities behind parallel computing.

Hadoop caught on both in media circles and in its results. The media loved the Big Data concept and showcasing examples of companies providing innovative solutions. This success led to demand from more companies looking to gain some advantage from these technologies and grow beyond their conservative RDBMS data architecture. This demand enabled the emergence of other new technologies and vendors in the "Big Data Landscape."[3]

Like any emerging technology that's experiencing significant demand, there was a significant talent gap especially in the late 2000s that could help enterprises and businesses take advantage of Hadoop. A whole class of companies, products, and services emerged to help businesses manage Hadoop infrastructure, map business problems to Hadoop implementations, or further simplify Hadoop's programming environment.

In addition, once entrepreneurs and data scientists recognized that there is a market beyond traditional RDBMS, additional Big Data platforms emerged with capabilities to match different workloads. Columnar databases in memory data stores, data stream processing, graph databases, and other engines emerged to solve different query, performance, and scalability challenges.

Beyond that, an entire ecosystem of other analytics, application, and other data service products emerged that either embed or extend Big Data technologies. Data integration technologies were enabled to move data into and out of these platforms. Content management technologies interfaced with document stores. Analytic and BI platforms were upgraded to handle Big Data platforms as a backend database technology. Capabilities like machine learning and artificial intelligence became more mainstream. Some enterprise systems moved off their classic RDBMS back ends to more powerful and faster columnar databases.

Flash forward to today, and the Big Data Landscape[4] is huge, consisting of 600-plus products and services. Today, there is the added challenge of not only implementing the technology and demonstrating competitive business value but also of selecting the most appropriate technologies up front.

SELECTING BIG DATA TECHNOLOGIES

Developers tend to be passionate about the platforms that they are most knowledgeable about and have had the most success with. Fifteen years ago, when there were fewer mainstream platforms, there were significant debates on Java versus .Net versus ColdFusion or MySQL versus Oracle versus Microsoft. It was rare to find someone who was technically proficient and objective about these platforms, and in most situations, one could substitute one platform for the other, leverage its strengths, and compensate for its weaknesses. The scope for selecting a platform was largely related to application development, maintenance, scalability, and performance.

I maintain that databases today are a different and changed domain. Their importance far exceeds internal and external application development needs: Database platforms are the foundation for most corporations' Big Data, analytics, and data-driven practices. The schemas developed will likely be connected to other databases and leveraged for many needs beyond their original purposes. They will most definitely be maintained and extended by developers that didn't author them, and ideally they will be interfaced by business users leveraging self-service tools to perform analytics.

Figure 3-2 is a simple visual that may help steer you in the right direction. In thinking about this transformation, here are some simple questions and guidelines on where to focus efforts:

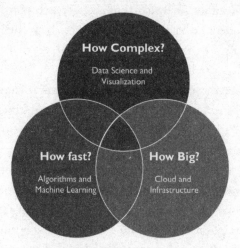

*Figure 3-2. Optimizing Big Data platforms based on
data requirements and priorities*

- **How big is your data?** The bigger the data, the more likely you will need to look at infrastructure to store, process, and manage larger data sets. You're more likely to select mature database technologies that have service providers that can help you scale and manage it properly in either public or private Clouds.

- **How fast is the data changing?** If your business derives value in presenting results faster for direct revenue, real-time decision making, or competitive advantage, it is likely you will need algorithms to directly churn data to drive other systems or decisions. If the intelligence required primarily looks at a lot of recently created data, then you're more likely to be looking at some of the data streaming databases.

- **How complex is your data?** Complexity comes in many forms. It may be unstructured data, data that has rich relational metadata requiring subject matter expertise, or data that's sparse and has other quality issues. If it's unstructured, then you might want to review document stores for this data. If it's semistructured or sparse data, then a document store might still work, but a columnar database may be a more versatile option. If you have a taxonomy or metadata and you have to store and process more information about the relationships between elements, then you might want to look at graph databases.

But most organizations' data can't simply fall neatly into one bucket, and you're more likely to have several use cases. In addition, you should experiment with applying these technologies to see what works best with the types of data, applications, and analytics.

To determine the appropriate technologies, many larger organization either developed Big Data labs or partnered with service providers to leverage their labs. The thinking behind the labs is to establish the infrastructure to run experiments, centralize the engineering expertise, and let business units leverage the lab to perform proof of concepts. The idea is to prove out both the business case and the underlying technologies.

The other extreme is startups where the CTO makes some quick decisions on the best platforms for the underlying business model and quickly builds up the environment. Startups that select optimal or near optimal database platforms may achieve an advantage over their competitors and is ultimately one of the success factors for these businesses.

This leaves a very fat middle of companies that must make some hard choices. These companies may not have the funding or skills to develop labs that don't have near-term ROI. They may also not have the ability to attract superstar talent that can come into the organization, work within its cultural boundaries to experiment, select the appropriate technologies, and demonstrate competitive value within an ambitious time frame. These companies are more likely to be laggards when it comes to implementing new Big Data technologies.

Which is more likely the wrong decision? Remember that digital transformation in an industry happens fast. Once the transformation is in progress, you might have as little as ten years to transform to a competitive digital business. If processing larger amounts of complex data is required to be competitive, and it more than likely is, the business needs to make some bets on new technologies and accept that "learned failures" are a better option than standing on the sideline.

If midtier companies can't easily fund labs or attract top talent, how can they best select and experiment with Big Data technologies? They should do a couple of things that are within reach.

First, you need to free up the top talent in your organization so that they can work on emerging opportunities and experiment with new technologies. As part of this program, you're going to have to get lots of training and time to prototype so that they are better versed in new technologies and how they operate. You also must consider how to reward and retain them because the last thing you want is to see them jump ship once they have training in these sought-after technologies.

Second, sign up with research partners that can provide both out-of-the-box research on the underlying technologies as well as expert advice. You're not going to get the organization smarter by just "doing it yourself," and you're likely to be able to buy basic knowledge rather than just build it up internally.

Third, tackle the culture issues up front that may become obstacles to investment and experimentation. It is likely that you have people in the organization who resist change or prefer the status quo and do not want to get involved in the risks of new technologies and practices. The best way to manage this is to identify new opportunities on the edge of your corporation's core competencies. Try to find use cases that don't disrupt existing business or challenge the status quo directly and use them to demonstrate new possibilities and hopefully quick wins.

Next, get some outside help that can bring in appropriate experience. You might not be able to fund a lab, but you're most likely going to need outside help to either select, experiment, or implement these new technologies. Even the act of shopping for a partner will help develop points of view on the appropriate technologies. Today, there are many options for midtier companies, including smaller service providers and boutique or industry-specific firms that might make suitable partners.

Finally, selectively hire some new talent. You might not be able to afford or have the wherewithal to attract top talent, but you can certainly find individuals who have had some expertise and ideally success with Big Data technologies. Find someone who's ready for a bigger challenge and ensure that he or she is a good cultural fit to the organization but make sure you give the new addition enough time and room to be successful.

Supporting Big Data technologies is a lot more complex than just having developers successfully using them and the infrastructure in place to support the workload. Think of all the operational responsibilities involved, such as existing relational databases including disaster recovery, data backups, archiving, performance tuning, scaling, and security. These operational considerations will be needed for every Big Data platform selected and used in production. What's worse is that the tools to perform these operations are often far more primitive than what's available in the far more mature RDBMS platforms, and the expertise is harder to attain. Managing the operations related to the Big Data platforms can be time–consuming, especially in the early years, and it's not trivial getting existing DBAs skilled in relational databases to learn the new technologies and support them over their existing responsibilities.

So you should pick your technologies as most organizations will not be able to support multiple platforms. That means you need a group thinking about the big strategic picture beyond what works in the lab today or where developers have had some success completing proof of concepts. You need to cherry-pick platforms and partners that have long-term viability, as well as proven business, development, and operational capabilities to back up your selection. Finally, you should think strategically about a roadmap of new use cases to make sure that Big Data platforms become strategic and provide sufficient business value so that the operational considerations and costs are not underserved.

Define Your Target Reference Architecture

The types, disparity, and volume of platforms can be overwhelming, and it is easy for IT organizations to get lost reviewing options or get sidetracked by going too deeply into any single platform. It's easy for technologists to debate platform endlessly or get lost on whether to support existing technologies or select new ones. Once platforms are in place, there may be debates over which ones to leverage in order to solve different challenges. How do you avoid getting lost in these debates?

Develop a small team that will begin proposing a reference architecture. This should be a simple communication tool that has a couple of components to convey to your team the past, current state, and future direction of technology.

The reference architecture should start with one or more conceptual diagrams of the system architecture. I like color-coding components showing "legacy," meaning technologies that you'd like to phase out over time; "current," showing technologies that are accepted in the reference architecture and will continue to be utilized in new investments; and "future," showing technologies that you plan to add into the ecosystem.

This diagram should be conceptual and stay high level so that it can be shown to any business leader that cares about the technology architecture. Figure 3-3 shows an example for a "self-service BI" platform. It includes (A) replacing a legacy BI tools with a modernized tool that enables business users to create their own analytics, (B) connecting the BI tool directly with exiting enterprise systems, and (C) instituting a new technology for integrating other data sources. The diagram shows what is legacy such as spreadsheets that will be replaced with dashboards, what's existing such as the CRM and ERP systems, and new systems and data like the self-service BI tool and social data feeds that are being introduced.

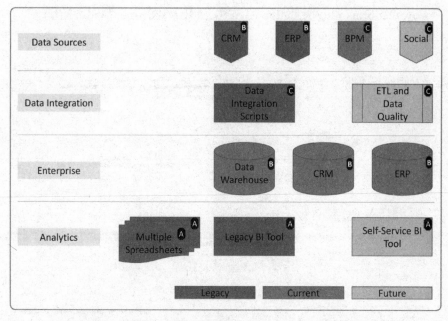

Figure 3-3. Reference architecture on modernizing data integration and analytics technologies

The second diagram should be a high-level table documenting some basic information on the current and legacy technology components. At minimum, I like stating the name, its version, key applications or processes where it is utilized, main capabilities used, future capabilities that will be explored, and, if known, when the next major upgrade is scheduled. For legacy technologies, this might highlight timing and high-level plans to migrate. You can use an ITIL configuration item standard[5] for cataloging existing assets, or better yet, leverage a configuration management tool. One note is that these standards and tools are designed for IT and need a simplified presentation when sharing with business leaders.

I like to have a separate table for future technologies documenting what problems it will solve, vendors being considered, and status of the selection process.

Finally, I like showing a roadmap in years, quarters, or months illustrating what technologies are being shut down, what new ones are being enabled, and what technologies are being upgraded. Figure 3-4 shows a more detailed roadmap illustrating the introduction of the two new platforms and the shutdown of two others shown in Figure 3-3.

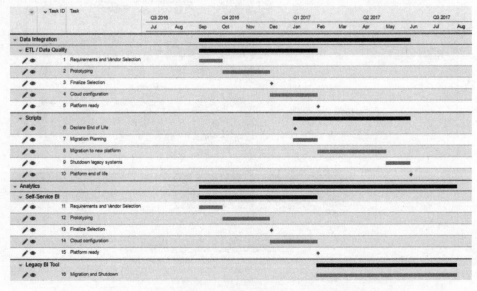

Figure 3-4. Example technology roadmap detailed with major transitions and milestones

The roadmaps you present should fit on one page and should have enough detail for the audience. If the one shown in Figure 3-4 is too detailed for an executive audience, you can show a rolled-up version like shown in Figure 3-5.

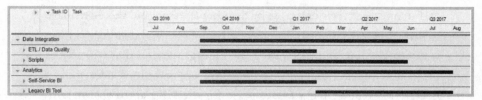

Figure 3-5. High-level technology roadmap

When developing roadmaps, I recommend using a tool rather than spreadsheets or presentations. Ideally, this should be pulled directly from your agile or portfolio management tools. Even when presenting to executives, I think it's important to acclimate them with presentation materials extracted from tools rather than investing the time to hand-build diagrams.

Some purists will argue that displaying long-term roadmaps is "not agile." Keep in mind that the near-term roadmaps should be completed using the agile estimated methods described earlier, but it's still important to include longer-term forecasted milestones. The full roadmap is a communication tool and should be used to convey the full vision.

The reference architecture should help tell the story of what digital technologies will become strategic, what will be phased out over time, and what will likely be added depending on whether there is sufficient business need. It is a picture to align the organization starting with the IT team and extending to the greater organization. A technical roadmap provides clarity on how to leverage existing platforms and capabilities with "big picture" knowledge of the technical landscape and what is likely to get implemented into the future.

CIO should update this document with some regularity showing what's been done, what's in progress, what's in near-term planning, and what's changed. The latter is important because today's technology and competitive landscape changes quickly, and future plans should adapt to these conditions.

Developing the reference architecture is a great opportunity to engage the top architects in the IT group. Most in the group inherited technology and architecture decisions made by their predecessors and should manage to these legacy decisions and systems. Planning the architecture roadmap is key to aligning and motivating the IT organization that will always prefer looking at "blue-sky" technology opportunities over today's operational reality. It's a key exercise for the CIO and IT leaders to change the IT culture.

IT Culture

What I have described in the last two chapters is the foundation of the new IT Organization. New practices like agile and DevOps along with a modern view of architecture will lead technology teams to deliver on transformational business practices and capabilities.

But practices and technologies will not get you there without considering the people and the culture. Culture is what brings people together to collaborate and solve problems without creating too much stress. It's what gets people motivated to work harder when there is a business need to go the extra mile. It's what protects the IT organization when it is facing execution issues and there are unhappy stakeholders. It creates safety when individuals need confidence that they can ask for help and get it without retribution. It celebrates small and big wins. Transformation is a journey, and it makes the ride worthwhile, fun, challenging, and rewarding.

Great IT culture is personified by the perks and drive portrayed in startups and successful Internet companies. These companies go out of their way to make technologists happy, excited, intellectually stimulated, rewarded, and competitive but not stressful. They design open workspaces and encourage open dialogue, collaboration, mind resting, and fun. Some provide meals and other perks to make it easier for employees to spend more time in the office solving problems.

While these steps don't by themselves creative a strong culture, they certainly make it easier for IT organizations and their employees to establish one.

Unfortunately, the environment and perks seen in these companies is not the norm and not the heritage of many companies. Many IT organizations reside in company cultures that are hard on teams and resources that are viewed as either cost centers or as service organizations to the primary revenue-generating departments.

IT puts in long hours to get things done. They are beaten up for the 0.1% uptime they miss, for the 5% of scope that fails to meet a minority of stakeholder expectations, for the poor user experience from one third-party application for an edge use case of a subset of users, by users that are unhappy with a technology selection and would prefer selecting their own, by the CFO whenever she needs to find a budget reduction, by legal when the data provided by IT for discovery takes too long to produce and doesn't tell the story they need to prove, by sales for anything that is perceived as blocking them from getting their bonus, or by the CEO for not having the latest innovation he read about on an airplane. I could go on.

As I write this section, I received a text from a colleague CIO struggling like other CIOs with cultural issues:

My issue and why I have been pushed so close [to burnout] is that my industry as a whole is still coming to terms w technology and my Mgmt doesn't care at all about my group, or to spend money on me and openly communicates that to others in the same breath they openly communicate all the IT things they want or are broken or lacking ... the spiral is destructive for me and I have never once been told I have done a good job at anything, not that I need a pat on the back or recognition I'm not in it for that but a little appreciation for the 80 hour work weeks for over a decade would be nice lol.

To which I replied:

I face the same issue. Many orgs don't know how to treat people. Period. It's worse when you are considered a cost center or services org. But the stress is the conflict created when you're challenging that assumption by having a stake and contribution in success or growth. Most orgs, leaders, and people aren't ready to treat a greater part of the org equally.

This divide can be a significant issue for CIOs that are charged with transformation. You can't easily plow through years of transformational activities if the organization throws you under the bus for the small misses. Negative behavior completely undermines the change management practices required to make transformational successful. How do you go to business users and have them do something better, more valuable, faster, but very different from what was done in the past, when the CIO and her staff have to defend their decisions, practices, and execution at every step?

My colleague points out that it's a downward spiral. The more value the IT organization is required to contribute to help the business grow, be more competitive, or transform, the more likely that they will simultaneously be creating a target on their back. Change-resistant individuals will take their opportunity to fire at this target, and that forces the CIO to defend. The issue is particularly challenging at the top where many leaders who have spent their careers getting to that seat don't want to share the spotlight or the rewards when they are available.

The added challenge is when this stress percolates down to the IT staff. It's fair to say that CIOs must develop a "thick skin" to handle cultural, change management, and transformational challenges. That is not likely to be the case for the CIO's lieutenants or the staff. The CIO is charged to get the IT organization to ramp up execution, partner with the business, deliver innovation, and sponsor transformation. And the CIO can make this successful in year one when there is little expectation, fewer challenges, and IT is asked to step up and deliver. But as time progresses, negative culture can impede progress, demoralize staff, increase stress, and probably lead to turnover.

While these are all company and business cultural challenges, I have found the best way to counter it is by working on the culture within IT. The CIO doesn't command a large enough sword to enact top-down cultural changes in one swing. This will take time, require demonstrating business success from transformational programs, and need investing in relationship building to gain supporters. But the CIO and IT leaders can do a lot of change within the technology department, and that can often influence other broader changes.

What Is the Culture of IT?

Your team's culture is unique. It has developed over time based on the nature of the business, the industry and market conditions you compete in, the geographies and locale of where you operate, the mission of the IT team and what is expected of them, how it hires and rewards individuals, and many other factors.

But I like to think of culture in terms of what is important for successful partnership, collaboration, and execution. If the team is aligned around similar values and principles, it develops a culture around them. Some of the values I think are important are tied to key practices like agile and DevOps, and the main cultural challenges are how teams handle issues that cross between operations and development. Some cultural elements should be tied to business expectations like the team's ability to interact with business leaders (business acumen) and the team's responsiveness to issues and requests. Finally, some should be aspirational, like the ability to deliver innovative solutions or to develop appropriate KPIs, metrics, and dashboards in order to be data driven. Figure 3-6[6] depicts some of the values I attempt to instill in the IT organization.

Signs that IT Culture Is Heading in the Right Direction

Once you have some principles established, here are some behaviors I look for that are signs of a strong IT culture:

1. **Agile teams get things done first, worry about process mechanics later.** When introducing agile practices or even when agile has been used for some time and the team is looking to mature its practice, I find that strong teams will think agile, focus on execution first, and address mechanics of the process second. For example, a new agile

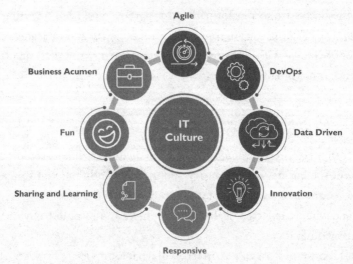

Figure 3-6. IT culture and the "digital" mindset that drives collaboration and results

team should get its backlog going first and commit, worry about story points and how to handle unfinished stories at the end of a sprint later. A mature agile organization, with multiple teams prioritizing stories, figures out the communication mechanics between teams during the sprint and formalizes communication practices later.

2. **Agile teams know how to use the business's products so that they can see where and how to make improvements.** User interface, workflow, and access to insightful, actionable data is so important to successful customer-facing application design and business system workflows that the technologists working on them should step into their user's shoes and experience the technology for themselves.

3. **Individuals are hungry to learn more and take the initiative to train themselves.** Sure, I can get individuals and a team formal training, but that's not where it starts. A strong IT team prefers rolling up their sleeves, experiment first, and ask for training once they know the basics.

4. **It's not always the business's fault.** Agile teams might blame the product owner for overpromising, and everyone has something critical to say about the business strategy, but strong IT teams will think through how to improve their own practices before blaming or being critical of other business functions.

5. **Speaking openly about where they suck and need to improve is important.** I want to hear about technical debt from software architects. Operations teams need to look at metrics and decide where improvements can have business impact. Quality assurance teams need to own up when their testing is inadequate. Most importantly, teams need to speak up when they recognize a problem because a problem well stated is half solved.

6. **Agile teams share information on how things work, document process, and educate colleagues on how to fix things.** IT teams that horde information, overcomplicate things so that business users don't understand how they work, or make it impossible for their colleagues to enhance their technical implementations are impeding organization growth and scalability.

7. **Agile teams want to get involved in understanding business priorities and challenges.** They ask the product owner questions on the priorities or want to understand how their efforts are contributing to growth or efficiencies. They'll seek out multiple solutions to a problem and debate which ones provide optimal solutions. They'll listen to marching orders but seek to participate in the debate on what and how the business should move an agenda forward. They are strategic agile thinkers and learn how to innovate.

8. **Agile teams leverage data and ask questions.** To become smarter about their own operations, they will collect meaningful data, convert it to metrics, look for trends, and prioritize improvements. They will learn to ask good questions about data and take other steps to help the organization become data driven.

9. **There is an interest in spending time together outside of the office and having fun.** One of my teams threw summer family picnics and assembled everyone for pot luck Diwali celebrations. Good teams want to spend time together, celebrate wins, appreciate individual interests, and be human.

10. **Agile teams are responsive when there are operational issues.** It's one thing to have all the systems monitored, ITIL practices to handle incidents, playbooks to recover from an issue, and strong technical skills to research root causes. These are all things strong operations teams work toward, but the best ones also develop a good bedside

manner, are responsive to even the most difficult users, find ways to communicate using language everyone understands, and make sure business teams receive regular updates when there are problems.

11. **Great IT teams refuse to fail, are willing to take on challenges, and find ways to make their initiatives succeed.** They are relentless to hit deadlines. They seek to keep things simple. They promote enthusiasm and heal downers and doubters.

How Transformational Leaders Can Drive Culture

What practices should transformational leaders focus on to improve IT culture and address bad behaviors? Here are three:

1. **Drive collaboration and communication behaviors.** Leaders should ensure teams are working well with their business colleagues on opportunities, solutions, and innovation. To irradiate the dividing line between "requirements" and "implementation," the number of people in the technology team who need to be able to communicate and collaborate with stakeholders is significantly larger than in decades past. Improving communication is an easy starting point to get developers, system administrators, engineers, and business analysts to be better prepared to collaborate. Here are some negative behaviors that transformational leaders need to course correct on:
   - Mentally says no, or actually says no to an idea or request without listening to the business need and priority
   - Communicates in technical jargon or overly complicates explanations back to a business user when responding to a question
   - Creates blocks and waits for requirements without engaging the stakeholder or proactively proposing opportunities, problems that need to be addressed, and solutions
   - Fails to regularly communicate status when resolving a critical issue
2. **Evangelize actions that drive efficiency.** It isn't going to be easy to justify investments to fix manual work or to dedicate application development releases in order to fix bad software. Both issues need

to be avoided before they are created and fixed incrementally over time. It's why addressing behaviors like the following are important:

- Fails to automate tasks and leaves significant manual steps
- Creates technical debt but does not itemize it in the backlog to be fixed
- Doesn't provide documentation, training, or other knowledge transfer to ensure that colleagues can support the technologies he or she developed

3. **Ensure technology decisions are data and quality driven.** IT is the hub of so much operational data, yet they often leave out the discipline required to review this data, develop metrics, and leverage in their decisions on priorities, problems, and solutions. If IT isn't using its own data, then how can it be a part of a data-driven organization? In addition, if IT isn't paying attention to quality or security, then how can it deliver reliable and safe solutions? These behaviors underscore issues that need to be course corrected:

- Chases rabbits when trying to diagnose performance issues without reviewing logs and metrics to guide efforts to areas of higher importance
- Overengineers solutions and inflates estimates
- Treats quality assurance, testing, and security as an afterthought and doesn't bake these paradigms into designs
- Doesn't implement unit tests, performance evaluations, or other test-driven practices to ensure that code is reliable and functioning properly

Are you ready to lead a cultural transformation?

4.

AGILE
PORTFOLIO
MANAGEMENT

Walk into a new transformation role three times in 10 years, and you get to see some patterns. In all three instances that I have done this, I start my review with leaders with one simple question. Think about the time you met your team or your colleagues for the first time in a group setting. Once you go through introductions, you're likely going to ask individuals and the team what they are working on. What are they doing today? Why are certain projects a business priority? How is everyone going about solving today's challenges, and what is being considered as the next potential business initiatives?

I do this with a very simple question that tends to unravel the fabric of how the business is functioning, whether there is alignment on priorities, where there may be execution issues, and whether the business has a healthy culture for taking risks and making investments. That question is . . .

What Is Everyone Working On?

The simplest of questions easily exposes the messiness of running IT, product, marketing, and data science organizations. The larger the organization, the more likely this simple question will lead to others that expose larger business challenges, cultural dysfunctions, execution roadblocks, talent gaps, funding constraints, process immaturities, and other considerations that impede transformation. This is not necessarily a knock on previous or current leadership, especially if you're coming in as a new leader with a different perspective or new priorities.

To answer this relatively simple question, you're probably going to get a plethora of answers. First, it's likely that some won't be able to answer this question immediately and will ask for time to get organized. Others will show you spreadsheets with incomplete and inconsistent information. You'll be given tours of different tools, maybe even an agile project management tool that will give you some sense of either development or operational projects. Some will show up with recent reports or presentations they made to management on the status of active projects. You'll find duplicate projects with different names, large multiyear programs with many subprojects, smaller to-do's that shouldn't be considered projects, projects that are already done, and others that have no hope of ever starting.

My absolute favorite is when someone shows up with an export and aggregation from the time reporting system. They will tell me, "This is the best system to record everything going on in the business or department because everyone is required to track their time in it." What do these reports typically show me? A list of projects, who's worked on them, and how many hours they worked. Perhaps it's granular enough to break projects into different tasks or task types, but I can bet there are many data quality issues at this level even without asking the team. In most cases, time reporting systems give me little information on what the project is, why it was prioritized, what business benefits are expected, whether success criteria are defined, how close to the target timeline is the current forecast, and whether expenses are in line with the budget. The data in these systems helps the accountant allocate costs and respond to auditor questions but provides little help when trying to understand the health of the portfolio or to identify opportunities for process improvement.

Imagine following this up with some more questions. Maybe I'll ask the CEO the same question: "What do you think everyone is working on?" Here I am more likely to get a slide or two from the last presentation to the Board of Directors outlining the company's strategy, a high-level list of projects, the business owner, and the current status. Now this is useful and a good tool for a top-down audit of the organization's priorities and working dynamics, but is the CEO's response a sufficiently complete answer?

The answer is no. It's a Board presentation intended to show a high-level view of a handful of strategic initiatives. What if I follow up with another question: "Is this everything that's being worked on at the company that's vital for hitting revenue targets, growing the number of customers in targeted segments, addressing business risks, or developing new organizational capabilities?" Good luck getting a detailed answer from the CEO to that question, and in many cases, you just lost the CEO's attention. If you didn't, chances are she's just assigned you to deliver that report . . . in a week. Good luck putting together a full enterprise view of everything in progress when your colleagues and predecessors have never aligned or collaborated to assemble this view in the past.

Now the Harder Question—
What Is Everyone Going to be Working On?

As hard as it is to get a picture of the current state of organization and individual priorities, how about asking this next few questions? "What is everyone working on next? . . . What are the priorities for the next ninety days and for the full year? . . . What do you think will spill over to next year?"

I'll probably get some answers from the CEO on this question. She'll whip out the three-year plan and the five-year strategy. It might be a nice deck showing market conditions, company opportunities and threats, strategic priorities, and the company's attempt at a forward-looking financial pro forma. Microsoft should add an Excel formula that helps the strategist draw the angle of the hockey stick of growth.

We can debate the usefulness of multiyear strategies when market conditions and technology capabilities have changed so drastically over the last few years and are unlikely to slow down. In 2010, did GM have a driverless car strategy? Did Marriott view condominium owners in large cities as a competitive threat? Did Honeywell look at Apple and Google as next-generation competitors?

Even when it is valuable, I find the ability to translate a multiyear strategy into executable plans a gap for many organizations. These plans serve a purpose aligning leaders and employees to a strategic vision. There may be some governance enabling the alignment of investments and projects to the strategy. There may also be a negative by-product, with some leaders pushing initiatives because of their alignment to strategy even when it doesn't have any tangible business benefits. But most important, many organizations struggle to define, communicate, and manage a defined process moving from strategy, to a portfolio of planning projects, to execution.

Capturing, vetting, and tracking an organization's initiatives may sound boring or be perceived as administrative overhead. Hire a project management office (PMO) to develop and oversee? Borrow a portfolio management process from one of the big consulting houses? Leave the definition of strategic projects to the CEO or key executives to manage at a high level? I would estimate that many organizations have tried one or more of these approaches and probably switched models multiple times over any ten-year period. Why? In simple terms, because top-down practices are too slow to match market conditions, too narrow in scope to ensure competitiveness, and too isolated from operating realities.

Who Is Generating the Best Ideas?

Strategies are most often top-down statements on the direction leadership is promoting to grow the business. While this is important and useful, it is not complete or sufficient in today's fast moving and competitive world. Millennials have a vastly different perspective on what's important now and in the future versus the boomer generation filling most of Board and leadership seats. Sales, on the front line of engaging new and existing customers, struggle to capture and keep up with the wants and needs of buyers. Customer service teams know the most frustrating complaints from end users. Aligning priorities to a top-down-driven strategy is no longer sufficient, and in today's digital world, it's more important to ask and solicit a larger scope of ideas from a greater pool of people.

Ask employees and leaders at all levels what their best ideas are for the firm to grow, win business, or become more efficient, and you'll get a wide range of answers. But you'll get answers, some of which will align to strategy, some of which will be good ideas but not worth pursuing, some that will be totally infeasible, and others that may just be the next big idea for your enterprise. But you won't know about this great idea unless you ask. When you do ask, be prepared for a number of responses.

Some of the responses will and should come from the sales team. Chances are that they've been given a portfolio of products to sell, a territory, a ranked list of existing customers and new prospects, sales tools to be successful, and a sales management process that has the accumulated organizational best practices on winning business. Now ask a group of experienced salespeople what they want to sell, and you should get a noisy response. Taken to an extreme, you might get a list of the optimal list of things to be sold to a small group of clients on the salesperson's list for him to exceed quota.

Ask the same question of someone in an operational role, and you'll get a list of frustrating, inefficient, manual, error-prone steps her teams must perform repeatedly. They'll want to automate steps, plug in new suppliers, capture better data, speed things up, enable greater configuration capability, and make other improvements that will make their key processes more efficient, reliable, and robust.

Ask the Security or Compliance Officer, and you'll get yet another very important list. If you're lucky, the marketing team has a list and partners well with technology leaders on vendor selection and implementation. Finance probably has a list, but don't even bother to raise their voices because they are last in line for funding or resources.

Here are the questions: Can these different organizations fulfill their needs in silos, or do they need collaboration from other departments to be successful? Is the change impact of any initiative understood sufficiently? When funding is required, how are these decisions made to align with strategy and ensure that there is some balance where funding is applied among growth, efficiency, research, and compliance driven initiatives? These are key questions that having portfolio management practices aims to address.

The Paradox—Why Businesses Fail at Portfolio Management

Every organization I've been a part of has the challenge of prioritizing resources toward the best ideas. The complication is that many projects and initiatives that are active or being planned are difficult to capture in a single place, let alone manage them. Compounding the issue is every business's need to prioritize investments in different categories. Most executives prefer prioritizing revenue-generating initiatives, but they should be balanced with others that provide cost savings, efficiency, compliance, security, and other operational benefits. Finally, all organizations and especially those that prioritize digital transformation should invest in R&D and innovation activities.

Why haven't more organizations looked to centralize the data, practices, and governance regarding their projects, initiatives, and investments? The need to have some idea of the organization's priorities and where funds and resources are being invested is so fundamental, yet so few organizations are successful at achieving a basic project portfolio. There are several reasons, and most organizations suffer from several issues.

There may be a lack of support from top executives who have interest in some of the more strategic initiatives and the ones consuming the most resources. They often have little interest reviewing the long tail of other projects that still require management and resources. These executives may not appreciate the importance and effort required to develop a comprehensive project portfolio.

To some executives, portfolio management is often viewed as an IT activity and delegated to the CIO to manage. The portfolio then centers on technology projects or ones that require technology investment and often falls short of representing other sales or other departmental initiatives.

Some business leaders are not interested sharing information on their initiatives especially if they have questionable ROI or do not require investment of resources out of their control. Many prefer managing these projects quietly and publishing their results of only the completed ones that yield successful results.

When CFOs drive portfolio management, they often align it with ERP and try to centralize the portfolio, list of projects, resources, and applied effort in these tools. ERPs are expensive platforms to develop on and are not the day-to-day tools used by teams to complete their work or manage projects. Centralizing project portfolios in an ERP is problematic if it requires the staff to duplicate data and creates additional administrative steps to report in a separate system.

CIOs have also made mistakes selecting and implementing project portfolio management tools. Pushing these tools in large enterprises often yields resistance when they are misaligned with team project management methodologies and tools. If the workflow is centralized, implementing in the tool is more efficient, but complications arise in defining KPIs, metadata, and workflow appropriate to all business types. Larger enterprises have the added complication of getting multiple businesses, spread globally, to collaborate on any centralized workflow or tool. In addition, organizations that outsource projects must decide how best to work with third parties. Lastly, some enterprises that invested in project management offices (PMOs) to take on portfolio responsibilities cut these programs when they are too slow to show meaningful results.

Another paradox needs consideration. Tools for managing ideation and innovation practices rarely have full portfolio management capabilities, and portfolio tools may not be the most user-friendly option to oversee ideation, innovation, or R&D pipelines.

Finally, project managers are often barriers to portfolio management when it's viewed as an administrative reporting tool. If the tool is also forcing them to replicate information that they use to manage projects or, worse, if management is asking them to standardize on tools that they don't prefer, then project managers can become the most difficult to win over.

So, lack of top-down support, complexity with regard to which technologies to use and how to configure them, and lack of organization alignment often lead many enterprises and businesses to complacency when it comes to portfolio management. It falls into an it's-too-hard-and-not-worth-it bucket, so they don't make tracking initiatives an organizational priority. They may capture high-level strategic priorities but leave it to individual leaders and businesses to manage the rest.

Portfolio Management Required for Digital Transformation

Looking at technology departments as a starting point, relying on ad hoc portfolio management practices doesn't work very well, and it becomes a real issue when additional investment is needed for transformational programs. Technology is partially about "running the business" and "keeping the lights on," but even operational teams have to take on initiatives. Many are small and scheduled like patching servers; some require investment like when storage is upgraded; others require business participation like when an enterprise system is upgraded; and others may be transformational, such as deploying new mobile capabilities that change workflow. These need to be scheduled, funded, resourced, and managed.

But digital transformation brings on a new wave of projects that have technology enablers, require new digital workflows, and ideally have new ways to service customers. They include integrating marketing automation tools, deploying upgraded mobile applications to customers, or enabling new data analytics capabilities through Big Data technologies. Initiatives that deliver new products require the participation of marketing and sales teams to be trained on the product, develop marketing plans, and establish sales practices.

I ask you, how is the CIO or CDO going to prove that the organization can execute a transformation strategy? How is she going to demonstrate where the organization can execute and where they need outside expertise and capabilities? How will executives know when an initiative is on course, is falling behind, needs outside assistance, or needs additional investment? What is the organization's single point of truth to view these activities and make decisions on?

This isn't just an IT need. Maybe some of the low-level IT projects have little business participation, but many of the examples I listed either need to be led by or have heavy participation by business leaders. How can executives know that their best business resources are aligned to the most strategic initiatives? Only if the other projects, the ones that do not require any IT role, are also represented in the portfolio so that resource alignment is holistic. In addition, it works only when the portfolio shows the scope, status, and resources in both IT and in business groups. It's only then do we see a business/IT alignment that has the best chances of executing on the most strategic projects.

In summary, here's why portfolio practices are important for transformational programs:

- ▶ Some of the best ideas come from employees and are not top-down driven from strategic priorities.
- ▶ Organizations need to pivot, speed up, slow down, and stop initiatives with more frequency and agility as market conditions change, new customer opportunities are discovered, and competitive threats become disruptive.
- ▶ Most strategic initiatives can no longer be executed well in silos and require staffing, expertise, and operational changes in multiple departments.
- ▶ Improving customer experience is not just about front-end customer interactions. Organizations also need to consider how to make operations more responsive, how to make data more accessible, how to address security or compliance requirements, and how to drive out costs to succeed at transformation.

Implementing Portfolio Management

Portfolio management practices fail because organizations try to implement too much capability with too many people in their organization too quickly. It's that simple. Because the efforts to centrally manage the portfolio tend to be top-down driven, the tools selected, workflows created, and rollout processes designed all aim to get the whole organization on board with the program. In doing so, they tend to bundle too many capabilities into the system and workflow up front and try to get people to adopt. The more capabilities and the larger the number of people, the greater the likelihood is that these initiatives will fail.

Technology vendors haven't been very helpful in this space. Enterprise project portfolio management (PPM) tools look and act like micro-ERPs and require significant configuration to adapt to different enterprise needs. Enterprises go through lengthy technology selection processes, then need to assemble teams that can determine the business requirements for portfolio management, then develop workflows that are easy for users to adopt, and then the team must figure out how to roll out and train users.

By the time the tool is rolled out to users, there's already a heavy investment in the implementation. At that point, change resistance emerges because working teams probably have some form of project or portfolio management process. It may be a bunch of spreadsheets or a PowerPoint, but to these teams, it's "good enough" for them. Lastly, by the time this is all completed, you may be several months into developing portfolio practices, and the sponsoring executives are likely to be well beyond frustration.

The centralized PPM system comes across as a complex, bloated administrative system. It takes significant time to get data into the system before its reporting and analytics capabilities become useful in decision making. But therein lies the final drawback: It becomes useful only if there is reasonable data governance in how individual project managers and teams use the system. Where there is inconsistency, any rollups or aggregation may enable decision making on low-quality, incomplete data.

Bottom line is that top-down, large-scale rollouts of portfolio management practices don't work. They take too long to configure and are too complex to roll out department by department. If you are in a command-and-control organization (which has lots of other issues), then maybe you have a shot at making this work using the stick. But here's the catch. It's hard to develop standards and enforce data quality if you roll out portfolio practices too quickly and without working examples.

Is there another option? Where can we draw inspiration from when we need to roll out an enterprise practice?

Learning from Social Startups

When Yahoo launched, it was a simple-to-navigate directory. Google was a search box and a button. LinkedIn enabled you to upload your contacts. Facebook first rolled out to college students only. Twitter started with 140-character text streams. What these consumer sites understood is that they had to do something fundamentally important in simple ways to get early adopters.

Social and collaboration tools usually follow a simple 1-9-90 paradigm[1] in user adoption. Typically, only 1% of users tend to be "contributors," 9% contribute passively, and 90% are information consumers or lurkers. Networks cultivate the 1%, especially if they are socially influential to drive content creation and adoption.

Many of you fall into the 9% of casual users when you post an occasional photo on Facebook or "like" an article on LinkedIn. The 9% will be influenced to contribute when a crowd is already participating and there is some benefit to their contributing. These contributions are also sought out by social networks because it gives them more authentic contributions (some of the 1% are self-promoters), and it enables them to have greater reach and relevancy to the last segment.

The 90% are consumers. They read the news on websites but never comment. They network on Facebook but rarely post a status update and almost never comment. You're sometimes lucky to get an emoji reaction from them.

For ad and subscription business models, getting this model is a good enough start. Even though 90% of users aren't active contributors, if the content is compelling and these users spend time on the site, then the network benefits.

Enterprises have this challenge of getting adoption and collaboration from larger percentages of employees compared to social network users. Enterprises won't be successful leveraging a CRM system with only 10% salesperson participation, so they use several tactics to ensure high levels of adoption. Best practices require executive sponsorship and tying sales compensation for both results and adherence to sales practices. Enterprise human resource functions require employees and managers to participate in performance management processes, and bonuses and promotions are usually tied to information put into these systems.

Enterprises can elect to implement strict, top-down governance to implement portfolio management tools and practices. That's one approach for command-and-control organizations, but there is an alternative, more collaborative approach to engage the organization.

What enterprises need to learn from social platforms is to start with small ambitions, less functionality, and targeting early adopters. Invest the upfront effort to get something working with a small group and a subset of functionality, then look to grow usage and capabilities over time. These social startups also recognize inflection points when they can accelerate growth, quickly add a new differentiating capability, or look to pivot when something isn't going as planned. Sponsors of projects targeting enterprise adoption should adopt similar philosophies and practices to enable the high rates of participation required for these tools and practices to be successful.

The Secret to Starting Small in Portfolio Management

The secret to developing the portfolio is starting small, gaining adoption and strong results from this group, then growing usage and functionality over time. I'm going to lay out the process I've done in three organizations to get basic portfolio management kicked off in the first 30 days of being a CIO. The heart of this practice is to make a 1.0 version so easy to use that it's criminal for any leader not to participate.

The rollout has five key steps:

1. Capture basic data on initiatives that are active or being planned.
2. Define your data integration process.
3. Identify and configure a portfolio management tool.
4. Gain top-level support for the program to enable you to scale it to other departments.
5. Run your rollout plan.

As with any process, the devil is in the details.

DEFINE YOUR DATA GATHERING EXERCISE

The first step starts where I began this chapter, soliciting some basic information across the organization. What you're looking to do is to understand what projects are in flight, what is their current status, who is leading them, what the strategic drivers are behind the project, and what tools are being used to manage the project.

A Portfolio of Initiatives

You'll notice that I use the word "initiatives" more than "projects." That's by design. Projects imply there is a start and end, whereas I steer most of the work toward agile programs that might have a beginning but then go into a phase of ongoing investment, not an ending. I like calling these agile programs.

Also, the word "project" makes some people quickly seek developing an end to end largely scoped project plan. This isn't ideal for agile programs, and is equally problematic for transformation programs and strategic planning exercises where a steering meeting must adjust priorities as they evolve their thinking.

Over time, I've used the more generic word initiatives to encompass traditional projects, agile programs, strategic planning, and all forms of activity that are non-operational.

That's my minimal data gathering exercise: answering the basic question of what project, who is in charge, what is the benefit, what stage is the project, and where can one go for more information.

Before embarking on this data gathering exercise, you'll need to better define these fields and decide whether these are sufficient.

- *What project?*—I require a short title. 140 characters max. Something that I can skim and read.
- *Who is in charge?*—I would suggest collecting email addresses for this field so that you have ways to look up additional information in your enterprise directory.
- *What is the organizational context?*—If you have multiple businesses, product lines, geographical centers, and other organizational context, then implement the minimal taxonomy so that you know the context of the initiative.
- *What is the benefit?*—Figure 4-1[2] shows four basic types that are driving either revenue, cost savings or longer-term strategic needs. You'll have to decide whether these definitions are sufficient for your

organization, but I would urge you to keep this simple. If your definitions are too granular, it will force participants to have to think a lot about how to best characterize their projects. More thinking implies harder to fulfill and less likely to capture sufficient data.

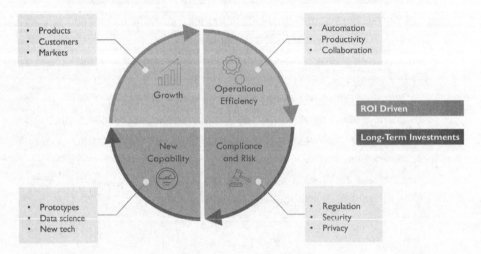

Figure 4-1. Types of initiatives that drive ROI, enable new capabilities, and address risk

You'll also have to decide how to respond to participants when they say that an initiative supports multiple strategies. If your tools enable you to collect multiple selections easily, then you can look to support multiple options. If you have a small number of types, then you could look to collect them as separate fields and ask for more qualifying information. So instead of selecting "Revenue driving," you could replace it with "Target revenue over the next three years" and Operational Efficiency with a similar metric on expected cost savings. While this is possible, I don't advise it because this adds to the complexity of collecting data, and it's likely that a single field of more detailed information isn't sufficient anyway.

▶ **Network**—Where I can get more information is ideally a link pointing to a document folder.

▶ **Stage**—If your organization doesn't already have a formal way of defining the stage of an initiative, then this is where you're going to have to propose one. I typically use the definitions in Figure 4–2.

Initiative Stage	Definition
Defined	A placeholder with no formal work done on it
Ideation	An idea that has a founder developing its business case
Planning	A business case has been established, and a small team is developing a businesses and execution plan.
Development	Active resources working on the initiative
Operations	Initiative is operational. The working team is taking steps to ensure success criteria are met and working on continuous improvement priorities.
Done	Success metrics have been documented, and the initiative was closed.

Figure 4-2. Initiative stages from definition to done

If you have a smaller organization, then there may be room to collect additional information that will help rank, group, and sort projects. But I would be careful about adding too many fields that may result in overwhelming or scaring off participants. Some possible options:

- More detailed description of the project and its benefits
- Planning questions that help steer planning teams to what open questions exist and should be addressed to validate the business plan assumptions
- Quantified revenue or cost savings targets—either year one, three-year, or multiple fields
- Strategy alignment dimensions if your organization has announced specific strategies
- More detailed resource information: Who is the sponsor? Who is on the initiative's leadership team?
- More details on initiative milestones to help develop enterprise calendars
- More specific details on whether and how the initiative requires any capital investments, new technologies, marketing activities, or needs from any shared services
- Link to any project management tool being used to track tasks and milestones

DEFINE YOUR DATA INTEGRATION TOOL AND PROCESS

Once you know what data you are collecting, you should decide an appropriate tool and process for collecting the data. You might have different strategies depending on how many people you are asking to participate, how many fields you are looking to collect, and whether the data already exists in another tool or needs to be created from scratch.

Organizations that already have some form of project tools in place can likely extract some information and fill in the gaps required for the portfolio. These organizations are going to want to specify both a data feed format and a spreadsheet template so that participants can share data.

Recall that in the last chapter, I highlighted data integration platforms as one of the key technologies used in transformation programs. This is a good example of where it can be applied. So ideally, if data already exists in another platform, consider how to automate pulling it, what data transforms are required, what quality validation is needed, and how to handle exceptions.

If you're building a portfolio from scratch and there are few tools used for managing projects, then you'll likely want to skip this step and focus on selecting and working with a portfolio tool.

IDENTIFYING AND CONFIGURING A PORTFOLIO TOOL

Once you know the data, then you can consider what tools you want to select, configure, and deploy to manage the portfolio. Here are some considerations:

- The portfolio must support the lifecycle of initiatives. Initiatives are created, move through stages, and some will be marked done. Some initiatives will start, pause, restart; others may get fully cancelled somewhere in its cycle.
- A portfolio does not replace tools used to manage agile initiatives and other types of projects. If you are a large organization, you'll want to consider whether you want to integrate data from these tools rather

than force participants to rekey data. The more projects, the fewer tools, and the more data available in these project management tools, the more likely it is that you'll want to consider whether you can automate some data integration.

- Consider UX capabilities of platforms. No one wants to click a lot to perform basic data entry. You'll want forms that can be configured to handle different use cases and grid entry so that batch entries and updates are easy. You may want to allow users to export, modify, and import.

- Make sure the tool allows you to track changes and approve ones that are significant. You probably need some controls to manage moving initiatives from one stage to the next and don't want participants to stage themselves.

- Make sure searching works well. If you're implementing many dimensions, then your tool should have easily accessible UIs to help drill into results. Modern tools should have faceted navigation and rely less on "advanced search" capabilities.

- Consider reporting needs for participants, leaders and executives. You'll want to make sure your portfolio tool has APIs or ODBC to enable external reporting.

- Develop a list of workflows and tools that don't exist in the enterprise and might be good enhancements to the portfolio. The next section has examples like centralizing status reports, tracking project costs, or engaging the organization on new ideas.

These seem like relatively straightforward requirements. You would expect that portfolio management tools should be able to support these requirements.

My experience is that this isn't the case. As stated earlier in the chapter, one chief reason why portfolio management often fails is that the tools selected are either too cumbersome to configure, have clunky user experiences and are too difficult to use by participants, or are too closed, making it difficult to import data or plug in external BI tools. If the administrative overhead to build, support, or use these tools is high, you'll never get the adoption. If the data collected and the workflow configured isn't developed to the specific needs of the organization, if it's too out-of-the-box, it will fail to deliver sufficient value, and the initiative will lose momentum.

It is for these reasons that I always elect to build rather than buy portfolio management tools.

But I don't build them from scratch. That would be too expensive to develop and maintain. The minimal portfolio I described is essentially a single table. You could build this capability in a spreadsheet, a MS SharePoint list, or even a simple database. But add in the next level of capabilities, and now you're going to need an application that supports multiple workflows and a larger data model. If you go down the home-grown route, it is very likely that you will need to dedicate development resources to maintain and extend capabilities. Most organizations can't afford to make this ongoing investment, unless the development is very inexpensive.

There are options to build custom applications rapidly and at low cost. These are so-called low-code platforms that enable developing web and mobile applications without the need to write formal software code. These platforms tend to be Cloud based and support limited workflow capabilities but still enable a wide range of lightweight organizational and departmental development needs. Some of these platforms are simple enough that they enable "citizen development," that is, applications, workflows, knowledge databases, and other tools developed and fully supported by business end users with minimal or no assistance from development teams. For many organizations, these tools are perfect for developing an organization-specific portfolio.

If you have a larger organization with more specific workflow needs or if the portfolio must comply with specific regulatory environments, then you can look at Business Process Management (BPM) tools to develop the portfolio. The downside of these tools is that many BPM tools are designed to be configured by application developers, so while this might be more efficient than developing a proprietary application, you'll still need to allocate development resources to in order build, support, or extend portfolio capabilities.

GAIN TOP-LEVEL SUPPORT

I have yet to meet a CEO who fully "gets" centralizing initiatives. They get it to a point but rarely understand all the value it brings to aligning teams and optimizing resources.

So having a prototype of the tool helps, especially if you can get some participants to input data. I'm not saying you'll be fully successful getting the CEO on board with a prototype filled with data, but the CEO will not see the value without a demonstration of how the portfolio will enable smarter investments and better execution. Don't forget to highlight simplicity because if the CEO associates the portfolio with bureaucracy and additional administration or if it resembles a previous attempt to establish PMOs, then you are likely to get bounced without the required support.

If you fail, your fallback is to launch it to your group as a beta. Guess what? That's more or less how I've rolled this out in my three trials, but it still pays dividends, and eventually you will get some support even if portfolio practices aren't fully embraced across the enterprise.

This step will help you determine your charter and scope. If it's embraced, you should prepare to roll this out to a wider net of participants and demonstrate its simplicity and value. If you're starting with your team, then you can focus on process mechanics and governance more than value proposition.

ROLLOUT PLAN

Regardless of your charter and how much data you're successful capturing up front, roll out your portfolio tool as you would any other enterprise tool. That is, roll it out as slowly as you can to get more volunteer adoption, to knock out any kinks in workflow, and to make sure you're getting the targeted data quality.

I've always kept the initial configuration incredibly simple because, in my experience, these tools need to roll out very quickly. At one CIO position, after showing the tool to the president during my second week in the role, he asked me to lead a prioritization exercise across the senior team at an offsite scheduled for the following week. In another role, we had to use the tool in month two to aid in a restructuring. In my third, we needed to define a charter for a transformation program and align resources very quickly to meet year one targets. If you keep the initial portfolio capabilities simple, you have a much better chance of demonstrating value.

Focus your rollout on the following principles:

- ▸ Make sure participants understand why you are taking on this exercise.
- ▸ Make it clear that this isn't a onetime effort and that they will be expected to participate.
- ▸ If your tool's user experience is cumbersome, strongly consider alternatives before you get started. Similarly, if using the tool requires a lot of training and isn't intuitive, you'd best slow down and look at other options.
- ▸ Ensure that data definitions are well documented and that the data quality targets are identified as success criteria.
- ▸ Encourage supporters so that you can use their efforts and results as examples to others. Let extreme laggards be laggards, and align them over an extended period.
- ▸ Set expectations on what you want participants to do in the tool and set a cadence for these updates. Expect to nag participants until using the portfolio becomes part of their habits.

Getting Value from the Portfolio

Once you have a basic portfolio in place and even if it's limited in scope it's time to add some capabilities that make it more useful. Remember, when you add capabilities, steer away from ones that are too complicated or replicate too much information that is already in project management and other tools. Continue to think of portfolio as a high-level aggregation tool that enables both decision making and collaboration.

The following sections describe a few capabilities that I have developed over time at three different organizations to various degrees of capability. I've always rolled out Status Updates, and these were foundational in my organization's ability to manage many active digital transformation initiatives. Smaller organizations may find value in using the tool for ideation and for resource management, so I've included some details on these workflows. Other workflow options include vendor management, hiring workflows, contract management, and asset management.

STATUS UPDATES

It drives me nuts to see project leaders send out updates on their initiatives by email—all that important knowledge buried in an email system and available only to the email recipients. Even worse are status updates delivered in MS PowerPoint, the ones that have big bold colors to indicate project status. While these enforce some uniformity in reporting, they are likely to be time-consuming to fill out and provide limited information to stakeholders. What if I want to observe the trend for an initiative? Is this initiative always status red? Is this leader more likely to label her initiatives red compared to her colleagues who prefer showcasing their projects as green?

Even worse is when there are no standards for updating leaders on the status of initiatives. These organizations operate with little information and request it only at key milestones or at specific organization events. How do leaders ensure that initiatives stay on track and don't require some remediation if there aren't regular status updates? What if an initiative needs to pivot, be delayed, or even accelerated? How are leaders going to recognize these needs without basic information?

A worse scenario is long drawn-out status meetings, the ones led by a controlling leader that isn't information driven, gathers all the leaders (or as many as can attend) into a room to do a readout of their initiative. Even if you only have a few initiatives, say five for example, the most efficient meeting is going to be 30 minutes in length and involve six individuals. Don't you think the same information can be conveyed a lot faster and more efficiently? Wouldn't it be more important to use the same 30 minutes toward decision making, planning, or coordination rather than just updating colleagues?

There is an answer, and I call them Status Updates, and here's how I've implemented them. A new screen in the portfolio tool asks project leaders to report a Status Level of red, yellow, green, and a text field captures a three to four-sentence update for each initiative that they manage. I ask project leaders to submit status updates weekly on a specific day of the week and time window. I set this schedule so that status updates are entered the day before any steering or leadership meetings. Reports help leaders view either all the updates for that week or updates for a specific initiative over a selected period.

I convene project leaders to walk them through the process, explain why these updates are important, and demonstrate the reports. I ensure that they understand their responsibility to submit them on time and to accurately reflect the key status of the initiative in language and terms that those not directly participating can understand. Also, I ask them to assign and train a delegate to submit an update for times that they are not available. Make it clear that they should submit even if there's no material change in status.

You'll need to nag a few laggards who miss getting there on time and coach everyone on when to set an initiative in yellow or red. Some junior project leaders will need assistance on how to improve their writing and to avoid internal jargon. Some will need guidance on what level of detail to include in updates that reach senior leaders.

Some will want you to formally define red versus yellow versus green status. I try to avoid this as I prefer seeing the leaders self-interpret these status levels. If they persist, I tell them that red means you've hit a material risk at missing a deadline, scope of a primary deliverable, or have identified a significant quality issue. They can use yellow to identify risks that the team is actively mitigating.

By that definition, many initiatives should be in yellow for periods of time. That's a good thing because it keeps the leaders and participants on top of the underlying issues and risks. If you see an initiative with green status for several consecutive weeks, it may be a good idea to take a deeper look and make sure the team isn't oversimplifying or missing key details.

SOLICITING IDEAS FROM EMPLOYEES

The best ideas come from employees, right? The salespeople talking to strategic customers, the new employee in operations who thinks there's a more efficient way to run a key business process, a digital marketer who has ideas on how to better reach a key customer segment, a developer who wants to prototype a new technology, the Compliance Officer who is looking for more support to address a key organizational risk, the administrative assistant who has an idea on how to enable better collaboration with remote workers, or the Security Officer who wants employees to learn about the latest threats. How do you capture those ideas and have the right people put effort into the most important ones?

If your organization is ready to use collaboration tools to capture ideas, then you might be ready to extend the portfolio to enable employees in the organization to submit them for consideration. If you've implemented a portfolio with an initial stage "Defined" as recommended, then you can use this as the default stage for ideas submitted.

From there, you should decide what data you want to capture on the idea. There's an art and a science to this because if you capture too little information, it will be hard to vet the idea without a lot of effort to consult with its sponsor. If you ask for too much information, it will look complicated, and you are likely to frighten off good ideas.

The other variable is how fast you roll this out. Do you share it with the entire enterprise on day one and promote a democratic process, or do you start with a select group and grow with some demonstrated success?

Learning from social startups, I recommend a simple start with a pilot group. The minimal fields I would capture include the Project Title, Who's in Charge (who submitted), the Organizational Context, and the single field to capture the Benefit. I would then add a single paragraph "Describe the Idea" field that I would limit to 400 words.

I would recommend partnering with head of talent, selecting two or three other leaders to form a steering group, and identifying the pilot group of innovators and change agents across the organization who can submit their ideas. The steering group should review the submitted ideas and assign one of three action-oriented categories: "Worth Considering," "Hold," and, "Pass." The steering group should then identify next steps for each category that covers how to communicate the results to the sponsor and provide guidance on formally moving the top ideas into the portfolio at the ideation stage.

RESOURCE MANAGEMENT

If you have a limited number of resources and they are largely employees, then there's probably little reason for the portfolio tool to have too much information on resources.

However, if your organization has a healthy mix of employees, contractors, and resources from outsourcing providers, you might find it useful to centralize a small resource database that's not replicating what human resources captures or what is required in your corporate directory.

There is some useful information for managing a portfolio of initiatives that you may not easily be able to store or access in an HR system, ERP, or corporate directory. You may also find that it is less efficient or reliable to ask project managers to record this information in their project management tools.

What information is useful at a portfolio level?

- ▶ Resource type (employee, contractor, outsourcer)
- ▶ Statement of work (SOW) terms such as start/end dates, contract type (time/materials, fixed, etc.), hourly rate
- ▶ Location
- ▶ Skills and skill levels
- ▶ Additional contact information (for example, instant messenger)
- ▶ Availability calendar (if you don't have one already)
- ▶ Links to initiatives they have participated in, roles they took on, and when they were participating
- ▶ Links to signed contracts

I find that organizations in transformation have a lot of flux in the number of running initiatives, budgets, and resources. Many resource management tools are optimized to handle relatively static resource pools and become difficult to leverage when you need to shift or add resources frequently. Centralizing a basic repository for this information, assigning ownership, and creating some basic processes can accelerate resource management practices in organizations that need to move smarter and faster.

Financial Portfolio Practices

At some point in your transformation, you're going to have to think through the financial aspects of how you will fund and ultimately drive a return on the investment. Unfortunately, most ERP systems are configured to run today's businesses and may not have sufficient detail to help model transformation scenarios. That's not to say they can't; it's just more likely that the financial teams only capture information at a high level and not at an operating level. Chances are that your financial system has a lot of detail on employee-related costs and high-level information only on costs tied to contracts, assets, and initiatives.

If you've implemented some of the portfolio practices that I've recommended, then you're on your way to capture some of the financial details on contracts (start and end dates, expenses, classifications) and external contractors (start and end dates, locations, hourly costs). Hopefully, you have an IT asset-tracking system that also enables you to capture financial details on any infrastructure or software assets. If all you're trying to do is keep track of existing costs and know when decisions are needed on an expiring contract or an asset going end of life, then you can select one of the many tools that handle this accounting.

But look around your organization and find out how individual departments propose and track their budgets. Perhaps the enterprise has selected a tool or implemented a component in the ERP to propose and then track departmental budgets. But I suspect that many organizations are doing this by working with their finance teams to review and transition costs as they are represented in the ERP from current to next year. Other departments will propose budgets by itemizing the details in spreadsheets. Budget spreadsheets are assembled, details are aggregated, decisions are made, and final aggregated numbers are loaded into the ERP. Once a quarter or month, depending on your organization, you sit down with the finance team to review spend and reforecast.

Why Legacy Financial Practices are Inadequate During Transformation, Growth, or Turnarounds

Budget tracking by spreadsheet is not sufficient for managing technology budgets, for multiyear transformational efforts, for budgets when an organization is experiencing significant growth, or for budgets for organizations that are undergoing a turnaround. These scenarios have a few things in common.

First, the budgeted spend on specific programs, vendors, and resources is likely to change through the year as more details enable better decision making. Most organizations formally budget once a year, yet transformational programs require making decisions and pivots throughout the course of the year. So if you want to make an investment midyear, you probably need a detailed accounting of current spend and forecast to determine where you can shift money budgeted from other programs.

Transformational programs are often multiyear, while corporate budgets follow a yearly accounting cycle. Investments, operational expenses, cost savings, and revenue often cross the accounting year boundaries, making it difficult to track. Eventually, sponsors of the transformation will want to understand ROI, and if you're relying on information collected in the ERP or data stored in spreadsheets, then you're going to have some difficulty tracking and reporting financial status.

Transformation programs also often require a spending shift. You might be automating operations and taking cost out, but the IT department needs new funding to support the underlying systems. You might want to boost marketing spend when new products are launched and want to consider curbing costs in other areas to offset.

Organizations experiencing growth or turnaround require looking at expenses across multiple departments to understand where costs can be cut or where growth requires additional resources. If your ERP has detailed scope and reasonable data quality, then this can be the data source for modeling these scenarios. The challenge is having the right tools to be able to model multiple scenarios, do so with frequency, and have a collaborative dialog with decision makers on what levers to pull. Try doing the modeling in a spreadsheet, and you're likely to go through hours of Q&A meetings with executives pushing for finalized numbers and operational leaders trying to reverse engineer calculations to understand the underlying decision.

There are times when you can make accounting cycles work to your advantage and other times when it can create risk. This is especially important for organizations with tight budgets or managing through a turnaround where every dollar matters. Perhaps it's better to make a purchase in a vendor's fourth quarter to get the best discounts? Maybe you are spending less on a contract than forecasted and there's room to squeeze another project within an existing scope of work? Both scenarios need leaders to track expenses at a detailed level to make tactical financial decisions.

Finally, organizations in transformation, growth, or turnaround should track variable costs at a detailed, operational level to make sounder financial decisions. Maybe there is a variable cost that's skyrocketing, while a business or operation is scaling and you need early warning signs from operational data before you are invoiced and on the hook for the cost overrun? Maybe there's a recurring cost for a service that's used episodically, and it may be advantageous to either renegotiate the contract or find an alternative service? Maybe you've surpassed a volume of operational activity, and there is opportunity to renegotiate? Maybe you need new controls to better manage an on-demand service that has significant cost factors? Decisions based on all these factors require a connection between financial and operational data, updated frequently and reviewed by subject matter experts to know when a cost factor requires a review and decision making.

If you're going to calculate ROI, then you also must project and capture financial benefits. The ERP should be the source of this information, but you're likely going to need some analytics or processing before plugging this into a P/L for an initiative. Maybe only part of the revenue from a new client can be associated with the initiative? Maybe you need some form of allocation of new customer revenue across multiple initiatives? Tools are needed to perform these allocations and ensure that the underlying calculations are transparent to decision makers.

You might argue that all of this is within the financial team's domain and they should step up with practices and tools to address it. The requirements outlined illustrate the need for financial and accounting teams to operate in real time with more operating data and with more transparency and collaboration with business leaders. Can they step up?

You're the transformational leader, so you can decide whether this team, its practices, and its technologies are ready to step up and take on this role. But in my experience, they aren't ready until you blaze a path for them. These teams are under-resourced and are last in line for technology investments. Few go out of their way to collaborate with them, so it's unlikely they have access or knowledge of the underlying operational data. It's also inefficient for you to fully outsource the scenario planning, cost tracking, and reforecasting to them when you manage a transformation program that is likely to require frequent reforecasts, pivots, and scenario planning.

Financial Planning for Digital Transformation

If your enterprise is doing over $500M in revenue, then you should consider leveraging an enterprise performance management application to perform profitability analysis and scenario planning. Gartner has several solutions in their magic quadrant that can likely be tailored to the type of ongoing analysis required for transformation, growth, or turnaround.

I am going to describe the scenario when this isn't an option. This may occur because your business is too small to afford one of these solutions, if your existing solution can't easily be used for transformation planning, or if it will take too long for your organization to acquire and configure a solution. This is the situation I've been in for my last three CIO roles.

There are three components to a solution that you can easily craft if you have the right basic tools and talent:

- ► A database to track budgets and expenditures
- ► A BI tool that can be used to develop dashboards connecting financial and ERP data
- ► A modeling tool for scenario planning and transitioning financials from current to future states

Let's look at all three in more detail.

TRACKING BUDGETS AND EXPENDITURES

Everyone has a budget spreadsheet. During budgeting season, it's nicely formatted and well structured to show the expenses, dimensions to help group them, and fields to align them to strategic drivers, owners, and timing. Larger departments will hand out segments of their budget to different owners and roll them up, sometimes manually and other times by versioning the worksheet in a document repository.

When completed, it goes through the corporate scrutiny process. Some items come out, others may get added, some values may change. It gets a little messy tracking these changes, but no one likes long budgeting processes, so hopefully this is over in a matter of weeks.

Once completed, finance has the job of rolling the data into their ERP. As reviewed earlier, most often this is done at an aggregate level. Likely, they will capture several categories of spend underneath every cost center. I have yet to see a finance department capture every itemized spend.

So that leaves the granular tracking to the budget owners. Some will elect to do this tracking. Others will manage to the overall number.

My experience with running digital and technology budgets is that managing the budget at a granular level must happen four quarters of the year. Sometimes I reforecast because the business climate changes or the priority changes, and I'm asked to submit an updated budget. Sometimes variable expenses come in higher than budgeted, and I look for other budgets to cover the variance. Sometimes the budget exceeds the technology organization's ability to execute, and I can drop the forecasted spend, while other times I want to increase spend where there is opportunity to deliver more value faster. There are times when I need to benchmark spends in specific categories to judge efficiency and need to be able to match spending categories to the ones supplied in the benchmark. Lastly, I need accurate low-level budget information to do bottom-up multiyear strategic forecasts. I likely must do this with a small team of lieutenants who have better knowledge of the various costs in the technology budget.

I've used tools outside the ERP to perform budget tracking of transformation programs. The tools have been relatively primitive but much more powerful than tracking budgets with spreadsheets. It's a second "use case" for the "low-code" platforms that I've deployed.

What does the tool look like? It starts with your budget spreadsheet, the neat one that you probably developed during the budgeting process. It then enables the following additional workflows:

- ▸ Assign an owner to the budget.
- ▸ Track individual budgeted items that roll up to various spending dimensions.
- ▸ Normalize a taxonomy for categorizing budgeted items.
- ▸ Lock the budget at the end of budget season.
- ▸ Enable workflow to request budget changes, have them approved, and reforecast.
- ▸ Interface with the ERP to capture invoice data.

This might look complicated, but it's not if you have a low-code platform. I've personally developed this tool three times to efficiently manage transformation programs.

I should point out that in all three instances, this tool, data, and workflow were shared with appropriate finance department members. It has cut down on meetings and complexities to track forecasting changes and enabled them to better accrue for expenses.

A BI TOOL FOR VISUALIZING FINANCIALS

Once you have a basic budget tracking process workflow, the next question is how you will report on the data. Your lieutenants need some basic dashboards to visualize spend and make decisions. You may also want to be sharing some of the data in aggregate forms with stakeholders, finance, and executive teams. I have found that providing this level of transparency drives trust with business leaders, showing that the technology team is making sound investments and are managing expenses.

This leaves you with a couple of options. You can either build some basic reporting out of the platform used to develop the workflow, or you can consider a reporting platform that connects to this data. I usually depend using a self-service BI tool for this reporting because it enables connecting to other data sources like the ERP and developing audience-specific dashboards.

FINANCIAL MODELING AND SCENARIO PLANNING

Tracking financials and visualizing them are not sufficient. The last mile is putting this data to good use to enable better short- and longer-term decision making. Some examples:

- ► Capture and track ROI against an initiative.
- ► Demonstrate a total cost of ownership of a service.
- ► Reforecast spending under multiple business scenarios.
- ► Benchmark your spending in specific categories.
- ► Model different investment scenarios when multiple solution options are possible.
- ► Show the ongoing operational costs against new investments.
- ► Forecast cost reductions when services or systems are decommissioned.
- ► Model the financial impact of reorganizations, outsourcing, and other strategic shifts.
- ► Implement a cost allocation when a service is applied to multiple business units.
- ► Calculate the impacts of increasing scope or accelerating timelines.

As a CIO, I have been asked these questions repeatedly. In small technology departments with understaffed finance departments, it has fallen on me and select members of my staff to do this level of financial modeling and presentation. So are you prepared to pull this off when you can dedicate only a fraction of your time to do this level of planning?

With baseline data in place and a reporting tool, you're halfway there. The last mile is to figure out what tool you'll use to do the modeling on demand or as needed.

This is where you must make some quick calls on the best tool for the job. In many cases, I'm resorting to spreadsheets that connect to the baseline data if I am putting together a onetime or low-frequency analysis. Other times, if I think something is repeatable, I may develop specific structures to capture and track the scenario or enable the modeling as a core capability. For example, ROI calculations are needed in multiple instances, so I am more inclined to develop this as a capability, whereas reorganizations are less frequent and probably best modeled in a spreadsheet. If the presentation can be done largely through calculations and data visualizations, then I will implement it in a BI platform.

Final Thoughts on Agile Portfolio Management

I hope this chapter didn't make your eyes roll. I know tracking initiatives, resources, and financials isn't the most exciting aspect of running transformation programs or technology organizations. But it is necessary and is far more important in successful programs, especially for smaller organizations where funding is not easy to come by and investments are not easy managerial decisions.

I've termed these practices agile portfolio management because they don't need to be in place prior to kicking off your transformation programs and should be designed to evolve where and when needed. Once you have the foundational structure to capture initiatives and financials and have a pilot team to work with, then you can scale capability and usage as needed.

How do I do this in practice?

I run my management team as monthly agile sprints. Our management meetings respond to "red" initiatives and plan the next set of organizational capabilities. They take the form of retrospectives, so when we discover a governance, practice, process, or data gap, we itemize it in our backlog and decide whether to prioritize its development.

Next chapters start entering the domains of new responsibilities. First, we must look at data, data science, the role Chief Data Officer, and evolving to a data-driven organization. Then we will look at how to develop product management capabilities to drive new sources of revenue and growth.

5.

TRANSFORMING TO A DATA-DRIVEN ORGANIZATION

am certain you already know all the hype about Big Data and may have even achieved some success with Big Data technologies. But I'm here to tell you that the Big Data opportunity is not just about the new technological capabilities to process and analyze large volumes, variety, or velocity of data. In some organizations, these technology capabilities may be a catalysts, but deploying them and even having the talent to leverage them are not sufficient to drive business value, enable new product offerings, demonstrate competitive advantages, or enable smarter decision making.

The Big Data opportunity is better described by how organizations get value from the data they already have, data that they can develop or create, or third-party data that they can integrate. Here's a definition of Big Data that I offered on my blog:

Big Data Defined—Big Data is not defined by its data management challenges but by the organization's capabilities in analyzing the data, deriving intelligence from it, and leveraging it to make forward-looking decisions. It should also be defined by the organization's capability in creating new data streams and aggregating them into its data warehouses.

This definition covers two elements of change. First, it's the skills and organizational changes required to analyze, derive insights, and encourage data-driven decision making. This is what is typically called the data-driven organization, and I'll be covering why this type of culture is critical for organizations driving digital transformation. More importantly, I'll cover how to cultivate a data science program and how to enable it through technology, practices, and governance.

The second element covers a capability that data-driven organizations must mature, which is the ability to source and aggregate new data sources, integrate in new analytics capabilities, and partner with third-party analytical services.

The final element is using data for strategic and competitive advantage by enhancing existing product offerings or developing new ones. It means embedding data collection into products so that you can personalize user experiences and delight customers. It implies that you can collect operational metrics and process in real time to improve the performance of a system or component. It enables you to deliver new intelligence to your customers by aggregating and anonymizing data that you collect.

Underpinning all of this is the new data technology capabilities even beyond the volume, the velocity and variety of Big Data that I covered in Chapter Three. It's aggregating data from massive arrays of sensors (IoT), processing for macro and micro responses, and sending real-time controls back to the appropriate environments. It's new predictive analytics capabilities, including machine learning, deep learning, and artificial intelligence, that can provide capabilities beyond human intelligence and the personalization of large amounts of disparate data. It's the ability to participate in the API economy and digital ecosystems where organizations can sell, share, and buy algorithms and capabilities.

To Become Data Driven, Start by Reviewing Our Past Data Sins

Before we can talk about becoming a data-driven organization, establishing Big Data capabilities, enabling data scientists, or developing revenue-generating products and services from an organization's data, it's important to look at the organization's underlying data legacy and culture.

It's not like more organizations have zero data analytics capabilities. Most do in some form and probably believe that they are data driven based on the existing talent, capabilities and tools. But the issue with data technologies and practices is that it's not just about the ability to produce insights; it's whether the underlying process is accurate, repeatable, efficient, and scalable.

Is the analytics accessible only to the person who performed the work, or can it be reviewed and extended by others? How many others can use the final analytics for decision making? How often is the data refreshed, and how many human and machine hours does it take to process this data? Are data definitions, calculations, and assumptions clearly defined and understood? Is there an underlying process to measure and improve data quality? And who has access to this data? How can the data legally be used, and what security, privacy, or other compliance is required for it?

Our legacy of data analytics and processing doesn't easily address these issues. The tools used in the past led to the proliferation of duplicate data, data silos that are hard to extend, and analytics that are hard to repeat. Data integration often requires manual steps, and the automated ones were rarely implemented with data validation or with scalability in mind. Most organizations don't know what data exists in their enterprise or how can they leverage it for competitive advantage.

Over the last few years, I've written on my blog about these different issues with more specific examples. First, let's look at the impacts of two of the most widely used data analytics and database tools across organizations of all sizes. Then I'll share some specific concerns of how most organizations implement data integration. Lastly, I'll provide my definition of an organization's "dark data" and its implications.

The Problems with Spreadsheets and Siloed Databases

How many spreadsheets do you have on your network? Do you champion analysts that demonstrate wizardly skills performing calculations, pivot tables, macros, and formatting spreadsheets? One of the most trafficked posts on my blog is a letter to spreadsheet jockeys[1] that they need to expand their skill set in order to leverage Big Data technologies, reduce human error, and collaborate in a data-driven organization.

The European Spreadsheet Risk Interest Group[2] published a number of *horror stories* coming from poorly configured spreadsheets.[3] *The Wall Street Journal* reported that a spreadsheet error cost Tibco shareholders $100 million. A $6 billion trading loss was at least partially due to modeling flaws in Excel.[4] A flaw in Harvard economists' Excel spreadsheet discredited their highly cited conclusions that higher government debt is associated with slower economic growth.[5] Barclays unknowingly picked up 179 additional Lehman contracts because the data was marked as hidden in a spreadsheet.[6] Genetic research incurred errors in their gene lists when Excel automatically converted them to calendar dates or numbers.[7]

How bad can it get? Think Enron bad. Felienne Hermans, of Delft University of Technology analyzed the 265,586 attachment files that were made public, of which 51,572 were Excel files and 16,189 were unique spreadsheets.[8] The full analysis is available in the published report, showing 2,205 spreadsheets that contained at least one Excel error and 755 files that had more than 100 errors.[9] If that wasn't bad enough, *The Telegraph* reports, "Some people were sending more than 100 spreadsheets back and forth on a daily basis which proves there was no agreed system or standardized way of working."[10]

This is not just a problem for big companies or researchers. As reported in *Inc.*, "Spreadsheets Are Destroying Your Business", "Spending valuable time working on inaccurate, static spreadsheets is a waste of your hard-earned dollars."[11] An estimated 88% of spreadsheets have errors in them,[12] so do you think your team of spreadsheet jockeys can beat the odds?

Think of spreadsheets as algorithms. Instead of "code," you have formulas and possibly even scripts but with few tools to debug or diagnose errors. Unlike a programmed application, there is also the potential for manual errors done through copy/paste or when a formula is applied to a range with missing cells. Most programmers today separate data, business logic, and presentation, but Excel merges all three, providing speed and convenience at the expense of manual errors and complexity. Finally, spreadsheet sharing is a pandemic that is very difficult to control. Even Cloud-based spreadsheet tools like Google Sheets or Excel in Office 365 cannot fully prevent people from copying worksheets and sharing derivative works.

But executives can't get off the juice of getting quick and cheap analysis. They can't see the impact of errors, the time applied to creating and recreating the analytics, and the lost opportunities when access to data is limited through email distributions. The need for business-created analytics is real, but ungoverned spreadsheets are no longer the solutions.

And spreadsheets aren't the only issues.

I also wrote about the SadBA,[13] the self-appointed database business analyst that creates single-purpose databases to address an analysis or a workflow. Many companies allowed business analysts to use Microsoft Access and other desktop database tools when they needed to do something more complex than what can be done in a spreadsheet. I inherited more than 40 of these siloed databases at one of my organizations, and I know other CIO and Chief Data Officers also struggling with them.

As big of a database mess as this is, the underlying data mess can be a daunting maze to get through. Considering even a single database, a trained database administrator (DBA) would need to understand the underlying data model, document any scripts or procedures loading data, and itemize reporting needs. If any forms were developed, especially if multiple people are using the database as part of a workflow, then you'll need a business analyst and possibly an application developer to consider how these business processes are accomplished.

Perhaps you've never had to read someone else's code? Rebuilding a database when it likely has poor naming conventions, missing data relationships, and a complete lack of referential integrity requires a DBA with the skills of a linguistic anthropologist. Now tell this DBA that there are multiple databases that contain duplicate and related data and that special software tools are needed to normalize the data model, load in data from multiple sources, and match, merge and de-duplicate records, before even considering how to replicate existing functionality.

Is this your company's sales data, customer data, marketing data, or financial data? More likely, the answer is yes because it's this data that business users work with the most. If the business user needed to perform a quick analysis and IT wasn't available or had the necessary agility to come up with a solution, then it is likely that a spreadsheet jockey or a SadBA established a solution.

Why Is Data Sooo Messy, and How to Avoid Data Landfills?

There's a paradox about the work data scientists take on. On one hand, data science is described as the "sexiest" job,[14] given the importance of the role in digital organizations. On the other hand, much of the work is messy "janitorial" work that data scientists have to perform[15] in order to be able to find "nuggets" in Big Data.

Why is the work of data scientists so complicated and messy, requiring them hours if not days to bring data together before they can perform any analysis? The history of data science starts with complicated data warehouses, expensive BI tools, hundreds if not thousands of processes moving data all over the place, and bloated expectations. On the other extreme, many organizations have siloed databases, DBAs largely skilled at keeping the lights on, and spreadsheet jockeys performing analytics in hundreds of files. The janitorial work data scientists are performing partially exists because of the mess of databases and derivative data sources created in the past and never cleansed into formalized data repositories.

And I'm not sure this generation will get it better. If spreadsheets and database silos are the data legacy issues, are modernized tools any better? How about your BI solution that has thousands of reports that are rarely used and others that are minor derivatives of other ones? Does your database look more like urban sprawl than a planned architecture, with hundreds of tables added over time to solve one-time problems? Have you replaced some spreadsheets with more capable data profiling, data integration, or visualization tools without having a defined practice of what gets created, where is it stored, and how it is documented?

With great power comes even greater responsibility. All the technologies and tools data scientists have at their fingertips also have the power to create a new set of data stashes—informal places where data is aggregated—or buried data mines—places where analytics are performed but not automated or transparent to future scientists. See Figure 5-1.

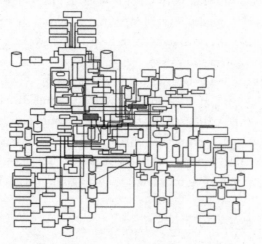

Figure 5-1. Illustration of a messy data architecture and unwieldy data flow

What can be even more challenging is the underlying steps to get data from point A to point B. Engineers call these ETLs, extract, transform, and load procedures, that move data from a source like a database, a file, a document, or a website, transform the data so that it is in a format that can be analyzed, used in an application, or shared, and then loaded to a destination tool or data repository. More universally, it's called data integration or data processing.

But those terms all largely apply when the process is scripted and automated. What you are more likely to find when an organization has ungoverned data practices is that most of the data integrations implemented have manual steps. Someone writes a query to pull data, loads it into a spreadsheet, and performs some manual data cleansing. They write formulas, pivot tables, copy/paste data, manually edit, and format the data—all steps that are very difficult to reverse-engineer. The data is then loaded into their personal data stash for their target business purpose.

If data scientists, DBAs, and CIOs are not careful, the data stashes and buried data mines can slowly transform into full-blown data landfills.

DBAs know what I'm talking about. It's a combination of data warehouses, reports, dashboards, and ETLs that no one wants to touch. No one understands who is using what reports or dashboards in what business process for what purpose or benefit. ETLs look like a maze of buried unlabeled pipes developed using a myriad of programming approaches and with no standards to help future workers separate out plumbing from filters and valves.

Data scientists and their partners, data stewards, DBAs, business analysts, developers, and testers need to instill some discipline in how they source, process, improve quality, analyze, and report on data. This is the heart of data governance, a term that makes some business leaders cringe and paralyzes many technologists when they don't know where to start. But before going into solutions, let's go deeper into a few other issues.

Clueless About Data Integration?

When someone says that the data integration process is automated, I suggest asking questions to clarify what they mean by "automated." You'll probably conclude that the process is anything but automated, let alone reliable, scalable, secure, or configurable.

To some, automation implies efficiency and reliability but can include manual steps so long as they are performed quickly and easily. Others assume that if the process can be completed without IT involvement, then it is automated. Still others don't care whether it's automated but are angered when there is a breakage in the process or if it doesn't scale magically as more data is piped in. There is also a bad assumption that the daily process running on a volume of data will magically scale when existing data must be reprocessed for a change in business logic or storage schema.

As hard as it is to modify software, modifying data integration can be even more daunting especially if the steps are not documented. For example, fixing data quality issues or addressing boundary conditions tend to be undocumented steps performed by subject matter experts.

So now you want to fix data integration. Take out the manual steps. Make the process more nimble, agile, reliable, and so on. Why is it so hard to get business leaders on board with the investment needed in data integration?

Big Data technologies like ETL, Hadoop, Spark, Pig, Hive, or IFTTT[16] are difficult enough for technologists to fully understand and apply to the appropriate data issues, but the jargon just frustrates business leaders. Many are clueless about the technologies (other than the overhyped term "Big Data") and are more surprised about the need to have them and invest time to build expertise in them. Information technology and processing data have been around a long time, so there is underlying assumption, even with Big Data, that integration is cheap and easy.

Now, unless you are doing very basic, point-A-to-B, straightforward plumbing, data integration can become quite complex as new data sources are added, logic is changed, and new applications are developed. Data integration may start off simple, but over time legacy data flows are difficult to understand, extend, or modify.

The complexity slows down IT, and if data and analytics are strategic to the business, it frustrates business leaders that they can't just add a new data source, modify calculations, improve on data validation, or strategically change the downstream analytics.

So now, whatever technologies IT selects and however it is presented to the business, it comes across as plumbing. All that time is invested just to have a stable data flow? Analytics, visualization, application, and for the most part doing anything useful with the data will cost extra?

The simple answer is that data integration is a key foundational technology capability if data is strategic to the business. It's not just a technology; it is a *competency*. Unfortunately, ranked against other data technologies like data warehousing and application development, data integration capabilities are often a distant third in staffing and funding priority. So it's no surprise that many processes are not fully automated and that business leaders don't *get* the importance of this capability.

Knowing you have a problem is the first step to solving it. Getting data in and out of primary data sources securely, efficiently, and reliably is as important as the underlying structure of the data warehouses and the analytics performed over it.

The scope of data integration is a lot greater today. It used to be that data integration had to do largely with internally hosted data sources and where DBAs and developers had many tools and ways to access the data. But what about data in SaaS platforms?

Enterprises are maturing their use of strategic software as a service (SaaS) or platform as a service (PaaS) and experimenting with innovative Cloud hosted services solutions that deliver new capabilities. On average, enterprises are using between five and nine SaaS platforms,[17] and the number is expected to grow to 30 over the next three years.[18]

But while top SaaS platforms offer advanced functionality, scalable infrastructure, speed to market on new capabilities, and often lower costs, using many platforms creates some new challenges.

Every SaaS platform captures content and data, enables workflow and collaboration related to its core capabilities, and provides some out of the box reporting capabilities. Ideally, these features should be "good enough" to unlock its primary business values, but is the platform "sufficiently open" to enable integration once usage hits critical mass and the platform becomes more business critical?

If you are evaluating an SaaS platform and ask the salesperson about openness and the ability to pull data out or push data in, you'll get the knee jerk response, "We have APIs." Business leaders are now overly sensitized to this response, and when they hear it, they assume that having APIs implies that it's easy to integrate and that the technologists should be able to figure out how to do simple operations like accessing or changing the underlying data. The salesperson may even go a step further and show additional capabilities like software development kits that enable using the APIs more easily in specific programming languages. Ideally, they should show you their app store showing example applications that were developed using their toolkits and present metrics on number of applications, developers, and other metrics to illustrate there is a critical mass of activity.

The more marketing around these capabilities, the more third-party apps available, and the more developers in the program, the more likely it is that these integration tools and the skills required to leverage them can be used to achieve a desired enhancement or integration. Even if the SaaS vendor is a small and emerging business, you can evaluate their commitment to this program if these integration capabilities are prominently featured on the vendor's website, if the documentation is easily accessible, and there is some evidence of external usage. When I evaluate technologies, I consider it a red flag if the vendor buries marketing, information, or documentation around their APIs or, worse, makes it available only to paying customers.

But APIs, SDKs, and the like are all tools for developers and require engineering efforts to leverage. In addition, APIs are proprietary, so there is a learning curve to everyone that is needed to fulfill integration needs. What if I am trying to implement a more simplified out-of-the-box data integration? Is there an ODBC connection that enables me to easily connect, and is the underlying data model easy to understand and leverage? Can I easily connect an enterprise ETL or data quality tool so that I can move data in and out of the platform? Do they have built-in web and mobile widgets that enable me to plug in their functionality into other platforms? Do they plug into IFTTT platforms such as IFTTT or Zapier, Tray.io, or similar platforms?

The better SaaS solutions will have mature APIs that have had significant customer usage. The better ones will enable direct integration with other platforms and simple tools for business users to connect workflows and data. The ones to watch are thinking three steps ahead and building on-ramps for your organization's future digital transformation priorities, IOT strategies,[19] and other integration needs.

Are you evaluating platforms on integration capabilities? Are you investing in integration where it is necessary or provides value? Critical corporate data is becoming more decentralized across multiple SaaS environments, so over time, a strategy is needed of if, when, and how best to integrate this data.

The Problems with Dark Data

Let's now look at one final issue and revisit the definition of Big Data:

Big Data Defined—Big Data is not defined by its data management challenges but by the organization's capabilities in analyzing the data, deriving intelligence from it, and leveraging it to make forward-looking decisions. It should also be defined by the organization's capability in creating new data streams and aggregating them into its data warehouses.

You can provide analytics only on the data that you know about, but what about the data that exists in the enterprise that data scientists don't know about or other data that is difficult to access? The industry call this dark data, and here is a definition that I offered:[20]

> **Dark Data Defined—**Dark data is data or content that exists and is stored but is not leveraged and analyzed for intelligence or used in forward-looking decisions. It includes data that is in physical locations or formats that make analysis complex or too costly or data that has significant data quality issues. It also includes data that is currently stored and can be connected to other data sources for analysis but that the business has not dedicated sufficient resources to analyze and leverage. Finally (and this may be debatable), dark data also includes data that currently isn't captured by the enterprise or data that exists outside of the boundary of the enterprise.

This basically demonstrates three conditions where data could be but is not leveraged in Big Data analytics: (1) It could exist in a sufficient format, but the business hasn't leveraged it yet. (2) It exists, but it is too costly to clean or process. Or (3) it doesn't exist, and it needs to be captured or acquired.

Why is this important? Well, you can translate dark data to examples of data that's difficult to find or access. Let's say you need employment records of the enterprise from the 1990s, and that data is stored on tape in an offsite vault. What if you found a presentation from a colleague delivered a year ago, you want to revisit the data that was used in the underlying analysis, and your colleague is no longer with the firm. Are you going to be able to find this data? Or let's say you are seeking a data set—let's say it's competitive data for a specific product—do you know how to find this data or the appropriate subject matter experts? How about scanning the network drives for instances of spreadsheets? Will you be able to identify key information on this data to know whether it is valuable in a new context?

These are all examples of detectable dark data, but my definition is expansive and includes data that the enterprise doesn't have but is valuable. Maybe this is data that could be captured, but the organization hasn't configured products and services to do so, or maybe it's third-party data that could be purchased, but no one in the organization has the role to identify these data opportunities. To the enterprise, this data is dark and may put them at a competitive disadvantage if someone else has it and is using it effectively to compete against them.

Dark data may not have been a business issue several years ago, but it is now. If you drive the organization to become more data driven, but no one knows what data already exists in the enterprise and what sources to leverage, then you run a risk of developing analysis and driving decisions on the wrong or incomplete data sets. If you ignore the ecosystem of publicly and commercially available data, then your competitors that do tap into these sources may develop a competitive advantage.

Do You Have a Nimble Data Architecture?

Lastly, let's consider the databases and data warehouses already developed and being used in the enterprise. I've seen databases developed in a few ways. A formalized data warehouse may have been designed using standard patterns or may have been assembled in a hurry for a specific business case. Application-specific databases may have been developed by a software developer with minimal assistance of a database engineer and designed to the specific requirements of the application being developed. Commercial data sources, the back-end databases to commercial software, may enable customer direct access while other databases have terms of service or technical mechanisms that prevent you from tapping into them. Then there are databases developed by business users that can have a wide range of quality.

Regardless of how databases are created, I've seen several issues that most fall victim to:

- They are poorly documented. Even when there is a formal database diagram, there is rarely data dictionaries and other documents to help users leverage these databases.
- The original engineers leave little information on how to maintain or extend these databases. When new needs arise, few guidelines are passed to a second generation of engineers to aid in implementing these enhancements.

- Many databases are developed for specific needs without aligning to a documented database and data strategy. The result is a lot of duplicate data, inconsistent naming conventions, and unclear understanding of where master data resides.
- There is little formalized on how to monitor these databases for performance or to track the impact of growth. DBAs are left to monitor them using generic database tools looking for growing tablespaces, slow queries, and other optimizations when they occur. This makes it difficult to know whether any database can handle a 10× increase in data, transactions, or other activity.
- Many were constructed before NoSQL, Big Data and Cloud technologies were widely available, so they may have constructs in them that underperform given today's modern database technology options.

In summary, most of our legacy is riddled with poor data practices. We enable ad hoc analysis by business users that easily pollute our file systems with multitudes of unstructured data. We develop data integrations on a need-to-need basis with little thought to strategy, maintainability, or vision to capture new data sources. We have both dark data and poorly maintainable data warehouses. This is our legacy, and this is what we should learn from before investing in and layering on Big Data and data science capabilities.

The Challenges of Enabling Big Data and Data Science

Your organization may have already invested in Big Data technologies and data science programs, and you can hardly call it an emerging technology anymore. Regardless of where you are in the adoption curve and ignoring the impact of legacy practices, there remains several Big Data and data science challenges that require consideration. They fall into some key areas shown Figure 5-2.

- ► Do you have business leaders ready to leverage data and analytics?
- ► Have you selected optimal and nimble data platforms?
- ► Do you have the talent, collaboration and practices?
- ► Are you thinking about future technologies that are enabled by Big Data?

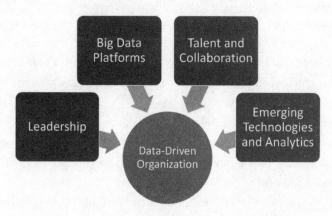

Figure 5-2. Factors that enable the data-driven organization

Challenge number one is leadership and the mindset of decision makers. Are decision makers in the organization leveraging data and reports that already exist to aid in decision making?

Every enterprise already collects lots of data but likely underutilizes it for intelligence, insight, and decision making. Data exists in disparate databases that can't easily be connected and analyzed holistically. Unstructured data in the form of documents, spreadsheets, and presentations exist that are largely used for individual or departmental needs and rarely coalesced centrally and analyzed. Enterprises that have deployed collaboration platforms could better leverage the networks and intelligence of its employees by analyzing relationships, contributions, and consumption on these platforms. Data collected in workflow solutions such as ERP and CRM are rarely merged and analyzed for intelligence. Email is certainly one of the largest repositories of unstructured data.

Also, consider that every enterprise system—ERP, CRM—has built-in reporting and analytic capabilities. Think about all the capabilities in web analytics available to track sources of traffic, segment users, pipeline activity, and track goals. Consider all the reports developed in enterprise business intelligence systems. How much of it is used?

The bottom line is that most organizations underutilize the data, reports, and dashboards they already have in their environment. Is it the lack of skill? Is it the lack of time? Sorry folks, these are underlying concerns, but the bigger issue is the lack of leadership and culture. If top-down leadership and cultural principles aren't instituted on becoming data driven, then the organization is less likely to shift to this form of operation even when there is a new generation of data enthusiasts driving change. Bottom-up culture change doesn't work on its own, and those trying to push a rope uphill will likely get stuck when they encounter a manager or leader who's never worked with analytical paradigms and capabilities.

Even when there are leaders pushing a data-driven culture, the next challenge is whether existing data practices, regardless of their technical sophistication, are scaled and get used by managers across the organization in decision making.

What I mean by "scale" is that data and insights need to deliver new intelligence deep into your organization and beyond the data scientist that produced it. Is your data used to adjust operational priorities? Is it influencing product managers on what products to develop, features to prioritize, or marketing strategies to focus on? Is the average salesperson adjusting their sales pitch or prioritizing prospects differently based on all the data available? Is finance using data beyond financial benchmarks in their forecasts?

You'll see many refer to this challenge as developing "actionable insights." In other words, taking data, finding insights, and taking action based on the learnings. *Driving action from insights is an organizational capability, not a technological one.*

Do You Have the Talent and Collaboration?

The single largest issue most organizations face when looking at Big Data, predictive analytics, and other data programs is whether they have the talent and collaboration to drive transformation. Talent must come from traditional technology teams that require the skills to properly select, install, configure, integrate, develop, and scale the underlying technologies. Talent must also come from the data scientists, statisticians, quants, and other data analysts that are going to leverage these tools to develop new insights, experiences, and products.

According to an *Accenture* study on the data science shortage,[21] "The U.S. is expected to create around 400,000 new data science jobs between 2010 and 2015, but is likely to produce only about 140,000 qualified graduates to fill them." Similarly, a McKinsey study on Big Data[22] predicts, "By 2018, the United States alone could face a shortage of 140,000 to 190,000 people with deep analytical skills as well as 1.5 million managers and analysts with the know-how to use the analysis of big data to make effective decisions." Finding the technology talent is also not easy, as reported in a recent *Computing Big Data Review*:[23] "It would be great to have more people with Spark/Cassandra and big data skills. They are out there, but they tend to be more seasoned developers who have been around the block a few times and have become involved as they became aware of it. But at a junior level, those skill sets don't seem to be there."

Even if you cultivate the talent, getting data scientists and the Chief Data Officer to collaborate with the technologists and the Chief Information Officer on technology, process, and methodologies is not easy. They both know enough of each other's responsibilities and skills to "be dangerous," and conflicts between these teams can lead to long debates or flat-out departmental wars. Equally challenging is having these departments adequately service business needs with results and insights while team members are debating the underlying technologies and methodologies. In the *Computing Big Data Review*,[24] 61% of their respondents claimed, "Company structure that allows data scientists to bridge IT and business departments" is the most important factor for data scientists to thrive.

This is a significant because in the war for top talent, most organizations will be challenged when larger organizations offer aggressive compensation, benefits, and notoriety for talent in hyper competitive areas. In other words, most organizations are going to have a hard time competing with Google, Facebook, IBM, JP Morgan, GE, and other companies making significant bets on Big Data and other emerging technologies. The rest of us are going to have to cultivate talent and teams to close the gap.

What Data Capabilities and Technologies to Invest in?

The second issue we should consider is what data capabilities and technologies to invest in. At some point, many organizations that truly want to become data driven must consider investments.

And therein lies a huge challenge for many organizations operating with small technology budgets or who are middle to late adopters of new technologies. In Chapter Three, I reviewed some of the Big Data technologies in Version 3.0 published by Matt Turck in March of 2016,[25] who has the technologies broken into six major capabilities, 60-plus types of technologies, and too many products to count. This is enough to paralyze many Chief Data Officers, CIOs, data scientists, or data architects left with justifying and then selecting Big Data investments. It can lead to long analysis and technology selection processes to identify the best-fit technologies and products that enable the organization. It's not uncommon for organizations to take six months or more just to select the technology, and, by then, the organization may be left behind by the competition.

The other approach is to go bottom-up and enable the technologists, data scientists, or ideally a collaboration between multiple disciplines to prototype Big Data technologies aligned with an innovation program that prioritizes experiments. This approach also has challenges. First, you need really good talent that is capable of prototyping with these technologies. Even if you do, they may not have all the skills or infrastructure needed to be successful or have sufficient knowledge of the technology to make quick prototyping with it successful.

As if all the legacy data issues, the Big Data technology investment needs, the cultural challenges becoming data driven, and the steps organizations need to take to develop talent that works collaboratively aren't enough of a challenge, along comes a new wave of emerging technologies.

I'm speaking about some critical technologies that represent the next wave of cognitive computing and transaction processing, including machine learning, artificial intelligence, predictive analytics, the internet of things (IoT), and blockchain technologies. It will be far more challenging to successfully implement these new technologies without a sound data management practice.

Big businesses are taking significant bets on these technologies, and the successful ones will realize a significant competitive edge. Think what happens when Tesla, Apple, or Google market the self-driving car if Ford, GM, or BMW lack a competing strategy. What happens to Honeywell, Philips, or Maytag if they are left behind leveraging IoT in home automation? Can Citi, JP Morgan, Chase, or TD continue to be the dominant banks if they don't have a way to replace existing banking systems with ones enabled by blockchain technology? Can the top medical research facilities continue to push medical science and drive down costs without considering the use of artificial intelligence to enable patient diagnostics?

The question is not if, it's when, by whom, and with what level of disruption. Recall from Chapter One that these and other emerging capabilities are driving many businesses to consider their future digital business and digital transformation. You should now be able to see that raising the bar on how the organization consumes and processes data is foundational to enable digital transformation.

So what are the solutions to today's challenges and tomorrow's threats and opportunities? There are some foundational data practices to consider in order to achieve competitive table stakes in the digital era.

Transforming to a Big Data Organization

If you worked with me during the last decade, you can attest that I tend to move fast. Time is not on your side if you are working for a startup burning cash to achieve critical mass and profitability or if you are an enterprise that needs to become digitally competitive. These businesses need to become data driven, to enable new data science teams, to leverage Big Data technologies, and to be ready for the next wave of competitive computing. Going slow, sequential, or waiting for a clear understanding of financial returns is not an option. You are bound to be sitting at a poker table with enough players that some will win with loose bets, more chips, or better talent.

The Startup Game of Poker

When sitting at a poker table, you're likely to face competitors with different skills, playing styles, and number of chips. A "loose" competitor plays more hands in the hope that they can get "tighter", more conservative players to fold their hands prematurely. Traditional business leaders often resemble tighter players who can struggle at winning poker against at a table with many loose players willing to take more risks with bigger bets. Many of these loose players will lose, but statistically, some that place the right bets at the right time will amass large amounts of chips and make it difficult for tighter players to compete with conservative playing strategies.

That essentially means that you must attack in parallel the challenges that I've laid out. You can't start with a linear approach and expect everything to fall in line as you develop capabilities and practices.

Digital leaders should follow these four lines of attack to develop their Big Data organization:

1. Begin getting the greater organization to leverage the data, reporting, and analytics that already exist in the enterprise. This is because anything that you do with Big Data technologies or advanced analytics is either additive or replaces existing capabilities. If the organization isn't prepared to leverage data in making decisions, driving priorities, improving customer experiences, or developing new products, then new capabilities will yield marginal results. It's like giving a high-performance automobile to someone who barely knows how to drive. Getting business leaders, line managers, and customer-facing teams to leverage analytics, dashboards, and data to better drive decision making is the challenge of becoming a data-driven organization.

2. Second, you must clean up the mistakes of the past; otherwise, a new generation of data scientists and database engineers will repeat them with a new set of technologies. You should clean up the spreadsheets, siloed databases, data quality problems, and master data issues that exist in your existing databases.

3. You must enable new talent, new capabilities, and new practices. How do you enable a new generation of proficient data analysts with competitive capabilities? How should they operate to solve new challenges in ways that are repeatable and maintainable? How do we prioritize this work to know that we are targeting resources to the areas of highest value?

4. More importantly, you should invest in data governance practices that define how data can and should be used across the enterprise. Governance should define the practices that help prevent the data quality issues of the past but also ensure that use of data can scale across the organization. Governance should also define strategy and priorities when it comes to Big Data investments.

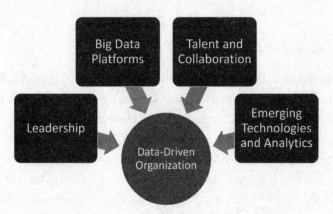

Figure 5-3. Collaboration among business leaders, data scientists, and technologists enabling the data-driven organization

Figure 5-3 shows that these practices represent two-way drivers. For example, increased consumption by business leaders in their journey to become more data driven will likely drive data scientists to increase the analytics they provide, improve data quality, and drive the business rationale to invest in more competitive capabilities.[26] Technologists should deliver new capabilities and operational performance but are also capable of defining data practices as they often mimic similar practices used in a software development lifecycle. Data scientists should demonstrate that their insights and tools drive both efficiency and growth in their business deliverables and must pass on technical needs and requirements to drive new capabilities.

The center box represents the function of a cross-disciplinary group of leaders that drive the overall practice by defining strategy, governance, priorities, and investments. For this to be successful, it will likely require representation from executive management, technology (the CIO) and data or analytics (the Chief Data Officer). If talent is a significant gap, then adding human resources is useful. If the primary mission is efficiency or cost savings, then the team should include the CFO or COO. If growth, product, or customer experience is a bigger driver, then the leadership team should include the head of sales, a CMO, the Chief Digital Officer, a Chief Revenue Officer, or a head of product management.

Data-Driven Practices: Part 1

Here are some very simple questions: Can you get business leaders to perform a review of their operations? Can you get them to do it without using a PowerPoint or other set of slides? How about getting them to do the review without using spreadsheets? One final question: Can you get them to do this review with less than two business days' notice?

You're probably going to get some hard stares with any of these requests because most departments are ill equipped without their bread-and-butter tools and with such little notice. It might be interesting to test leaders to see, if they can get one exception, which one would they select? Would they want more time, the ability to repurpose existing spreadsheets, or a preferred presentation format?

Inability to respond to any of these three requests indicates that a business is not ready to become data driven as manual effort would be required to perform an analysis or report results. The impact is that they can't perform this analysis with any frequency and likely the department's ability to share this data with individuals in the department, their colleagues, or senior management is inhibited.

But there is a reasonable answer to this challenge that most organizations, at least in theory, should be able to perform. Does your sales team have a CRM? Does your finance team operate an ERP? Can your digital marketing team report out of the customer engagement tools that are yielding the greatest success? Can your operating teams pull reports directly from the systems managing workflow? Do you already have a business intelligence system or reporting tools that can be leveraged? Unless you are an organization using Microsoft Office, Google Docs, or another competitive office suite as your back office system of record, then ask yourself why is it that most organizations elect to process data manually instead of pulling reports directly from the appropriate tools?

There are a few practical answers. First, some of these tools do a lousy job of reporting and analysis. They are often the last investment made by software vendors, giving users clunky user experiences, ugly visualizations, inadequate functionality, or slow performance. It's why so many businesses are forced to abandon out-of-the-box reporting capabilities and often invest in having custom reports developed.

Whether you use custom reports or out-of-the-box ones, the next issue is training. Some organizations are good at training users when a system is rolled out, but the practice typically fades over time, making it difficult for new employees to leverage the system to learn new capabilities when upgrades are performed. If a manager has to access data in multiple tools, if she's been barely trained on them, and if these tools are upgraded with reasonable frequency, you might see how using these tools over time can become a challenge. It's easier just to export the data and use the few spreadsheet tricks she knows to clean data and make it presentable.

The third issue is the reality of garbage-in/garbage-out. If the CRM or the ERP has data quality issues, then reporting directly out of these systems becomes a lot more challenging. Sales has 3,000 contacts? No, it really has 1,900, and the others are duplicates or records with missing data that are hard to filter. Your department is under budget? Well, no, you haven't submitted invoices for the last 90 days, so it's unlikely the report you generated is accurate. These examples are ones that the business leaders know about, but the issues that they don't know about are what ultimately frighten them. These issues keep them from reporting to senior management directly out of systems without manual intervention.

Lastly, there is the reality that meaningful business metrics and KPIs are valuable only when connecting data from multiple sources. Want to know whether the revenue forecast is at risk in Q3? You probably should analyze CRM and ERP data. Want to know which marketing campaigns are generating the most profitable customers? You likely need to pull data from at least three systems.

These barriers encourage many business leaders to go back to basic tools. They ask someone to get exports, cleanse data, and run numbers in Excel, email their team results, and paste finalized insights into management presentations.

Addressing this issue isn't trivial. To make the switch, you're going to need to get some supporters and pick a spot or two where you are more likely to have some marginal success. Maybe it's sending department P/Ls out of the ERP or sharing year-to-date sales figures from the CRM? In any example, you're going to need top-down support to help drive behavioral changes.

PROCESS: ANALYTICS PLANNING PROCESS

You need to pick a spot where you can challenge the status quo by pushing the use of existing enterprise tools and leaving manual practices behind. In rolling this process across multiple businesses, I've found that you must find an early adopter and collaborate on new practices. In one organization it was marketing, in a second it was operations, and in a third one it was sales. It doesn't matter, so long as that you have a leader who's willing to partner with you on the journey.

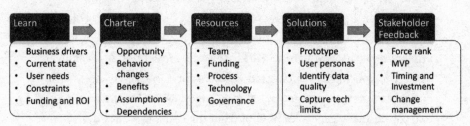

Figure 5-4. Data discovery process to ask questions and drive insights

Figure 5-4 shows the basic planning process to develop a new analytics capability. The planning process starts with *learning* current workflows, opportunities, and issues:

1. What's driving the business leader to make changes? Is it efficiency because performing the analysis and publishing it is too time-consuming? Is using data and reports in the current format too cumbersome? Does someone need the information more frequently? Does the current approach expose data quality issues?
2. How is the report generated today? What is (are) the data source(s), and what system and manual steps are taken to generate final outputs? Who does this work, and how much effort is required? Can they tell you why it was set up as it was, and what are some of the challenges? What would people do if they had the opportunity to redo the approach? What existing tools are being used?
3. Who uses the reports and data? Are they being used individually or in a group setting? What are some of the actions they take based on the data? How frequently do they review the data? What's the impact if this report were no longer generated or if it were to be delivered late? What would recipients do differently if the report was generated more frequently, and what would be the impact? What are some current pain points and what are some suggested enhancements? Ask users what other reports they use on a frequent basis and where the report in question ranks in importance versus the other ones identified.
4. Are there any business constraints that need to be considered up front? Is it important for the business leader to have a solution in place in front of a key deadline? Are there timing constraints or opportunities for rolling out new practices? What are the security, privacy, or compliance considerations?
5. Are there any funding opportunities for this program? Are there cost benefits to any legacy practices or systems that can be shut down? Are there any existing KPIs that may improve with better reporting?

Coalesce the information you gathered into a *charter*. Who are the process owners that use the report? Can you create a diagram showing how the report is constructed? How would users change the report to be more insightful or efficient, and how would they benefit from these improvements? Are there any technical or process dependencies that need consideration if you were to rebuild or upgrade this report? What other assumptions need validation?

Agree on available *resources* that can be used to formulate a solution. Do you have access to funding that will enable bringing in additional help or expertise? How will the team collaborate and share results with stakeholders and end users to ensure a successful solution and transition? What technologies currently available to this group will likely be used in the solution? Which leaders will help drive priorities and decisions during the implementation phase?

Brainstorm to get the team and stakeholders to form a solution. Develop a prototype, then look to see how different user types (personas) or roles affect functionality and workflow. Identify existing data quality issues and how they impact operations, as well as other technical considerations.

Present top options to stakeholders for *feedback*. Get consensus on a minimal approach and what is out of scope. Rank most promising options and see whether there are any timing constraints or funding opportunities. Lastly, think through the people and workflow impacts of implementing this upgrade.

When you kick off this practice, you're going to have a limited number of technologies available to deliver analytics from, but as you add new Big Data platforms and develop expertise, you'll have more options. Similarly, when you start this program, you might have a small team with limited expertise and little practice collaborating. As you invest in data science and agile data practices, you will see them mature to deliver insights more frequently and with more capability.

As you expose more data and deliver new insights, business leaders will ask questions that spur additional analysis. They may also want to see dashboards shared with appropriate decision makers and expect department leaders to amend processes in order to leverage them. This, in the best of business situations, will help provide funding to add technologies, expertise, and develop practices.

Don't be afraid of charging forward with humble beginnings. Your goal in this first stage is not to get a data science program going or to get value from Big Data technology investments. Your goal is to get the greater organization, the frontline managers and business leaders to better experience leveraging data in their decision making. Plus, you need them to get away from manual processing data and moving toward leveraging data to make proactive decisions.

EXAMPLE: BECOMING DATA DRIVEN BY DEMOCRATIZING ANALYTICS

Here is an example from my past with an organization that was charged to source data that we would process and sell to customers. They would call on businesses, ask them a series of questions, request access to some of the underlying documents, and input all of this into a data capture tool. This data would then flow through a series of data processing steps and eventually end up in platforms that delivered analytics and data back to customers subscribing to this data.

Their challenge was to collect more data faster with higher data quality and with fewer resources. This seemed like a daunting challenge, especially since the executive team could not afford to give them outside investment in technology or in practices to achieve their goals. We were too busy improving the end user experience for subscribing customers, and working on our data sourcing and processing practices was a distant secondary priority.

It turns out that the group already had a ton of data capturing productivity and quality metrics. The problem was that the data was locked in complex spreadsheets and siloed databases that took too long to distribute, and it was too complex for the average person to interpret. So, while they had plenty of data, they weren't 100% data driven. They needed to simplify the analytics so that individual managers could drill into their metrics and make recommendations and decisions based on their team, region, and mission.

The good news for them was that we had already made an investment in a "self-service" BI tool that we were using to improve the analytics to subscribing customers. The question was whether this team could leverage the same tool to develop visualizations against their existing data and whether using these analytics would help them achieve their goals.

Flash forward several months later, and I was pleasantly surprised at the results. I attended one of their semiannual meetings where they made operational decisions regarding targets, process, and people. Instead of looking at prepared presentations and complex spreadsheets, presenters shared their insights by navigating the analytics directly in the BI tool. When someone asked a question, they made a couple of clicks to find answers. They could see whether a specific issue or opportunity was a local condition specific to a single manager or a macro issue. Managers made collective decisions on what to do in the upcoming months to achieve their goals.

We'll visit other approaches to get the organization more data driven. But let's recall that this is one of four streams of activity to become a Big Data organization. Let's turn our attention now to the some of the other disciplines that need cultivating.

Developing Data Programs: Understanding Roles and Responsibilities

If you're going to scale your data practices, then you need to consider people and process. Let's start with people and review roles and responsibilities that are part of a data practice.

Figure 5-5[27] gives you a sense of the main functions in a data science program. Data scientists have the primary function to develop analytical models, construct dashboards, and perform data analysis aimed at improving decision making by leaders, managers, and individuals. More importantly, organizations in a digital transformation program should rely on data scientists to enable products and services with real-time analytics capabilities that demonstrate value to end customers.

If data scientists are primarily involved in modeling and delivering analytics, data stewards are responsible for sourcing data and managing overall data quality. Sourcing data can come from a new business relationship, for example, when marketing departments acquire marketing lists and take steps to nurture them into qualified leads. Data sources can also include data captured directly from products and services such as operational data, clickstream data on websites, or purchasing data from transaction systems. These internal data sources need owners responsible

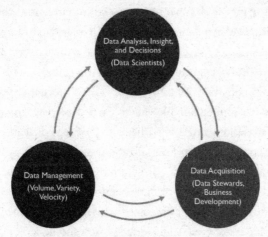

*Figure 5-5. Relationship between data science, stewardship,
and management*

for documenting data definitions and owning the overall data quality. Finally, more organizations are taking steps to create proprietary data sources. This could include market research, data that is crowdsourced, or web scraping efforts.

The last major function is what I broadly term data management. It would be a mistake to equate this only with running the underlying technologies because a big part of what makes data practices successful is how data is stored and processed. Your data scientists will be a lot less successful if the data is stored in disparate database silos rather than a holistic data architecture. Data pipelines can be robust and provide data stewards the ability to monitor data quality, or they can be dumb pipes without monitoring or management tools. Data may be marked with known master data records, or you might have a lot of duplicate data. Systems may or may not be secure, with high availability and disaster recovery capabilities.

The figure shows that the success of these roles is interdependent. Data scientists can't perform meaningful insights if data quality isn't documented and managed. Data stewards are limited to what they can do to improve quality if the underlying technology and data architecture doesn't enable them to manage it. Technologists spend more time maintaining disparate systems if data scientists do not partner with them to help consolidate to a defined data architecture and set of platforms.

The other reality is that people rarely fall squarely into these defined responsibilities. I've seen data scientists design basic databases and perform data steward tasks to be successful. There are technologists with sufficient math and statistical background to write meaningful *R* models and display results in powerful data visualizations. There are data stewards that, without modern tools available, have learned to perform wizardry in querying databases or using spreadsheets to profile and cleanse data.

The other issue is that most organizations have a lot of people who have some skills working with data but who have never been educated on the practices and responsibilities of data scientists or stewards. In addition, with the research presented earlier on the shortage of data scientists, hiring from the outside is not a sufficient strategy. You should look to convert the spreadsheet jockeys into bona fide citizens in your data organization.

So now that you've fostered some demand for data capabilities, let's look at some options on filling the talent gap.

Identifying Internal Talent and Evangelizing the Data Mindset

If you want to find potential data talent in your organization, create an environment for employees to review operational data, ask questions, and seek out answers. Good questions lead to discovery efforts that produce insights and intelligence regarding the gaps between what data exists and what is needed.

A colleague and I accomplished this at a town hall we hosted to introduce our organization to becoming a data-driven organization. It's not as if the organization didn't understand data because we sold subscription and data analytics as a business. Like most businesses, analysis of internal sales and operational data was a second priority because of the underlying complexities. After showcasing some of the "quick wins" on new analytics developed and being used in different departments, we left participants of the town hall with one very simple request: "Go ask questions and try to find data that helps provide answers." We didn't say what to do after that and were relying on human curiosity to drive some individuals to seek answers.

I like to find individuals who ask good questions. They tend to be analytical and data driven but don't necessarily have the technical skills to perform data discovery work to find answers on their own. Ideally, they are business decision makers or are highly influential to drive others to review data.

These people aren't necessarily the ones asking for reports from IT systems. IT systems tend to serve a single or a small number of departments, so requested reports tend to be narrow in focus. Reports that show the health of a sales pipeline (CRM), trends in purchasing behavior (e-commerce), velocity of the development team (agile tools), or P/L performance (financials) are all examples of basic reporting. They all help answer questions on performance, alert people if there is risk, or provide evidence if specific activities are changing performance.

The best questions are usually more strategic and often require correlating information from multiple data sources. The answers may demonstrate collaboration opportunities by showing how an activity performed by one organization affects others. They help connect customer behavior to operational activities or decisions regarding the supply chain.

It has been my experience that identifying individuals that ask the tough questions is a key step to becoming a data-driven organization. Their curiosity often leads to new discoveries.

When you find people asking questions, your job as a digital leader is to motivate, enable, and mentor them in data practices. These are emerging leaders who are probably subject matter experts in their departments, are willing to challenge the status quo by asking questions, and are looking to leverage data to back up their hypothesis. You've motivated them enough to take a step forward, now you need to enable them.

Your new recruits are what are called *Citizen Data Scientists*. They are not data scientists, quants, or statisticians by training with analytics, machine learning, or programming skills but have stood up to be citizens in the program. For organizations that cannot hire enough data scientists or find adequate partners to outsource analytics needs, cultivating these citizens is an approach to increase the number of analytics produced and drive the data-driven organization. If they ask data-driven questions, are skilled in Excel, are willing to learn new skills, and are disciplined to follow basic data practices that you will lay out for them, then they are good candidates to be citizen data scientists.

When a citizen data scientist in marketing aggregates data from multiple marketing tools to determine what approaches are yielding the best leads, the CMO must listen. When a sales operative shows that account reps who proactively engage their clients at least once a quarter have the highest retention rates, then that should grab the attention of sales leadership. They are insiders in the mechanics of how the department operates and are likely to be trusted. So, in addition to growing the skill set, you are also indirectly growing a department's reliance on using data in decision making.

Principles of Self-Service BI Technologies and Services

There's just one potential problem once you begin recruiting citizen data scientists. Do your new recruits have the skills to be data driven? Do they know how to use analytics, visualization, and other tools to drive at answers? The answer to this question largely depends on what tools you have available. To enable citizen data scientists, you need tools that are easy for them to learn and be successful, especially on simple analytics. Their drive will enable them to learn more complex analysis over time, but if they can't get started with the basics then they will either lose confidence, lose interest, or lose any support from their managers to take on data challenges.

I label these tools as "self-service BI" and they are a form of citizen development technologies. The makers of these software tools not only target the expert data scientists; they also target the citizens.

They certainly won't be targeting IT as that's the sin of BI tools of the past. Legacy BI tools enabled developers to program the analytics, develop dashboards, or create custom reports. The problem with these enterprise tools is that they are too slow and expensive for most organizations to operate. They follow similar design pattern as custom software where business analysts document requirements and developers implement. To be competitive today, most organizations must do more analytics faster, and these tools fail to enable the greater organization. See Figure 5-6.[28]

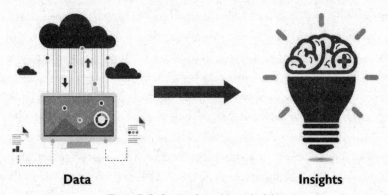

Data   **Insights**

Figure 5-6. Getting from data to insights

"Self-service implies that the analysts can do all or much of their work without IT resources or with services from other organizations or experts. These tools have intuitive user interfaces and help analysts develop data visualizations without the need of a lot of (or any) programming or SQL. They help data stewards profile data, remove duplicates, merge records, and perform other data-cleansing steps without having to call in IT to develop scripts. The tools are easy to navigate and enable the novice to "click and learn" rather than having to go through extensive documentation or training classes to learn how to do the basics. There should be lots of examples, either with the tool or online. Ideally, there is some form of app store showcasing other work. When some training is useful, they have a library of publicly accessible short-length videos that enable users to learn concepts and step through the implementation.

They require some built-in constructs to make it easy for novices to make mistakes. Some capture the full clickstream of the user to enable several "undo" steps in case they make mistakes. Some document all the steps taken so that a "pro" can understand what was developed without having to examine the underlying implementation. Most will have some capabilities to enable reusing chart configurations, formulas, and algorithms. They must have collaboration capabilities so more than one data scientist or data steward can work together using the tool.

These are the basics, and I then look at what happens when we need to do something a little more complex. Ideally, these tools have low-code paradigms that enable citizens to perform basic automation, data validation, analytic calculations, or data manipulations. What coding language is optimal for these users? Here's a hint: If it's based on a programming language used by developers like SQL or JavaScript, then the software company probably didn't have citizen developers in mind when it was created. Look for dialects that are intuitive and are not overly expressive. If you have to write a lot of code to simplify things, it's going to be too cumbersome for citizen development.

Finally, I look at the last mile. Does it have a plugin architecture, APIs, and other constructs to extend the software vendor's implementation? You must evaluate these APIs and extensions carefully. If these constructs are there because the software is underdeveloped and they expect developers from your organization to program as needed, then that's a huge problem. Again, "self-service" implies that you probably don't need to call IT in for doing more than 80% of common work, so if configuring basic visualizations or performing common data-cleansing steps ultimately requires a developer, then this tool isn't ready to be called self-service.

One exception is if the tool has hit critical mass and there is already a healthy ecosystem of developers who have extended the application and made their extensions available in an app store. If the citizen developer can shop for plugins, download, test, and request an internal approval for using it in production, then that is certainly a positive endorsement for the technology.

What Technical Services Enable Citizen Data Scientists?

These tools are only one aspect of establishing a self-service analytics capability. Here is my definition of what users should be able to do "easily" to deliver on this promise. A user wants to:

1. Know what data repositories exist in the organization and what type of data exists in them.
2. Make requests to get access to data, get tools installed, or find out where documentation is stored without significant delay.
3. Understand individual data repositories by leveraging easy-to-understand documentation that defines data fields, data flows, connected applications, and data sources.

4. Comply with governance and rules on the proper use of data.
5. Connect with "owners" or subject matter experts on data repositories to ask questions.
6. Develop their expertise with analytical tools. Know how to request support from internal experts or from technology providers.
7. See working examples of dashboards, reports, or analysis performed on the data.
8. Have some understanding on data quality issues and any efforts under way to make improvements.
9. Escalate and resolve technical needs such as performance, linking data, or loading in new data sources.
10. Leverage organizational best practices on implementing visualization standards, collaborating with other data scientists, publishing and referencing insights, and sharing information with colleagues.

These requirements will shape the data services that technologists and data stewards must fulfill in the Big Data organization. I'll be covering this in the next section because a successful program requires an IT partnership and maturing their data services practices. We'll then turn back to getting the cross-disciplinary team structure and enabling collaborative agile data organizations.

Transforming IT with Data Services

Traditional IT teams have many more responsibilities in a Big Data organization beyond just selecting, installing, configuring, and running databases. If you look at so-called citizen data science programs through the lens of an IT skeptic, then all I've done is arm business users with more powerful analytical tools that will create a new generation of data silos, dashboards, and reports on top of the legacy data warehouses and spreadsheets that already exist in the enterprise.

The skeptics would be right if we stopped there. The solution is to instill governance and management practices while providing business users and citizen data scientists process capabilities that work with their analytical tools. As the previous section noted, they need these capabilities to be successful, but will ask for practices only when it is too late and they are either struggling to get something done or are overwhelmed with a problem. IT must be proactive partners in this program, suggesting and influencing new governance, practice, and data capabilities well before business leaders require them.

Prioritizing data service practices ahead of business need and demand is a primary role for IT in digital transformation programs. It must sell business leaders on implementing new practices like change management that are IT-centric. They should shift data quality from being an "IT issue" to one that business leaders need to manage by accepting data stewardship as a new responsibility. Success will likely require additional collaboration because a single spreadsheet jockey working in isolation will not be as successful as an aligned, collaborative, and organizationally distributed analytics team.

Let's look at some of these practices in more detail. My objective in prioritizing these practices is on scaling the organization's ability to train or hire new data scientists, introduce more analytical capabilities, improve data quality, and aggregate new data.

Provide Collaboration Tools and Practices

Almost nothing frustrates me more than seeing a complex spreadsheet being emailed between colleagues with the intent to collaboratively edit them. The sender is emailed back multiple versions of the original spreadsheet and will have the arduous task of merging them. When the spreadsheet is completed, it is then emailed to a larger number of decision makers to review the results.

There are far better ways to work on documents together or to share access to them, including capabilities in Microsoft Office 365, Google Drive, Jive, Box, Dropbox, and many others. This isn't a technology issue today, it's a training and change management issue getting business users to phase out behaviors that create duplicate data and cumbersome, email-driven workflows.

The problem with email sharing could get worse as you enable new analytical tools beyond Excel. Imagine that creating dashboards in BI tools and having business leaders request the reports sent to them in PDF format by email or creating screen shots and pasting them into PowerPoints is the status quo of how business leaders want to review their results.

Therein lies the core of the problem. Going off emails, PDFs, and PowerPoints and onto clicks directly into analytical tools is a huge challenge in changing executive behaviors. They are the ones largely stuck on email powering everything, and it is very difficult to change this behavior. It may be impossible with some leaders, and you might have to work around them and not let it force delivering new capabilities back into outdated practices.

The newest tools have sharing built in; for example, tools like Tableau and Qlik have Cloud and server versions to enable publishing analytics and make them accessible. Both enable bookmarking results and creating "stories" from different views of the data. Your executives are unlikely to see these in action until they've been to a conference and seen a presenter tell a data story through a visualization tool instead of a presentation tool.

Don't let these executives become the bottlenecks. Remember that becoming a data organization requires both top-down and bottom-up changes, and instilling collaborative practices is definitely a bottom-up transformation.

Think through two primary forms of collaboration:

1. **Collaboration during the "development" process** where citizen data scientists, data stewards, and technologists are going to need some vehicle to work together and at other times to make service requests. This can easily be done in the agile tools that you're using in the IT organization and now extended within citizen data science programs.
2. **Collaboration with consumers** who will be using analytics to perform their work or make decisions. How will dashboards be shared to this group? How will documentation be provided? What example "stories" can be used to illustrate specific use cases?

If you've ever managed application development, then you'll recognize that both are collaboration practices typically implemented as part of a software development lifecycle. Developers need to collaborate, know what's being worked on, and know how to task one another. When software is ready to be released, end users need to be trained and taught best practices on using the new capabilities being introduced.

The main difference here is that you're extending this collaboration beyond the formal walls of IT to less technically trained business users. Tools for citizen data scientists must be simplified and easier to use than what software developers use, and the ones targeted to the software development community may not be good fits for use by business teams. There are exceptions, so you should look at the underlying user experiences.

When it comes to collaboration with consumers, my recommendation is to lead by example and expect a lot of pushback from laggards. Send emails with links to tools and without attachments. Provide some context so that you can get successful "open rates" but lead users to click through to additional data. Hold internal sessions to demonstrate the power of using the tools and telling stories through data rather than just how-to sessions.

This practice needs to evolve over time, so be realistic about the pace of the change that you drive. If an executive refuses to look at data that's not in a PDF or PowerPoint, then appease him while you get others to change behaviors. Help the ones using the tools frequently to be successful, then have them encourage middle to late adopters to get on board.

Change Management Practices

There are other IT practices that need to be considered in data science programs as citizen developers begin developing more sophisticated models, algorithms and visualizations. Does the new *R* script, analytics dashboard, or upgrade to data quality go live without some form of change management practice? It might, unless this discipline is enabled, promoted, *and required by* everyone working in the data organization.

Change management practices must be enforced because it is unlikely that data scientists, citizen data scientists, sponsors, or leaders will automatically sign up for these practices. Remember, they come from the world where when a spreadsheet is done, it's just emailed out to everyone. What's change management?

But the better analogy to explain change management involves the editorial and publishing of formalized PowerPoint and other presentations. A presentation sent to the Board probably goes through dozens of edits and reviews to ensure the accuracy of the information, the simplicity of key messages, and sequencing. Deploying changes in data artifacts should be validated for accuracy and quality of results, boundary condition issues, dashboard performance, data privacy/security considerations, and other potential risks. I once quoted a famous movie line in my blog, "With more power comes greater responsibility," and analytics need to be embedded in a basic change management practice.

What goes into this process? Just the basics to start:

- Who tests the artifact before it is ready to be released? Is the data accurate? Are the analytical calculations selected appropriate and implemented correctly? Do the results make business sense? Are the business rules for data quality engineered appropriately? Does the new artifact reduce the performance of a key system resource?
- What kind of compliance and communication checks are required before sanctioning the release? Are you releasing new data to end users that comply with privacy and security policies? What documentation needs to be updated? Do users understand any new or changed dimensions or measures and how to use them in decision making? How are you communicating the change and making sure end users and stakeholders understand the timing and impact?
- What system environments are being used to support development, testing, and production? How are new artifacts transitioned, and what automation is developed to ensure that it can operate smoothly? What are the business rules on synchronizing data between these environments?
- Who ultimately signs off on the release? Where is the change log captured? How is the change monitored for any unexpected conditions? What are the steps to roll back and under what circumstances is a rollback triggered?

For those of you well versed in change management practices, you'll note that I am only scratching the surface with these principles. Like the previous section on collaboration, change management practices need to mature over time as the data organization grows in size, capability, and impact.

Document Databases and Data Flows

Now let's consider documentation. Relational diagrams, data flows, defined calculations, data dictionaries, database connection parameters—how many of these do you have documented across critical databases in simple formats that *business users*—not DBAs—can consume? How many of these are in formats that make it easy to update and maintain?

Databases and data flows are the foundations for Big Data organizations, yet documentation is often lagging, especially on legacy data warehouses. For the business to take better advantage of this data, it often requires some form of documentation to help them recognize what data is available, what the data fields mean, and how the data can be used.

If you're successful getting the business interested in using data from a legacy data warehouse and demonstrating value from it, then you are more likely to get funding for cleaning it up, improving it, or rebuilding it. If the data warehouse is underutilized, then it effectively is another form of dark data.

Unfortunately, without some basic documentation for the new citizen data scientists you are grooming, knowledge and usage of data are limited to the few subject matter experts who have used it before and maybe were part of the team that originally designed the databases. You can't easily mature a data organization if knowledge of key data warehouses is limited to a few experts.

What types of documentation? I look for very basic starting points:

- Asset details on data systems identifying the databases, data flows, underlying technology and version, and what systems they are running on in production. I also want the inventory of systems identified with some basic attributes like cores, memory, and accessible storage. Finally, I like to see what external applications are interfacing with the database and some basic information on the connection type, data consumed, and data transacted.

- Database diagrams including a high-level entity diagram along with a more detailed one that is developed from an entity relationship tool.
- Data dictionaries that provide more context on the fields in the databases.
- Data security considerations should also be documented answering some basic questions like what information is deemed private (PII or other), what are the different group- or role-level access types to this data, and what are the underlying business rules and approvals on who gets access to each role.
- Data flows showing movement of data from source to destination and identifying primary processing steps.
- List of analytics and calculations that are computed either in data flows, database stored procedures, or applications.

This documentation is either a diagram (like database diagrams) or a database itself (asset lists, data dictionaries, list of assets). A governing team should decide up front what tools will be used to manage this documentation. The team should also decide where these documents should live so that they are accessible and may even come up with a tagging taxonomy so that documents are easily searched.

Equally as important to having documentation is to decide when and who will maintain them. Usually this can be done as part of a change management practice, so when changes are being deployed by either data scientists or technology, the underlying documentation is updated appropriately.

One last note is that some of these documents are better developed and maintained by the Chief Data Officer or by the data scientists. Data dictionaries and catalogs of reusable analytical calculations are created and consumed by this group, so getting data scientists to "own" them has the added benefit of ensuring materials will be written and maintained by the target audience.

Provide Data Warehouse and Data Integration Services

Now that data scientists have tools and a change management practice and existing data assets are documented, the next step is for IT to provide specific services related to the existing data warehouses and integrations, as well as the ability to create new ones.

The self-service tools deployed to data scientists only go so far in functionality. They are often point solutions to enable specific analysis and data integrations. Once created, a mature team will review what was created and decide which elements should be refactored over time and implemented directly in the data architecture.

The main benefit of centralizing it is to enable reuse, to secure it, and to scale it for larger volumes of data. But the downside is that it often takes longer to update data models, analytics, and data integrations when they are centralized versus what data scientists can do independently. The team needs to collaborate and decide when it is appropriate to centralize data in the enterprise data warehouses and when it is reasonable to have it managed privately for one-off analysis by a handful of data scientists.

Sometimes, there is no choice or the choice is obvious, and the team needs to centrally implement from the get-go. You might be developing a new data warehouse for petabytes of data or integrating a new data source that needs to be joined with multiple data sets. Even in these situations, it often makes sense to prototype against a subset of the data before implementing it directly into the central systems.

What are some of these services? You might take this out of technical terms and make this more business friendly. "I need help with . . ."

- Getting access to a data asset
- Reviewing a new data source and how to best integrate it
- Improving performance of a query, a database, a dashboard, a data integration
- Writing a query to pull the required data
- Identifying and resolving a data quality issue
- Regenerating any documentation that is system generated

You'll notice this list looks more like a service desk's practices rather than an engineering practice. That's by design because if you're working with citizen data scientists, they will more likely get stuck and request help than directly ask an engineering team for implementation services. Once the request is made, then the data services team can assess the opportunity and determine the appropriate course of action.

Larger organizations may call this a center of excellence rather than just a service desk and engineering practice. This is a smart way to position and market these services; however, it has a couple of implications that need to be considered. First, the center of excellence needs to be staffed with experts on the various tools being used by both technologists and data scientists. Second, you need a service commitment from the individuals who will be fielding requests and a time commitment from management. This may prove more challenging than expected since many organizations would prefer seeing their best data scientists and technologists working on business problems rather than participating in the center. Organizations that are truly committed to becoming data driven should see the benefit in having experts spread their knowledge, but they must recognize that it requires an investment and commitment by their best people.

Proactively Monitor Database and Data Integration Performance

Now let's review operational considerations. No one is happy when a query is slow, a dashboard takes too long to load, or there is a delay in processing a data feed. Not happy is putting it mildly—more like furious and frustrated.

Your database operations are primitive if you are only monitoring at the systems level showing whether resources like CPU, memory, disk, or network resources are performing as expected. You need to be tracking actual database performance, application performance, dashboard performance, and data integration durations to better sense when there is a performance issue. You also must be able to sense an episodic issue like a slow query bogging down the system, or a slowly emerging one such as a data integration that's getting slower week to week.

Database performance is the dependent variable, so you should be able to track some of the inputs that drive poor performance. Are you tracking the size of the database, the amount of data flowing through ETLs, or the number of simultaneous user activity on primary dashboards? These are common inputs that may affect both episodic and longitudinal performance degradations.

Performance should be reviewed with the collective team because issues likely require collaborative decisions. If data integration has episodic slowness when it is processing large quantities of data, then perhaps it needs to be moved to a Cloud computing environment where computing resources can be ramped up during the period. If a database performance is slowing, then the easiest thing may be to archive data rather than add resources or performance-tune the database.

The main transformation is that if you're driving the organization to be data driven, then consumption will rise, complexity will increase, and tolerance for subpar performance will decrease significantly. Your operations teams need to be more knowledgeable about how resources are being utilized and measure performance to resolve issues, find the root causes of recurring problems, and scale computing resources.

Define Data Quality Measurement Practices

More data quality issues will be identified as consumption of data and analytics increases. The analysts and data scientists working with data often work around the underlying data quality issues. Sometimes that means ignoring issues by filtering out "bad" data; other times they will create complex formulas and other operations to cleanse data. Vocal analytical teams will highlight data issues so that there is a better chance that they can be addressed earlier where the data is collected or processed. They will say, "Let's fix the data upstream" because they know correcting issues at the sources or early in the data flows benefits all consumers of the data.

Many business leaders are oblivious to data quality issues until they are knee-deep in them. There's an underlying assumption that "the system" will prevent duplicate records, bad street addresses, formatting issues with emails, and other data validations, not realizing that it takes investments either to prevent bad data at the source or to implement data-cleansing practices.

Like any other below-the-surface issues, the best way place to get started is to build awareness of the issue by publishing some basic metrics.

How many bad emails have come in from different marketing lists? What salespeople are entering the least amount of prospect metadata? What are the primary sources of duplicate records? How many records are missing values for critical dimensions?

Once there is awareness, then solutions can be implemented either by providing data stewards with data quality tools and practices, by implementing data cleansing within data integrations, by creating the right incentives to drive end user behaviors when entering data, and by formally creating master data repositories.

But onetime awareness isn't sufficient, and IT should consider how to establish and publish metrics. Many data integration tools have this capability built in, and they are worth considering. But it's a key consideration because organizations need their data scientists performing more analysis and less cleansing. Furthermore, new data quality issues emerge when data sources are added. By building up awareness, you're helping the organization recognize the need to create and assign data stewards, a fundamental role in a growing data organization.

The Agile Data Organization

You now have many of the building blocks to develop a data-driven organization. You have some business leaders consuming existing data, an emerging citizen data science program, technologists that are taking on greater data services, and an emerging role for data stewards. How do you put this all together into one cohesive process and collaborative team that can deliver frequent business results?

Now that we've defined some roles, a primary governance challenge is in balancing responsibilities. Who does what steps in the data management practices, and how are key decisions made?

Figure 5-7 gives you a basic model of the different responsibilities with technologists handling the data management practices and governance while citizen data scientists handling the analytics. Now how can we get these people working together on prioritized questions and opportunities?

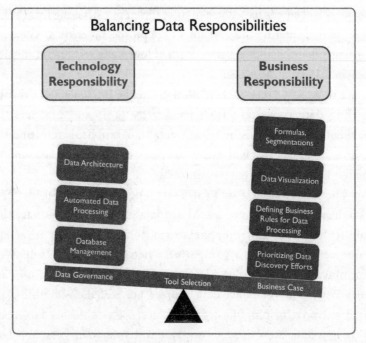

Figure 5-7. Balancing data management and data science responsibilities to enable collaboration and drive results

Getting a Collaborative Data Science and IT Data Team

The answer is agile. In software development, the agile product and software delivery teams are almost always cross-functional between business and IT. The heart of agile is the product owner managing a backlog of features and enhancements, defining minimally viable solutions, working with IT on implementation scenarios, and prioritizing planning and development stories. Strong agile teams also have mechanisms to express and prioritize technical debt, larger business investments, and more significant infrastructure changes.

The same practice can be applied to agile data teams, except that, instead of prioritizing features, teams prioritize Big Data questions. What questions provide value to stakeholders and customers that are worth answering? How do we attribute value and estimate feasibility on answering the question? How do we factor in other work such as loading in new data sets, data-cleansing efforts, upgrading data security, or improvements in data processing?

The next step is to get a team working together on discovery efforts. Once a multidisciplinary group understands priorities, there is a stronger likelihood that they will work together and disregard organizational boundaries.

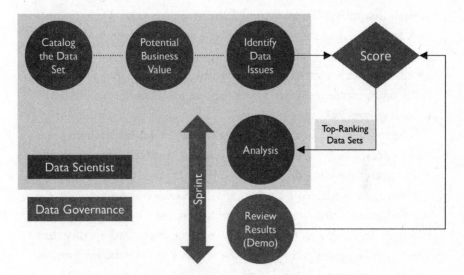

Figure 5-8. Agile data discovery process that enables data teams to prioritize analytics and demo results

- Figure 5-8[29] shows an approach to align data science with agile practices. It starts with a single data set that is either part of the organization's dark data or may be a new data set. The first step is to catalog the data so that business users can learn about its existence. Break the data into basic entities, dimensions, metrics, and metadata to provide more details to business users looking for data sources.
- Identify three to five potential questions, target insights, decisions, or activities that can be researched using this data should someone commission a data scientist to investigate.
- List known issues (defects) with the data source. This can be measures of data quality, information on how the data is sourced, and other feedback that might undermine any analysis of the data.
- *Score* this data set based on its potential versus known issues. Absent of any easy way to quantify value, scoring by a voting committee can at least rank what data sets look attractive for further analysis.

- Commission agile sprints on data sets that have the highest scores. Review results and rerank based on findings.
- Demo the insight and adjust the score based on its business value.

This reinforces that the data scientist's work should be grounded in analysis that answers questions and delivers business value. Data scientists look at the value of data before investing too much time in discovery. Imagine that all the friction in the analysis because of the data set's size, speed, complexity, variety, or quality can be "solved" given sufficient skills, tools, and time—what do you hope to get out of this data analytics or mining exercise?

The approach can be applied to other cases beyond just analyzing new data sources. There might be business units looking for specific analytics, models, and dashboards. This should be expressed in the form of questions, scored based on value, and have solutions provided by the team. Another case is addressing technical debt by taking steps to eliminate legacy artifacts or simplify existing ones. Data quality debt efforts can be prioritized by data stewards to address data, integration, and other processing issues.

The key to the approach is to enable the prioritization of questions, a cadence to deliver results, and a theater to observe the results.

Now let's put this in the context of the *analytics planning process* introduced earlier in this chapter. If you recall, that process enabled you to learn and develop a charter and then a planning process to identify a team, solutions, stakeholders, and scope. The agile analytics delivery process in Figure 5-8 then defines how this team can deliver iteratively. Figure 5-9 brings this together to show you the full lifecycle of strategy, planning, and delivery.

Figure 5-9. Data discovery practice: strategy, planning, and delivery

You'll notice that in delivery, the team needs to continue to ask questions and reset priorities. This is because, as the team works with the data and technology, they will likely reshape their scope. Some questions determined during agile planning will be less useful, and new ones will emerge that will be of greater importance.

In fact, one way to judge the health of an agile data team is how quickly they can go from strategy to delivery on a data opportunity. In other words, agile planning in a mature organization should be fast because teams are easy to assemble and stakeholders are acclimated to the process. The main planning tasks are related to scope and solutions or, in agile terms, to developing the initial backlog of questions for agile delivery.

So getting the team structure is key, but how you go about it will change as the agile data team matures.

Agile Data Team Structures

You might be wondering how to structure "multidisciplinary" agile data teams considering the skills include trained data scientists, citizen data scientists, data stewards, and technologists. There isn't a simple answer to this question as a lot of this depends on organizational structure, objectives, competing objectives, and the maturity of the overall practice.

Figure 5-10 shows the first two stages to mature the team structure.

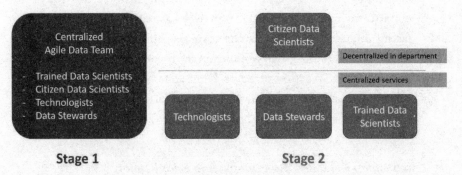

Figure 5-10. Stage 1 and 2 data organizations

In *Stage 1* when you're just getting started with data science it helps to centralize a cross-disciplinary team while Big Data technologies are still being evaluated, and the overall agile practice is still being developed. Centralization enables the highest degree of alignment of the team that is optimal for both technology selections and process adoption. Roles can be sorted out at a more detailed level, and missing skills can be identified more easily. Finally, if data stewards are on the team, then they can be tasked to address data quality issues in parallel to the analytic solutions.

Stage 2 should begin once an agile planning and delivery practice is established and some technology in place. Focus then should be to help organizations that want to be data driven to be the most successful. When this happens, I'd rather see citizen data scientists work independently in their organizations delivering the analytical results and aim to be "self-serving." If you've established a center of excellence, then they can make requests of the technology organization for either technical assistance or upgrades to the underlying technologies.

Similarly, in many cases where data sources are shared across the business and the skills of data stewards harder to fill, it makes sense to centralize data stewards in a service organization that can independently monitor and upgrade data quality. Lastly, if the organization requires trained data scientists to work on analytical models, then it makes sense to separate this out as a separate service.

Stage 3, as shown in Figure 5-11, is when a business has the opportunity to leverage data and analytics as part of a customer-facing product. In this case, the team working on the product should be part of the group working on the user experience. It is an add-on to the structure of Stage 2 but adds complexity in that centralized services can now receive "requests" from multiple internal- and external-facing organizations.

Establishing Releases, Roadmaps, and Prioritization

You can probably guess that the structure in Stages 2 and 3 can lead to complexity if multiple organizations are participating and multiple products are being developed or supported. How does work get prioritized

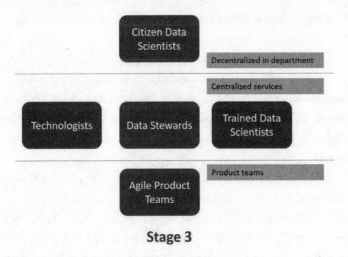

Stage 3

Figure 5-11. Stage 3 data organization, illustrating shared services and decentralized data science teams

and coordinated between these teams and the services that they may have dependencies on?

This is where the concepts of "change management," "releases," and even "estimation" become important. Sprints give the teams a process for working on short-term priorities. Releases promote change management formalities but also help dependent teams have some visibility over a team's midterm deliverables. When teams can estimate well, then they can be used to provide roadmaps beyond the upcoming release.

Prioritization can be a bit more challenging as it is difficult to define "minimal viable" for analytical services and difficult to compare "business value" between the deliverables across different organizations.

To solve this, you can leverage ideas from portfolio management. The governance group can be given authority to set priorities for each team either at a release level or at a roadmap level (multiple releases). Each team can then use voting mechanisms to judge the business values of the deliverables requested by different business and product teams.

Summary of Data Governance

You can't lead with governance. No one understands what governance is, and if you try to explain it, it comes across as an administrative bottleneck. Business leaders understand corporate governance and are beginning to appreciate IT governance, but data governance will be puzzling to executives in organizations that are just embarking on leveraging their data assets.

But once you have collaboration and a basic set of practices among data scientists, technologists, and data stewards, instituting data governance is demystified. Instead of a hard-to-define "governance," it becomes a set of business rules that define the underlying practice. The rules to focus on what will emerge as the teams collaborate, instead of having to define everything up front or through a commercially designed data governance maturity program.

Here are some responsibilities for the data governance team:

- ▶ Determine and approve strategies on what organizations to prioritize data services and to approve charters.
- ▶ Oversee financial aspects of the agile data organization; justify investments and demonstrate ROI where applicable.
- ▶ Review and approve standards for technologies, agile practices, data definitions, documentation formats, metrics, security, privacy, quality, and performance.
- ▶ Review roadmaps, releases, and priorities set by teams and ensure alignment with strategy.
- ▶ Review the current state of talent; identify gaps where new talent or training is required; align incentives and rewards.
- ▶ Oversee data or technology R&D priorities; prioritize where new data sources, technologies, or quality improvements are required.
- ▶ Handle disputes and bottlenecks across teams.

Two key responsibilities that should be the focus of the leader overseeing this transformation are to:

1. Own data security policies and prioritize its implementation.
2. Manage stakeholder expectations and nonstakeholder derailments.

Data Security

Several key policies fit under data security. What are the organization's data classifications? Who "owns the data" to define its policies, such as who gets access and defines the permissible use cases for the data set? Are there specific entitlements related to row or columnar views of the data? What kind of auditing is required to track viewing, changing, and distributing the data? What are the business rules for replicating, retaining, and archiving data? If the data contains personal or confidential data, what level of encryption, data masking, or anonymizing is required? What rules should be implemented to prevent data loss? What are the legal and compliance requirements on where the data can be physically stored?

This is a subset of security considerations that requires significant attention when organizations transform their data practices.

Managing Stakeholders

A key reason for having the transformational leader involved in data governance is that you need senior leaders to be involved as stakeholders in the transition to a data-driven organization. We've reviewed how important it is to get some early adopters to sponsor analytics charters and partner with the agile data organization. Once partnered, you're likely going to need the transformational leader's partnership to help set realistic expectations.

Stakeholders don't always understand or embrace agile principles when it conflicts with their priorities. They'll remember all the things you signed up for in agile planning but forget that it's an evolving process that prioritizes every sprint based on learnings and implementation realities. Some will look at charters and scope like contracts and bury teams if they underdeliver, yet provide little acknowledgment for additional scope taken on or for other complexities encountered along the journey.

If teams feel this pressure, they will be less likely to take on additional work for this stakeholder. If forced to, they will become more conservative in their commitments, and the stakeholder will likely be dissatisfied with the results given the investment. Things can get really bad when stakeholders challenge the underlying talent, technology selections, delivery practices, or data governance when they aren't getting everything they want.

It kills the culture. Instead of getting a data-driven culture, you can end up with one that pits business stakeholders against the people and teams that are providing services.

The data governance team needs the transformational leader to step into these situations. Maybe the team miscalculated the complexities, oversold their stakeholder, or didn't execute efficiently. Maybe the stakeholder wasn't listening to the team's recommendations or didn't fully grasp tradeoffs in priorities. Maybe the data governance team didn't handle conflicts efficiently, introduced too much governance too quickly, or empowered teams with inadequate funding or skills.

The transformational leader needs to best handle the situations from the perspective of getting the culture and alignment right first, execution considerations second. This means being the final arbitrator when it comes to disputes but also helping everyone in the program see the big picture. If something is systemically wrong, then the transformational leader should draw attention to it and make sure leaders are assigned to address it.

But what about the other issue of working with nonstakeholders? The leaders who are satisfied with status quo and don't want to become data driven. The passive-aggressive ones who are sitting on the sidelines waiting for the first sign of execution issues to bury the program. The ones that may be losing power, clout, or budget because data-driven decisions are driving priorities out of their domain? The ones who are hostile to the program because they would rather have more control over it.

In "The Reason So Many Analytics Efforts Fall Short,"[30] researchers revealed "that leadership issues were often at the heart of the problems" and "the commitment to advanced analytics disrupted [the C-suite] equilibrium" and "in all too many cases, the CEO devoted little time to trying to manage this dynamic." They have a number of recommendation for the CEO to keep their analytics programs from being a waste of time[31], including managing the C-suite and getting the right leadership and governance instituted for analytics programs.

But the researchers highlight two other key responsibilities to "challenge existing mental models" and to "create an environment of rapid innovation" that are key to successful programs. The first is a change management exercise that takes significant time to nurture, while the other is more tactical, encouraging team members to take calculated risks. Both are key elements of becoming a data-driven organization and reforming both leadership and culture.

Data-Driven Culture Summary

A data-driven organization is a cultural statement. So, what does this "look like"?

- A defined business strategy helps people focus their data discovery efforts.
- People ask good questions, challenge assumptions, and have healthy debates on where to make improvements, investments, or other changes.
- Many people in the organization have the skills, access to data, and sufficient expertise with BI tools to perform data discovery tasks and are successful extracting insights from data.
- Meetings kick off with a display, discussions, and a dive into data first to help shape opinions and the dialogue based on facts.
- Presentations reference their data sources—and these data sources are available to appropriate people in the organization to review, challenge, and conduct follow-up analytics.
- The IT organization provides a defined set of data management and BI services to assist the organization in their discovery efforts.
- There are already efforts to drive organizational changes, improve communications, and to get bottom-up contributions. Becoming data driven is a key but not the only cultural priority.
- Efforts to leverage data in decision making have measurable results—improvements in operations, sales, new revenue-generating products, happier customers, and so on.

▶ Data is shared and leveraged across different businesses, organizations, and products.

▶ There is priority, demand, and hunger to address data quality issues, to integrate multiple data sources, to capture new types of data, and to leverage third-party data to become smarter, faster, and more competitive.

Why is being data driven important in a digital business? Why is it critical to transformation? The answer is that you need organizations to help shape the future based on rapidly changing market conditions. They should be smarter and faster to compete with new competitors. And to do this, the products and services delivered to customers must be smarter, more efficient, more convenient, and more reliable.

Leveraging data and analytics is the core competency to enable this transformation. It's not just the job of the technologists or data scientists, it requires the entire organization to be data driven.

6.

DRIVING REVENUE
THROUGH
DIGITAL PRODUCTS

Strategic Planning Digital Revenue Products

The last few chapters brought your execution, decision making, and data practices to levels that enable you to manage digitally driven projects and transformation programs. You can use data-driven practices to make better decisions and to analyze customer needs. Portfolio management practices help to ensure that you have balanced priorities that target short-, medium-, and longer-term benefits. Agile methodologies help you drive execution, keep alignment, manage change, and improve quality.

Now you can apply all this capability to operational excellence and become a more efficient organization delivering higher-quality services to customers. Many organizations can drive significant bottom-line improvements through automation, digitally enabling workflows, and integrating third-party capabilities. Any organization that's been lagging investing in digital technologies and still performs a lot of nonphysical work manually should be able to find lots of opportunity to become more efficient.

But digital transformation isn't just about improving the bottom line. Efficiency plays will enable businesses to be more profitable and operationally competitive but still ripe for disruption from new competitive services that offer customers new choices and opportunities. Garmin isn't going to survive by becoming more efficient while improving their automotive GPS tools given that most consumers will get "good enough" capabilities from alternative inexpensive mobile applications.

Many businesses will be able to get a lift in customer satisfaction and revenue by providing digital, self-service capabilities in their products and services. Newspapers provided subscribers with websites and mobile applications to read content and advertisers a digital medium to target customers. Banks enabled business and consumer customers with online and mobile experiences to perform common transactions. Existing retailers added e-commerce channels to sell alongside their brick-and-mortar stores.

Digital Product Extensions

Let's put ourselves in one of these situations so that I can illustrate a point. You are a newspaper, and you built a website or a bank that has built a mobile application. It's less interesting to look at how the original channel got justified and developed, and the relevant question is how has this channel been supported over the years after its initial launch. What was the organizational approach to product improvements? What level of investment was made over time to ensure that the product remained competitive? Who drove the product priorities? How were improvements measured for success?

A few patterns emerge when you consider how organizations supported their initial investments in digital products and channels:

- **Big bang, infrequent upgrades**—Many financially driven institutions look at digital investments as onetime events. You scope, plan, build, release, and hopefully reap the benefits. If improvements are required, someone has to make an ROI case or prove there's a competitive threat to drive new investment.

- *Sales-driven investments*—If your product is being sold by a sales force, then many businesses become "sales driven," and priority investments are driven by their needs. Sales-driven product priorities can be very ad hoc when the loudest or most experienced salespeople drive the priorities.
- *Customer-driven investments*—These occur when products and services are sold directly to their consumers and there is a voice-of-customer feedback loop providing insights on their wants and needs. For example, I can go onto Atlassian's website, vote for a feature, and hope this feedback will drive priority.

There are some benefits and weaknesses in all three approaches. Big bang investments work best in industries that are very slow moving and where disruption from new entrants is least likely. In theory, these businesses can wait for a more aggressive competitor to demonstrate what capabilities are driving success, then look to replicate.

The problem today is that fewer industries and businesses can operate with little threat of disruption. Everything is being challenged today, and if you wait too long between investments, you have a lot more work to catch up before driving any new innovations. What's worse is that you are less likely to have the culture, practices, and skills to engage customers and develop products. Lastly, technology is changing so rapidly that businesses playing a wait-and-see game have a larger hurdle replacing legacy technologies or finding new technologies to enable innovation.

In my opinion, big bang product upgrades are a dead-end strategy at least for the next several years, as just about every industry faces some form of digital disruption.

A sales-driven strategy sounds good if you have evidence that the sales team can retain customers or drive incremental sales from the investment. There might be customer-specific requests like, "If we don't have feature X, then customer Y might switch to a competitor, but if we do, I can get us additional revenue." Or more generically, "I have customers that require A, B, and C."

These requests look appealing to CFOs and CEOs who look for investments that have near-term ROI but suffer from other issues. First, the expression lacks a true understanding of customer need and value proposition, so it's unclear whether the solution is solving a strategic long-term need or a short-term tactical challenge. Second, since the request is expressed through a salesperson, it's unclear whether the investment and solution can scale across multiple customers. In today's digital world, it's hard to get a single or small group of customers to fund the upfront investment and ongoing support of any solution, so sales-driven priorities tend to drive small incremental improvements in the product.

Customer-driven strategies tend to have the reverse problem. You may be collecting direct feedback from your customer through engagement, surveys or actual product usage metrics. In aggregate, they may provide an expression of what enhancements key customers and segments want from your product, but they may not provide sufficient context to drive significant investment or change. Depending on how you collect the information, it may be difficult to ascertain whether customers are willing to spend more on the improvements, measure the urgency of the request, or capture what alternatives they are considering.

When a business or a product is operating at smaller scales, it is possible to be sales or customer driven. There's a finite demand coming into the organization, and very often a decision to invest is driven by whether customers are willing to pay for the enhancement.

But for most products where there is a larger number of customers, discerning the true opportunities from disparate voices of multiple salespeople or directly from customers can be complicated or misleading. Even when priorities are easy to ascertain, there is still the issue of whether the enhancements developed for the needs of a few customers introduce complexities to mainstream customers or to the teams supporting the products. You can easily see this issue when applications have complex user experiences, forcing you to enter more data through more steps, and were designed to support several use cases. One way to measure this is to collect product usage statistics. Many products with long histories of having customer-driven enhancements show a few primary features with heavy usage and a long tail of secondary features used by a small minority.

Sales- and customer-driven organizations often view the role of product management as a proxy to make sense of all these needs. If the primary source of priority is sales, we often call them "*stakeholders*," and if they are specific customers, then we label them "*strategic customers*." One of the roles of product management is to sort through stakeholder and strategic customer needs, develop priorities, and drive organizational buy-in for implementing them.

Digital Strategy

Sales- and customer-driven product improvements are essentially bottom-up, tactical approaches employed by many companies to prioritize enhancements to existing products. There's nothing fundamentally wrong with sales- or customer-driven prioritization so long as there is some governance in the decision making. In addition, a user experience strategy is needed so that product interfaces don't evolve too complex experiences as new capabilities are added.

Beyond just extensions, some organizations can buy time by focusing on nondisruptive digital products. They complement existing "analog" products, and consumers will buy analog, digital, or both. For example, you can buy a print, digital, or both experiences of *The New York Times* or *The Wall Street Journal*. You can pay Netflix for DVD subscriptions, streaming movies, or both. These work well when existing businesses can offer new digital capabilities to existing customers and also attract new ones.

Although these digital products may look easy for businesses to manage internally, the reality may be quite different. The executive team first should determine whether digital product sales and support will be new responsibilities added to existing business lines or managed as separate digital businesses. Many media and retail organizations opted for the latter because selling and supporting digital is often a different skill set and business dynamic then their analog equivalent. Still there are often conflicts on branding, go-to market strategies, pricing, and sales strategy once businesses have to manage both legacy and digital. Overseeing this can be a distraction for the executive team and is one reason disruptors can sometimes come in and blindside incumbent businesses.

Product extensions and nondisruptive digital product offerings may not be sufficient to drive digital transformation depending on how fast your industry is changing and how easy it is for new disruptive entrants. In this environment, organizations must be more market driven and strategic and looking at brand-new product and service opportunities, partnership opportunities, and new investments. This isn't easy for many organizations that have been selling and delivering the same products the same way with well-defined competitors for long periods of time.

A digital strategy reimagines a new digital business with potentially all new products and service experiences based on market opportunities, the blending of physical and digital capabilities, and leveraging emerging technologies. In this transformation, the existing business is broken down to its assets, organizational capabilities, and other building blocks. Additional building blocks are then considered, some that the organization might develop internally, others it might buy through services, and others where it will establish partners. This future "digital business" is conceived, and then leaders have the very difficult task of strategically planning a transition from a legacy company to digital business.

The executive team should form a product leadership team to develop a digital strategy and align a process to other strategic planning efforts. Who will lead the product leadership team, and who else should be on the team and fulfilling what roles? How often will this team take on planning activities? How will the plans be communicated, and what elements of the plan will be public, shared with a limited audience, or private depending on its risk of disruption. Finally, they need to consider where to bring in outside partners to aid in the research or analysis, perform tasks outside the skills of the organization, bring in tangential capabilities, or lead change management and training activities.

There's a lot to cover under strategic planning digital transformation, so let me suggest that there are a few key tenets that organizations need to focus on to develop their digital strategy. First, product management needs to focus on strategic activities like determining target markets, quantifying market opportunities, and determining longer-term customer needs. Second, they need to conceive new digital products that deliver value to existing customers and new markets. Lastly, they need to conceive go-to markets strategies, digital marketing approaches, and sales processes to sell digital products.

This may sound daunting, and it is for many organizations that struggle with organizational change management. Therefore, articulating a digital strategy is a critical step in the transformation as becoming more of a digital business is likely to affect the entire organization. The strategy should set a future direction of the business but also provide some guidelines on how leadership plans to get there. Thus, the strategy is a communication tool to the extended executive team, employees, the Board, and selected strategic partners.

But the strategy doesn't have to be developed top-down in an ivory tower. Also, contrary to what experts tell you, it doesn't have to be developed as a first step before anything else can be considered. I prefer setting the strategy only after some other factors are considered, such as target markets, customer segment opportunities, and even potential products.

So, for the remainder of the chapter, I'll break this down starting with product management's role in digital transformation.

Product Strategy in Digital Transformation

As stated earlier, many organizations view the product management role as a tactical role aiming to listen to customers and stakeholders and manage the product with the goal of growing revenue and the number of customers. But project management disciplines go well beyond managing everyone's wish list. Product managers drive changes in sales process, marketing, tiering, bundling, pricing, discounting, partnerships, and enhancements to achieve their goals. The product management function is usually broken down into several key disciplines:

- *Product strategy* involves identifying and quantifying target markets, market needs and opportunities, market sizing, competitive considerations, industry transformation considerations, economic, legal, or geopolitical factors that help businesses determine the primary opportunities for growth.
- *Product ownership* is the role in agile practices and is responsible for setting priorities for developing or enhancing products, measuring customer satisfaction, and engaging internal stakeholders.

- **Product management** disciplines oversee the P/L of either a customer segment, product family, or single product and drive priorities on revenue, growth, profitability, quality, and customer satisfaction.
- **Product marketing** is the skill to define, execute, measure, and modify go-to-market strategies along the lifecycle of the product.

It is often very difficult to find product managers that have skills and experiences across all these disciplines, but the revenue-generation elements of digital transformation programs do require them at different stages in the transformation. This means organizations must consider how to apply internal resources and bring outside help in weak areas. You might bring someone from the outside to help quantify target markets and to review competitive offerings. Perhaps the organization has ill defined or outdated pricing and some research is required to determine price elasticity and value propositions. You might have a defined product strategy but need outside help to develop talent to assume product ownership roles. You may have developed a product but lack the data or marketing knowledge to market it optimally.

More importantly, it requires organizations to recognize the strategic importance of the product management function. The executive team needs to give product managers the charter and backing to review the end-to-end business and to propose blue-sky options that might include options that disrupt existing products and services. They need to blaze paths to get them access to data, ensure that business leaders are accessible, and require that sales leaders provide introductions to clients and prospects.

The Smarter/Faster Approach to Product Definition

Redefining business strategy, target markets, value proposition, and competitive landscape is a daunting task, especially for companies that feel competitive pressure to transform or are already experiencing declining revenues. Most organizations can ill afford multiyear programs to do encompassing strategic reviews as a gating step in transformation. The world just moves too fast, and by the time a long planning exercise is done, the market will have moved significantly.

So where to start and how to simplify? Most organizations need to consider executing along three simultaneous paths shown in Figure 6-1 to help drive some conclusion.

Figure 6-1. Parallel product management activities that facilitate developing a digital strategy

One activity looks at the world through the market and customer lens, the second reviews existing products and services, and the third brainstorms and ideally pilots new products or partnerships. When an organization gathers baseline data across all three tracks, it is more ready to host a guided discussion on digital strategy. The intersection of target markets, existing products and customers, and potential new products and partnerships are the basis for forming the digital strategy.

My approach to defining the strategy is to prioritize a set of questions, reviews, and information-gathering exercises according to the track that the product leadership team should pursue. It's important to be realistic about the number of questions and scope of research assigned to this team. Conservative organizations are more likely to want a lot more answers up front, and it's important to expose this because it takes longer and more expense to answer them. These organizations need to reflect on these desires because decisions on strategy, transformation, and product development often require making assumptions and validating them over time through a process.

However, more aggressive organizations can fall victim to being "serial starters," looking at and committing resources to too many opportunities, failing to get a good number of them to market, and struggling to achieve critical customer interest in many of them.

DEFINE TARGET MARKETS

- What data can be gathered on existing customers, the products they buy, and their spending with the business over the last three years?
- Align internal and external data to any existing customer segmentations. Are they still relevant, or are there new orientations based on the impact of digital transformation in the industry? Who is likely to benefit from digital and who is likely to contract?
- Based on the data available, look to agree on "strategic" customer segments and key customers and top prospects.
- Can a set of buying personas be defined that represent the buying decision makers? Can a separate set of user personas be defined? What other stakeholder personas are needed that are parties to either buying or using the product?
- Looking at the list of target markets, define a list of product offerings that may be competitive, substitutes, or complementary.
- What industry trends, regulation, or other factors will factor into whether this market will grow or shrink over the next decade? What research should leadership review?

AUDIT EXISTING PRODUCTS

- Develop a multiyear P/L that has the underlying revenue details by customer and a high-level breakdown of the operational costs, especially variable ones. What are the attributes of larger, longer running, or growing customers versus smaller, shrinking accounts?
- Capture the rate card expressing sales channel, price points, discounting, and incentives. Is product discounting trending better or worse?
- Define buying, user, and stakeholder personas. Map existing contacts to personas and rate health of the relationship.
- What does the competitive landscape look like today and how does it compare to the existing product offering?
- Interview key users and buys. Determine their successes using the product, pain points, and opportunities. Identify whether they are using any competitive or complimentary products. Validate value proposition.
- Capture journey maps showing how prospects and customers navigate. Identify pain points and opportunities.

TEST NEW PRODUCTS & PARTNERSHIPS

- Who are you targeting with the product or service? What customer segment or segments? What are some example customers from the existing client base and some new potential customers?
- What is the core value proposition and convenience you are addressing for these customers?
- What is the product vision expressing how the solution will address the core value proposition?
- What is known about competitive offerings, price points, and size of the potential market? Forecast the first year's revenue potential and identify the underlying assumptions.
- What are some of the inputs needed to enable the product offering such as components, capabilities, data, and processes? Of these, which ones are assets of the company, others than can easily be acquired or developed, and others that require up front R&D?

Figure 6-2. Example questions to discover target markets, audit existing products, and assess the impact of new product concepts

Figure 6-2 shows a sample of questions that you can start with and adapt to your business context. Some will be relatively straightforward to answer, while others can call for entire projects to properly research or implement. Because this strategy will evolve, it's best to define a minimal target, other activities that can be resolved over a longer period, and others that can begin once other questions are resolved.

My strong suggestion is that this strategic planning exercise be limited to a very small group that has some history of collaborating and that brings different skills and experiences to the table. The product leadership team needs to meet frequently and likely for lengthy periods of time so that ideas can be fleshed out and documented. When documenting findings, this team must be particularly careful separating out facts from insights. Once they have a version to share with the executive team, this group will have the difficult task of bringing them up to speed on the facts, reviewing to see whether they agree with insights, and convincing them of any proposed strategy.

Building Consensus on Strategy

I like to think that 1.0 of the digital strategy should attempt to answer the following questions:

- Which markets and customer segments should we target, which should we maintain, and which are least important to the future?
- Of the existing products, which ones are worth growing, which should be maintained, and which ones should be shut down over a period of time?
- What types of products are worth investing in? What statements can be made that provide context on the target market, nature of customer experience, and financial assumptions that can bound ideal products versus others that are less strategic or others not worth pursuing.
- What are the key customer experiences that we need to enable to drive value, satisfaction, and loyalty?
- What are the recommended next steps regarding strategic planning, planning on specific initiatives, and any initiatives that are in development?

When the product leadership team has sufficient facts and insights to report on these questions, then it has enough material to present a 1.0 strategy. The team next needs to decide how to present it to the executive group with the hope that that they don't dispute facts, largely agree on insights, and are open and honest on whether they agree with your recommendations.

You can't just show up at the executive meeting and expect this level of buy-in. The only way to get there is to review this one-on-one or in small groups so that executives have time to absorb the material and can express opinions freely. Your primary objective is to determine where everyone stands once you formally present it and believe that you have sufficient buy-in from enough executives on your recommendations. You may need to adjust your position based on learnings from these dialogs.

Even when you have presold this to all the key executives prior to any formal review, be prepared and expect the unexpected when you formally present. Executives will change their minds, attempt to add more considerations to the scope, use the data and insights that you present to push their own agendas, or even distract other members of the executive team if your plan conflicts with their objectives. It's rare that you'll get the positive head nods you desire even after you've run it by everyone.

Hopefully you can drive the dialogue to some concrete decision and follow-ups if required. If the conversation is going off agenda or if strong conflicting arguments are raised, then there's only one answer to this situation. Get the CEO on board and make sure she knows that her role is to manage the executive team to some form of consensus.

The product leadership team should then consider how best to document the strategy and formulate a communication plan. A best practice is to start with minimal documentation and communicate with a small group of change agents that will have critical early roles in the transformation. Over time, materials can be expanded to help bring a larger audience in on the journey. It's a delicate balance because communicating too early raises questions the team won't be ready to answer, whereas waiting too long will create speculation and fear.

From Strategy to Product Planning

With a digital strategy 1.0 in hand, the organization can take on several parallel activities. In this section, I will concentrate on developing products and partnerships.

Let's go back to Chapter Four where we discussed portfolio management. The art of product development is to move product ideas through the pipeline. Initially, the portfolio should have lots of ideas in the "defined" or "ideation" stage, but we want to narrow them down to the most promising ones before we get to the "planning" and "development" stages that will require more effort from internal resources and investment.

We can use our digital strategy and framework to help gauge whether a product is worthy of going to the next stage and to define the governance in each stage. To do this, the product leadership team should take on several responsibilities:

- ▶ Define governance by stage.
- ▶ Judge or vote on whether product ideas can move to their next stages.
- ▶ Define and review constraints that limit the number of simultaneous products active in the pipeline.
- ▶ Manage funding aligned to product development.
- ▶ Propose and measure KPIs associated with the health of the product pipeline.

Since the portfolio should be holistic containing revenue ideas (products) and other types of initiatives (operational excellence, new capabilities, risk/compliance), the executive team should determine whether the portfolio is governed by a single steering group or there are different groups reviewing and judging initiatives depending on their initiative type. It's certainly easier to manage the entire portfolio if the steering group is skilled in reviewing initiatives of all types and has a holistic mindset to balance what is moved forward.

Managing the Product Pipeline

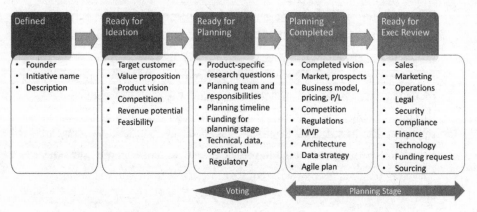

Figure 6-3. Product development lifecycle through planning stages

Figure 6-3 shows the product planning process from *defined*, to *ideation*, to *planning*. When a product is a concept, or an idea, it should be listed and put into the "defined" stage. The *founder* of the idea should be listed, and the instructions to him should be to answer some questions like the ones used to define the digital strategy. Specifically, here is the initial *product charter* and what the founder should be able to answer when proposing a product for ideation:

- ▶ **Target customer**—What customer segment or segments are targeted? Who are some example customers from the existing client base and some new customers?
- ▶ **Value proposition**—What is the core value proposition and convenience being addressed for these customers?
- ▶ **Initial product vision**—What is the product vision expressing how the solution will address the core value proposition?
- ▶ **Competitive landscape**—What is known about competitive offerings, price points, and size of the potential market?
- ▶ **Revenue potential**—Forecast the first year's revenue potential, and identify the underlying assumptions.
- ▶ **Feasibility**—What are some of the inputs needed to enable the product offering such as components, capabilities, and processes? Of these, which ones are assets of the company, others that can easily be acquired or developed, and others that require upfront R&D?

The ideation questions are designed to be relatively easy to answer, and what the product leadership team should be doing is determining its alignment to the digital strategy, validating revenue potential, and considering feasibility.

The founder should then be asked if he has his manager's commitment to work on this idea and whether he is "signing up" to take steps to bring it to a planning. If the answer is yes, then a target date should be selected to have this completed, and the founder should be armed with materials that outline the digital strategy. From there, the product can be moved to the "ideation" stage and the founder enabled to go and capture the information requested.

The product leadership team should establish some guidelines on products that are in ideation. What's the maximum amount of time for this stage? What resources do they get access to during this stage? What kind of help can they get from sales, marketing, finance, and technology when their products are in ideation? If you enable a large part of your organization to promote product ideas, do they need additional levels of sponsorship or product management mentorship when a product is in this stage?

They should also set expectations on the level of detail required. Product visions at this stage should be intentionally vague to enable customer, competitive, and other forms of research to better align it to market needs. A founder may be able to give only high-level information on the competitive landscape and feasibility depending on his skills and access to resources.

What Goes into Planning Products?

During ideation, the founder's job is to follow up on any questions on the *product charter*, then take steps to define a backlog of what needs to be done and delivered in the *planning* stage. This to-do list should be in the form of a list of questions, and the goal of planning is to get answers, ask more follow-up questions, and develop a business plan for high-potential product ideas.

When drafted, the founder should prepare a readout for the product leadership team with a formal request to move the product into the planning stage. This founder should come prepared to answer the following:

- What key questions need to be answered during the planning stage? These questions are typically product specific, and the founder needs an extended team of experts to answer them.
- Whom does the founder want on his planning team, and what are their responsibilities?
- What is the timeline for completing planning?
- What other resources are needed to complete planning? This could include funding requests for market research, prototypes, and other external expertise.
- What are the technical, data, and operational considerations for the product?

These last few questions force the founder to think a few steps ahead and propose what needs to happen in planning, who he wants on the team, and for how long. This information also gives the product leadership team some context to evaluate the initiative on its merits but also gives them a sense of cost and potential resource bottlenecks. Three founders on different initiatives can't easily work with the same technologist to plan their initiatives. Initiatives that require longer planning durations, larger teams, and more resources to complete planning should have to demonstrate more revenue potential or strategic value.

What are some example planning stage questions and materials the founder should count on answering during the planning phase?

- A completed product vision indicating inputs (what raw materials are needed to make the product) and outputs (what is produced and consumed by customers)
- Completed research on the target market with more details on the organization's reach into this market and what steps, if any, are needed to expand this reach
- The target user personas of the product. Who are the buyers, the users, and other key players having a role in the customer journey?
- An overall design of the user experience highlighting key flows, screens, transactions, events, forms, dashboards, and other interactions that make up the product.

- A proposed business model, price points, and how the product will be packaged and sold
- Identified competitors and alternatives and how the product's value proposition will win over customers
- Identified regulations, constraints, and other risks that need to be considered
- A proposed minimally viable product (MVP) and the product roadmap beyond the MVP detailing the agile backlog for its development and proposed release plan
- A technology plan identifying the architecture, computing needs, usage assumptions, and operational requirements
- A data strategy identifying what data assets will be utilized, what new data needs to be procured, and what data will be collected with the product
- A proposed P/L
- The beginnings of a go-to market strategy for the product

The founder should account sufficient time and resources to be able to answer these questions. In addition, the product leadership team should clearly identify the list of question and any presentation formats so that the founders have a clear idea of what's expected of them when presenting a product idea for planning.

The product leadership team should be trying to determine whether there is alignment to strategy and if the product idea is worth investing more time and energy. My recommendation is to implement a voting mechanism to capture steering members' feedback. Scoring the initiative provides detail beyond just yes/no and gives a business value that can be compared to other initiatives in the pipeline. Since initiatives will consume resources, these scores should be transparent and are indicators to individuals, teams, and departments on prioritizing their resources. Scoring also helps to audit individual product leadership team members to ensure they balance business needs and don't give priority only to initiatives that benefit them.

Scoring by itself may not be sufficient to move a product into planning. First, the leader of the product steering team should indicate whether it does meet the criteria to move forward. Second, any constraints such as funding, lack of availability of requested planning resources, or departmental constraints should be identified and resolved before clearing a product for planning. But once the product is moved into planning, the intention should be that, if the key assumptions on market, customer need, competitive landscape, revenue, level of investment feasibility, and regulatory considerations check out, the organization plans to invest in its development.

It's worth noting that in my experience, every organization is culturally different in terms of how many questions need to be addressed, what level of planning is required, and what degree of assumptions or unknowns is reasonable before making a concrete investment in either planning or development. I've tried to present a balanced approach between what can be planned up front versus other activities that can likely occur during the development phase.

It's good to set some guidelines. For example, for digital products that don't have many legacy dependencies, integrations with the physical world, upfront R&D for new inventions, regulatory considerations, safety, or significant internal workflow changes, my rule of thumb is that I like three- to seven-month MVPs that require one to two months of planning. Anything longer, and you may miss the market or overinvest, and it can be shorter if you have an experienced team working with known practices and platforms.

Planning "Digital" Products

Up to now, I've described a basic process to plan products. Before I review how to close out the product planning products, let's consider what makes a product "digital" and have the potential of transforming to a digital business? These are certain things product developers should consider if they want to achieve this lofty goal. Here is a starting checklist, and you'll notice that a good number of them relate to creating winning customer experiences:

1. How will you provide a customer experience that people love? Digital products must be easy, fast, consistent, and intuitive to use. They should provide the user conveniences and balance between activities that require user input versus activities that provide customers insights, utility, and value. This is where all that work on user personas becomes important because product developers need to validate that the experience provided enables the needs and expected use cases for each

persona. How are you personalizing the experience by persona and for individual users? In what ways are you connecting emotionally to prospects and customers? How fast and "real-time" is the information that you are providing? Is it memorable that customers are likely to refer their friends or business colleagues to your product or service?

2. Great product experiences not only map experiences to personas and then personalize, they look to provide other conveniences based on context. Location and time are obvious context, but great products try to leverage other variables to provide more relevant information or more specific experiences. Inputs should include recent information the user already indicated, including the products reviewed, what online content the user reviewed, what newsletters were opened, how long and how frequently the user visited your site or store, or whether the user is at home or traveling. Context can also include other local and global conditions, such as weather, traffic conditions, what's happening in the news, the state of financial markets, and other factors that might change customer needs or behaviors.

3. Digital customer experiences offer consistency. Customers navigating to different parts of your site or using different tools have some consistency in navigation and available tools. Search functions work across all information assets but personalize the response based on context. Performance needs to be fast and consistent.

4. Regarding the user's identity, digital products must offer extreme conveniences registering and logging them in while being responsible about security and privacy. Are you asking for a reasonable amount of information when registering on the site? Are you taking advantage of registration and authentication mechanisms provided by social platforms? Do you have single sign-on securely implemented across all your applications? Are your forgot-password functions convenient and secure? Do you offer two-factor authentication and enforce standards on password length and complexity? Do you notify users in multiple ways that there were changes made to their personal or account information? Are you properly encrypting and securing passwords and other personal information on your servers? Are your customer service representatives trained and taking the proper steps to validate identity?

5. How will the product be designed to enable on- and offline networking? Products today can't survive in a digital silo, and consumers expect some ubiquity and interoperability with other platforms. How is developing this network going to impact the business?

6. How will you build trust with customers, prospects, partners, the media, and with the public on social networks? Trust must be a factor in how you message, how engineers implement data security, how you implement privacy, and in your terms of service.

7. Many product developers have experience and a comfort zone in developing products for the physical world and the web, which is why many digital specialists advise them to think mobile and location-aware experiences first. Products that can offer better conveniences and insights to mobile users are more likely to provide value when users are behind a screen or in a physical environment. Are you taking advantage of mobile-specific capabilities such as notifications?

8. How are physical and digital experiences integrated? This is particularly important for retailers who have high bars to ensure that a customer can start their journey shopping in the store, complete a transaction on a mobile device, and elect to return to the store if they need to do an exchange.

9. How is pricing handled on digital interfaces? Do you offer a reasonable number of purchasing options? Do you make it convenient to compare different products or pricing options? Are you transparent with conditions that might affect the price over time?

10. Do you offer multiple payment options, and are the interfaces to input payment preferences convenient? If you store payment information, is this information secured properly in your computing environment? How easy is it to make changes to payment information, and do you proactively inform users of any expiring payment methods? Do you provide reports showing what transactions were made and make it easy to report payment issues?

11. How are you providing customer service across all your experiences? How easy is it for customers to reach out for help? How convenient is the self-service help that you are providing, and are customers successful using it? When a user reaches out to a customer service representative, how knowledgeable are they about the customer's

product usage, and are they able to resolve questions or issues quickly and with high satisfaction rates?

12. How are you leveraging the customer's social network to provide additional capabilities, convenience, and intelligence? How are you using it to drive usage, enable repeat business, or reach new prospects? Do you make it convenient and rewarding to share information? Does your product offer digital collaboration and social function that enhances my overall utility and experience? How are you rewarding top contributors or providing incentives to users that are highly influential on social platforms?

13. How is your product leveraging the data it collects and data that should be easily accessible without violating privacy constraints or becoming creepy to the end user? Where are proprietary algorithms including those leveraging predictive analytics, machine learning, or artificial intelligence being developed that will give customers added convenience, intelligence, or insight?

14. What kind of services, benefits, and directives are you providing employees on their use of the product? Are you providing financial incentives to use and promote the product? Are there capabilities and training so that all employees can provide basic customer service tasks?

15. How are you interfacing with the ecosystem of machines, sensors, things, third-party services and the physical world to add intelligent data gathering, responsive outputs, or other conveniences? Where are you developing APIs to enable additional business services and ways to deliver new customer values?

16. Where can your product leverage automation, digital partnerships, crowdsourcing, and other methods to ensure operations are scalable, require minimal assets, and have efficient cost models?

17. What is the opportunity to enable recurring revenue sold as a subscription? What additional products and service capabilities are going to be needed over time to enhance the value proposition and to enable retaining customers and increasing fees?

18. How can your product/service evolve to a platform or develop marketplaces that enable developing additional products and services? Both platforms and marketplaces enable customers to extend how

they're using your product or service with new options made available by third parties.

19. Where are there opportunities to develop and promote the product toward social good? In addition to the contributions you are making, aligning customer involvement to donations and other places where you demonstrate social responsibilities drives a higher emotional response and satisfaction. Sometimes, even simple messaging such as encouraging users to print less can drive brand loyalty.

How are you measuring the customer experience? Do you have a full 360-degree view of all the interactions made with the customers? Can you sense issues in real time and provide services to customers struggling or others that have reported a bad experience? How strong are the analytics on customer experience to help identify who, what, and when there is evidence of great experiences and poor experiences that need improvement? Are you leveraging surveys to capture satisfaction, net promoter, and other metrics to help drive improvements?

This is not to say that every product requires all these considerations, but it's hard to imagine digital products today without some of them. Many of these are foundational capabilities, so it's very important for a product developer to consider the appropriate elements during product planning.

Quantifying Sales and Marketing and Gaining Buy-In

The last step of product planning, shown in Figure 6-3, is gaining whatever approvals are required to either develop a product or invest in new enhancements.

The most crucial part of gaining approvals is to get the commitments from sales and marketing to the business plan. This plan usually calls for closing a defined amount of business over a period and the sales team's responsibilities for hitting revenue, pricing, and customer targets. The marketing team should commit to the metrics that support this growth especially if they are responsible for delivering qualified leads to the sales team.

Every product manager will tell you that getting these commitments is the hardest part of their job. Trying to get their agreement before the product is even developed is harder since the sales people have only a limited picture on what the product looks like, what it does, how it will be marketed, and how their best prospects will react to their early sales efforts. This is even more daunting for products being developed using agile methodologies where there is only a commitment to develop the MVP and where the product owner can adjust priorities.

How much of a commitment is required at this stage? Is having a business plan sufficient, or does your organization require a full sales commitment prior to approving product development? How does the organization's need to protect against a product manager's overly optimistic or unrealistic sales plan compare to the need to protect against a highly conservative estimate from the sales team? This can become a significant leadership challenge depending on how conservative the executive team is, the availability of funds to make product investments, and how the organization handles successes and setbacks.

Here's my best advice on this subject. First, the objective is to get any sales commitment. If they attach a $0 to a product, then that's clearly a red flag. Once they agree that there is some product they can sell, then that should be considered an endorsement of the product.

Second, to quantify the sales opportunity, ask a different question that will help back into it. Find out their top prospects who will have at least a moderate interest in the product. You now have a potential sales pipeline.

Next, leverage data to model this out in a very fact-based, transparent way. Use data from the CRM to determine metrics on typical time frames to prospect, develop relationships, and close business on similar products. Use third-party benchmarks if your CRM does not have this detail. Second, consider using third parties to research price points for the product. Develop a financial model that enables you to plan both an aggressive scenario (high price, high close rate, short sale cycle) versus a more conservative one.

Perform similar steps with marketing, especially on the steps to acquire and qualify leads. Marketing will have a significant role from branding to lead generation to attracting new customers and will likely be conservative in the number of qualified leads they commit to passing to sales. If the number of leads modeled is overly conservative, sales leaders will use this to negotiate a lower commitment.

Follow a similar approach by modeling lead generation. If you have similar products, determine the lead conversion ratio and back into the number of leads required for both your aggressive and conservative models. Then look for either internal or third-party benchmarks to map out time frames and costs to produce these leads.

Make sure your finance team reviews this model and plans to present both scenarios to sales and marketing leaders and later to the executive team. Make sure that you parameterize and disclose any other assumptions baked into the model.

Finally, present a conservative product development roadmap, and develop milestones that link future and ongoing investments to revenue and other marketing or sales KPIs. This will help present a lower upfront financial commitment and demonstrate to the executive team the controls you are proposing to gate additional investment.

Putting this together, you are presenting a product where the sales team agrees that there is a revenue opportunity, where you can show modeled conservative and aggressive business plans, and where investments are gated on successful revenue generation. This should take a lot of the emotions and haggling over the business plan with the hope that the executive team is ready to make a guided and rational business decision.

Gaining Approvals for Development and Investment

The executive leadership team needs to endorse what the approval steps are, what materials are required, when reviews need to happen, who needs to participate, and how investment decisions are formally documented. If this doesn't exist in your organization, then the product leadership team should propose one and get the leadership team's approval. Not having these guidelines can lead to a lot of ambiguity, overplanning, or underplanning when these expectations are not grounded with governing principles.

Care should be taken here to define some boundaries. You don't want to overcomplicate the information required and steps to follow to gain approvals. The signoff should have parameters that differentiate what's required for "small" or "low-risk" product offerings versus others that are "larger," "higher risk," and other parameters requiring more rigor. This is where larger organizations should consider developing standards and checklists so that smaller, low-risk offerings can go through any approvals efficiently.

Product leadership should look at this stage beyond just getting the necessary approvals. This is a critical stage to get the organizational buy-in to what is being developed and to finalize their commitment on their responsibilities bringing the product to market. Product leadership should spend time in all relevant departments to make sure all steps are captured, included in the development plan, and appropriately resourced from the applicable departments.

When presenting to the executive team, the product founders should provide a factual and emotional case on the time urgency of investing in the product. Why now? What conditions make bringing this product to market now rather than delaying? What's likely to happen or possible if the executive team elects to delay? You certainly can present financial, competitive, regulatory, and other factors to make this case, but this is one place where an emotional, passionate case is warranted.

In my experience, risk-averse leaders who prefer comprehensive research, highly detailed product plans, more conservative investments, and perfect alignment between departments will use delay tactics rather than directly oppose a good idea. The product founders should address this directly by making a clear argument that delaying is a bad business decision and should show as much evidence demonstrating why building the product now is optimal. Translate and negotiate the final objections to things that you will follow up on, but press hard to get the approvals, even conditional ones, so that you can drive digital to the next stage.

From Product Planning to Development

As you begin to transition from *planning* to *development,* you should be starting to formalize your agile backlog that defines the project plan. You should also be deciding who will play the product owner and other roles in the program. These artifacts, along with an approved budget, a go-to market strategy, technology architecture, target timeline, and resource plan are some of the things that I look for before moving a product into the development phase.

The backlog should contain all the major epics and stories required to bring the product to market. In other words, this isn't just a technology backlog. It is likely going to contain epics, stories, releases, and possibly defects covering marketing, sales, and other operational changes. By putting everything related in the program in one place, you enable every member of the team to have visibility on everything prioritized by the product owner required for a successful launch. An aligned, collaborative, cross-disciplinary team is absolutely necessary to drive digital products.

But this isn't always easy. IT operations may be working out of an IT service manager tool. Sales may have a mandate to record all activity in the CRM, and marketing may be using spreadsheets to track their work. Are you going to take on the challenge of centralizing transformation and product development activities?

It's your call. You can manage everything centrally but without all the active participants collaborating in your backlog tool. This will likely require you to have a project manager in addition to the product owner to keep track of activities performed by people who can't or won't collaborate in a central tool. If you're up to the challenge, getting everyone on the project looking at one backlog, one news feed, and one set of reports and updating their activities has significant advantages.

Agile development was covered in Chapter Two, but let's review some concepts from the perspective of a product owner. There are many books and articles about product ownership, so I am going to focus only on some important concepts.

The Product Owner's Fundamental Agile Principle

Product owners start a development project with a vision and a list of everything that they want the product to deliver. In many cases, the vision, strategic requirements, and primary functional requirements have been gathered by soliciting information from customers, prospects, and key salespeople. It also likely includes requirements driven by competitive needs, compliance, operational, technology, and security requirements. In some cases, the product owner has made commitments to have certain capabilities available in the product, sometimes to enable sales to an early buyer, others because of minimal compliance requirements, and others because the product owner made promises to internal stakeholders to get their approval.

Product owners also made commitments to deliver a product on a timeline, budget, a defined set of resources, and an agreed-upon technology architecture. In effect, these are some of the constraints the product owner has to manage to in order deliver the product.

So, given the variables of scope, timeline, budget, and quality, how is the product owner going to manage tradeoffs, conflicts, risks that materialize, and new needs that are learned or discovered during the development phase.

A fundamental principle of agile practices is that, given these multiple interdependent constraints, agile practitioners advise on *managing to timeline and budget first, quality a very close second, and scope third.*

Now it is counterintuitive to many product owners to accept and manage to timeline first and manage to scope last, given all the work they've done learning customer needs, convincing stakeholders, communicating vision, and even documenting some fundamental requirements. Why is scope last?

There are a couple of tactical and strategic answers. First, agile provides a framework for the product owner to see iterative improvements. You might see a skeleton of a product in sprint one and more capabilities in sprint two. The product owner may then look to go "off plan" and adjust scope and priorities because of something that was learned through a demo or from engaging customers during the development period. You can't expect a development team to hit the *original scope* when the product owner has a license and authority to make some degree of scope changes.

Second, estimations are inherently just that. They are best-effort estimates based on what the development team knows, what they assume, and what they understand behind the technical implementation. What happens when the estimate is off and something is going to take longer to implement than forecasted? At times, you can make up the time elsewhere or ask the team to work harder. But in general, if something is taking longer, the product owner should make decisions on whether to maintain scope and extend the timeline or keep to the timeline and modify the scope. In most situations, agile practitioners will advise to compromise on scope rather than extend the timeline.

The strategic rationale is that you almost always have a second chance to come to bat if you miss on scope. You can have a customer lined up ready to buy that will buy anyway even if the scope isn't exactly what was promised. In this situation, the product owner has made the right decision on deferring scope because there is little business impact in missing the feature. Maybe you learn that the feature isn't that important anyway. If it is and the customer is upset, as a product owner, you can offer to discount the purchase until the missing feature is ready. Worst case, you can attempt to close the sale but only fulfill it once the feature is available.

But miss a deadline, and the product owner now has some harder issues to overcome. First, there's a loss of credibility with stakeholders and potential customers that often requires significant energy from the product owner to overcome. Second, when the product owner misses on a delivery date, it often implies a budget impact. Third, most product plans use the delivery milestone to drive other business activities such as marketing, training, and sales activities, so missing a date can have significant implications working with business teams and schedules. Finally, the best product owners will align delivery dates with other business events that enable them to get a marketing boost or a more efficient internal rollout. Maybe there's an industry event that will enable a large number of prospects to learn about the product. Maybe there is a manufacturing schedule and penalties for delays. Maybe the sales team is coming in for training and is the best opportunity to get them ready to learn and sell the product.

Missing on quality is a close second because it's harder to define minimal, acceptable, and superior quality. A big part of quality is the underlying user experience, and if it isn't easy and convenient to do the most important things, then buyers are more likely to consider alternatives. In many cases, it's better to deliver a superb experience on a few things rather than a clunky one on many things.

There are other forms of product quality, including stability, performance, security, and reliability that need some form of minimal acceptable criteria. But even these criteria have some variability depending on how their acceptance criteria are expressed.

Responsibilities of the Product Owner

You need a product owner to have guiding principles that are aligned with digital product delivery.

- **Define an achievable minimally viable product defining strategic capabilities and quality criteria required to bring the product to market.** The key word here is *"minimal,"* and the product owner should challenge whether she can address a sufficient part of her business plan with every additional capability or quality criteria introduced in the MVP. In my experience, the single biggest mistake a product owner does is either not expressing the MVP or over-subscribing it with too many capabilities, quality criteria, or other requirements.

  Let me illustrate this by example. Let's say you are targeting to sell 12 customers over the first year of a new product and expect a ramp-up with only one customer in the first quarter. Is the MVP what is needed for 12 customers, one customer, or something in between?

  The answer should be what you think is needed for one customer, but to do this properly, the product owner should plan and budget a full-year agile program. First, the product will need funding for ongoing development so that capabilities can be added and improved on to hit the full sales target. Second, the product owner needs sales to have several active prospects in the first quarter to increase the likelihood that one will close.

- **Set reasonable expectations with customers and stakeholders on the scope of product delivery.** Product owners should consider themselves as members and leaders of the delivery team. Most of the organization will not understand the concept of managing to an MVP or leveraging market research and agile practices to enhance products over time. Many won't care about the complexities of product development, adhering to security or compliance requirements and just want to know that a product that customers want to buy will be done on time and budget. Smart product owners set reasonable expectations up front, knowing that they need flexibility to manage unknowns and changes.

- **Partner with your leads, and follow a methodology for prioritizing.**
Product owners should use their vision to make sure that the whole team
has a shared understanding of what they are trying to build, for whom,
why it will provide value, and what they will need to win. That's the big
picture the team needs to understand, but after that, they should be more
focused on what they are doing today, this sprint, and this release. To
make teams productive, the product owner should be working with their
leads to force-rank everything that goes into the product development
backlog. Product owners can reorder, add, or delete from the ranking
based on the governance agreed on, but the ranking needs to be explicit
to drive alignment and productivity. Most people can't look at ten
number one priorities and implement solutions that address everything.

  There are a couple of other ways product owners can help your
leads. First, they can learn agile and other technical lingo, which
fosters better teamwork, more efficient collaboration, and a respect
that helps everyone perform better. Second, they can thank the team
frequently because today's triumph will be forgotten tomorrow when
a new issue needs resolution. Finally, they should listen and value the
team's opinions and ideas. Product owners should be careful not to
overly fall in love with their own solutions and must engage the team
to provide ideas, feedback, and innovative ways to address challenges
in smart efficient ways. Lastly, leads should be telling the product
owner about operational needs, technology standards, defects, and
technical debt that need to be considered for prioritization.

- **Own communications, and communicate frequently because
things move fast in an agile process.** When are demos, what
priorities have been lowered, what new considerations have been
added to the scope, how can others recognize the team for their
accomplishments, where is help needed, and what material risks are
being mitigated?

  One word of caution is that communication requires some art and
science. You don't want to communicate every hit or miss because the
swings may be hard for stakeholders to comprehend. Sharing too
much detail might overwhelm colleagues, but being too generic or
lacking any drive may risk losing the audience over time.

For this reason, product owners need to have a plan for engaging and communicating with stakeholders. The primary goal is to set reasonable expectations up front, then to communicate status frequently to ensure stakeholders are not surprised later in the development process.

- **Get into the weeds, and expect to spend a lot of time with the team.** The agile practice requires a strong commitment from product owners to help set priorities, communicate requirements, and listen to the team's ideas and needs. Gone are the days of giving the team all the requirements up front and asking them to manage and deliver it. Product owners should be attending release planning, sprint planning, brainstorms, and demos at a minimum, and many agile teams want the product owner at daily standups. My target is that the product owner should be spending at least 40% of their time working with their teams.

Product owners need to spend considerable amount of time reviewing with the team customer needs and what drives value. They should share the overall product vision but also break this down to the vision of the release and the vision of the sprint. This helps team members understand goals and objectives in the context of the stories that they are working on.

From there, product owners need to express what they need in the form of problems and ask the team for solutions. "What's the best login experience that we can implement in one sprint that allows very busy users to leverage their LinkedIn or Twitter accounts?" "How can we best enable users to search by geography when some users want to look at large, multistate regions and others want to narrow down to cities, counties, or even zip codes?" These problem statements should be enhanced with why it is important to users or how a solution may impact the value they get from the solution.

Nonetheless, you can see how the product owner is expressing what she wants but avoids the specifics of how to implement it. She should be giving the team the responsibility of identifying one or more solutions and expressing any advantages or disadvantages in them.

So how can the product owner influence solutions? Work with the team is to be as expressive as possible with the acceptance criteria related to solutions and agile stories. For example, "It must allow registering users from their social media accounts without keying in any new information." If the team doesn't have a solution, the product owner should consider prioritizing one for a brainstorming session or look to schedule spikes to help work out technical approaches.

Product owners should avoid the urge to add/change stories inside the sprint, which can be very disruptive to the team. Agile teams work in rhythms. At the beginning of the sprint, they are in thinking/planning mode; during the sprint, they are focused on fulfilling the story; and at the end, they are closing out defects. Changes midstream create an imbalance and can be particularly disruptive if there are multiple teams or if the teams are distributed geographically. Now most teams are flexible (being agile) and will accept some changes/additions, but this should be managed as an exception, not the norm.

Product owners should set the agenda for the demo and look to have key stakeholders attend. They should capture feedback but avoid letting the demo turn into a brainstorming session for any issues raised. They should work with the team to accept stories that are done and be specific on where the team fell short of expectations.

But the most important mistake I see in product owners is when they don't thank their teams. One release leads to another, and when one sprint ends another begins, so it's easy to lose sight of accomplishments. Team members don't forget.

- **Product owners need to be exceptional collaborators and know where their responsibilities end.** In most organizations, team members do not report directly to the product owner, and how the team allocates work should be left to the team. In addition, most product owners don't have the skills to measure the productivity, quality, or overall skills of team members. Stepping into the realm of managing the team is a critical mistake product owners make, and it can create significant negativity and disruption when this happens.

  Instead, product owners must manage through influence and bringing the right people together to collaborate on priority opportunities and solutions. In some cases, product owners should drive multiple stakeholders to consensus; other times they should drive teams toward solutions that meet multiple needs and constraints. Driving consensus, pushing team velocity, and nurturing optimal customer solutions can't be done consistently by demanding product owners who don't listen and collaborate.

- **Product owners should present data before analysis or opinion.** Everyone has opinions on what to invest in, what to prioritize, what customers want, and what solutions are optimal. Product owners in businesses should help drive consensus and coalesce opinions to investments that grow customers, increase revenue, and drive customer satisfaction. A product owner without data to back their analysis, ideas, and solutions is just another stakeholder with an opinion.

What data should product owners pursue? They need to be looking at product usage data to understand how customers are interacting with them. They need to interview existing clients to see what is and what is not working for them. They need to couple this with information from prospects and from customers no longer using the product to determine gaps and points of dissatisfaction. They should be using market research firms to gather more data about the competition. They need to be looking at financial data on how the product is performing and review its profitability, along with marketing data on the successes, failures, and learnings on attracting prospects.

- **Product owners need to become product evangelists.** They should be out in the market speaking at conferences and events. They must visit key clients, see how they are using products and services, and learn about their opportunities and issues. Most important is that product owners need to be an expert in how the product works and its configuration capabilities. They should be versed in running slick demos on the spur of the moment and tailor them to the audience.

They should go on sales calls to different types of customers and learn what's working and not working in the sales process. They should also be well versed in competitive offerings and specify to sales members how to respond to questions about things the product doesn't do today.

In the process, product owners should update their vision with a roadmap. The roadmap helps employees understand the future direction of the product that includes a statement of priority and a forecast on timing. The best product owners will engage their teams to help develop the priorities and any forecasts tied to the roadmap.

- **Product owners need to balance capability with operational and compliance-driven requirements.** Product owners that only drive the development of new features, capabilities, and configuration options are doing a disservice to their customers and organizations by underinvesting in the underlying operations, security, performance, scalability, and analytics of the product. That's one difference between getting an MVP out, to growing the customer base, to getting the product to become a stable, reliable platform.

    Product owners should also be listening to their technical leads, architects, and delivery managers on getting technical debt addressed. Technical debt is a list of improvements in the underlying software that the technical team recommends addressing. In some cases, these are shortcuts they've taken to ensure that they can hit a delivery date; other times, their implementation needs an upgrade based on new learnings, operational considerations, and the availability of new technical capabilities. Regardless of cause, products that address technical debt systematically are less likely to have operational issues or degrade into legacy.

    Product owners should also be reviewing the overall quality of the product. Defects need to be addressed. Data quality issues should have automated solutions or workflows addressing them. Teams must understand the impact of quality issues on customer experience.

- **Product owners need to identify partners and join the ecosystem.** Today's digital products cannot survive in isolation, and organizations developing new products are unlikely to succeed over the long term without successful partnerships. Product owners should consider doing SWOT analysis (strengths, weaknesses, opportunities, and threats) to help set some guiding principles on where to consider partnerships and where collaborating with third-party services provides strategic advantage.

Product owners need to leverage their technologists to look beyond business partnerships. Where can third-party APIs provide capabilities, and where can developing them enable revenue opportunities? What third-party services provide additional data, algorithms, analytics, machine learning, artificial intelligence, and other capabilities that increase the intelligence, insights, and conveniences in the products and services being offered? Are there new attractive distribution channels in promoting applications in third-party app stores or even evolving the product into a platform of its own?

Some of the more advanced capabilities help organizations evolve from digital channels, to products, to evolving businesses.

Developing the Go-To Market Plan

The last major role for product management is in developing the go-to market plan and overseeing its execution for the product. This is an entire discipline that lies in the intersection of marketing, sales, and general management. The exact role the product marketer needs to take on varies considerably by organization structure, the availability of specialized talent, and the exact needs of the product.

What are some elements of this strategy and plan that are critical for organizations building digital products as part of a transformation?

- *Branding of digital products and services* is important if the products are target new markets or help position the business in a new digital context.
- *Pricing, bundling, unbundling, repackaging, and discounting* are all important considerations especially if the product is bought directly by end consumers or if the product is an extension of an existing "analog" product.
- *Marketing plans* need to factor how to introduce the offering especially if there are new or evolving brands in scope. They should consider digital marketing capabilities to promote the brand, bring in leads, and nurture leads to be primed for sales activity.

- **Sales process**—Product owners should work collaboratively with marketing and sales leaders on an overall sales process. Who is selling the product between existing and new field reps, inside sales reps, and direct? What are their targets? What activities should be performed from first interaction to close? What sales materials should be used, and what guidelines are you providing reps on whether and where they should tailor the presentation?

- **Sales relationship and pipeline management**—Many organizations that have long standing products and services are less likely to have structured sales governance, pipeline management, forecasting, and measurement practices. Worse, many organizations must transform sales teams that were successful selling analog products that "sold themselves" with few competitors.

  Sales of digital products can be super simple when they are direct to buyer and offer freemium or try/buy options. Digital products being sold by inside reps or in the field can be more complex versus their analog predecessors requiring salespeople to develop new relationships, understand buying personas, capture disparate customer needs, and distill all the information in an orchestrated sales process that leads to a closed/won, captured in a CRM.

  In addition, sales leaders need more advanced analytics from their CRM to understand the overall health of the pipeline, to manage salespeople effectively, and to make macro and micro planning decisions on territories and assignments. They need to provide constructive feedback to the rest of the organization on what is or isn't working well enough in the product, in marketing's leads, and in the sales process.

- **Working with distribution partners**—Product managers need to look at opportunities to enable resellers, product integrations, and other business development opportunities. While some of these may be traditional business development opportunities, product owners need to consider other digital partners. If you're selling a product to a sales or marketing team, then you'll want to consider developing a CRM application sold through a vendor's app store. If you're developing a data product, then you'll want to develop APIs and partner with developers to conceive new applications.

- *Legal, financial, and compliance considerations*—Product managers need to work with their legal and financial teams on everything from developing contracts, identifying terms of service, and ensuring that compliance considerations are identified and managed. They should be working with finance teams on developing product codes, reviewing order-to-cash practices for any new requirements, and identifying any new considerations for invoicing and charging customers. This is not a onetime effort because adding new customers will require deciding what terms can't be amended, others that can change based on customer need, and others that need to be considered for global changes made on a periodic basis.

- *Establishing credibility and trust*—Lastly, product managers must bring some rational thinking about what the business should do more of and should not do in selling, marketing, or developing the product that influences the sentiment, credibility, and trust that consumers have with the business and the product's brand. In this regard, the product manager must partner with privacy officers, security officers, compliance, and marketers to determine appropriate guidelines. Product owners have to recognize their level of authority in these discussions as many security, privacy, and legal guidelines are enterprise-wide and not negotiable for a specific product.

Final Words on Establishing Product Management

As noted at the start of the chapter, establishing product management practices and enabling them within the structure of the organization can be a difficult transformation. Leaders aren't always aligned on the roles and priorities of the product team and can become defensive when the team drives changes against established practices. Furthermore, product management needs commitment from resources in sales, marketing, technology, and other departments, so leaders have to be willing to allocate their resources to these efforts. When a product isn't selling as expected, leaders should listen to product managers on adjustments or even pivots to strategy. However, when products have conflicting priorities from customers and sales, leaders have to respect the prioritization decisions empowered to the product team and accept answers of "later" or "no" to some of their needs.

The pressures and tensions can be very demanding on the product team. I've seen talented product managers crack under the pressure. Others have been in the trenches so many times that they may revert to demanding, confrontational behaviors because of the ongoing pushback they receive.

Product managers fall into traps that can make their hard jobs even harder.

The first trap is when they do a good job of listening to customers and stakeholders but then try to give everyone what they want. Product owners in this camp fail to recognize that they are working with finite budget, time, and skill and that their role is to digest the input, then communicate a set of realistic priorities, strategies, and requirements. These product owners need to communicate the rationale behind these decisions and accept the fact that they aren't going to make every stakeholder equally happy. Their job isn't to make people happy but to make decisions that drive customer adoption and growth.

The second trap is when the product owners fall in love with their vision to the extent that they fail to listen to stakeholders, including the technologists that they need to partner with on solutions. Product owners need to constantly reshape their vision and priorities based on feedback. Second, product owners need to share and communicate their vision repetitively and gain buy-in over time; otherwise, stakeholders will communicate their objectives, often loudly and forcibly and probably late in the development process when changes or pivots are costlier. Lastly, product owners need to shape their vision at least partially based on the organization's capabilities, so they need to be presenting opportunities to their team and learning feasible solutions from their team.

A third trap is when they become overly demanding of their engineering teams or treat development estimates like a contract. Agile estimation is a key tool to form a dialogue about solutions, to drive a discussion on MVP, and to help teams plan releases. Agile product owners should use estimation as feedback to make decisions, but some fall into the trap of using estimates to manage their teams to fixed timeline, fixed-scope releases. Sometimes it works, but when estimates are done early in the process or performed by less mature teams, they will have degrees of inaccuracies. Agile product owners that "box in" their teams to fixed schedules and deliverables will lose their ability to adjust priorities, or, worse, they may degrade the culture that drives both execution and innovation.

The fourth trap is when product managers underestimate the power of using data in driving decisions. When product owners present data first, it becomes a lot easier for them to drive priorities and decisions. Why are we working on these features for the next release? Because 30% of surveyed users requested them. Why aren't we discounting the product more aggressively? Because we're still 10% less expensive than our competitors, and 20% of prospects that say no come back within 60 days and say yes. Responding with facts backed by data often diffuses passion-driven challenges and is the best weapon product managers can master to gain alignment across multiple responsibilities.

The final trap is when product managers don't recognize that they must master multiple personas. Most of the time, they have to be highly collaborative and be able to manage everyone's ideas and priorities. Later, they may need to be humble to get help understanding a technical concept or need a department's help getting specific tasks completed. They have to be mentoring, especially with senior executives to help them understand strategy, customer needs, and product decisions. Lastly, they need to be demanding drivers to ensure that deadlines are met and key customer needs are fulfilled.

The trap is when the product owner fails to separate out these personas and applies the wrong temperament to the wrong situation. Worse is when they get locked into one or two personas. A demanding product owner will come across as a bully and will fail to inspire a team to greatness. An overly accommodating product owner will get run over by leaders who are more driven by their next paycheck or have very little incentive to enable a longer-term strategy.

What Digital Leaders Should Do to Enable Product Management

Digital leaders should recognize that the product management function is critical to driving digital transformation. If you're a CIO chartered with transformation or a CDO brought in to enable one, the responsibilities outlined in this chapter need to be at the top of your priorities once you have a baseline agile practice established.

How you go about this in your organization largely depends on the existing culture, organizational structure, how individual leaders view their responsibilities, and to what extent product management practices already exist.

As a digital leader, establishing a product management function may be the most difficult undertaking compared to agile, portfolio management, or becoming data driven. Developing products and services is critical to all organizations and affects all departments, so it's hard to imagine leading this without facing confrontation, obstacles, passive aggressive behaviors, and other reactions.

You'll need to elicit the executive leadership team to sponsor and support the product management function. They need to be explicit about where organizational boundaries lie and to provide guidance on instituting product team members into the organizational model. You'll have to decide how fast to push the organization and whether you are driving too fast or too hard.

And since many leaders don't fully appreciate how fast digital can disrupt your business and industry, you're going to need to educate them on the need to move smarter and faster.

7.

DRIVING DIGITAL: SMARTER AND FASTER

You've recognized the need to transform your organization. You have agile practices evolving and a target technology architecture. You're making the organization smarter with data and providing them self-service tools and practices. You're establishing product management disciplines to listen to customer needs and bring new digital products to market. You are also balancing product development with a balanced portfolio of operations-, compliance-, and research-driven initiatives.

If it took you several hours to read through this book, it's going to take you a lot longer to implement these changes in your organization. It's not an easy transformation, and I've seen some organizations adapt in under six months, while others took longer than 18. It largely depends on the culture that you're working with and how quickly leaders and managers are willing to leave sacred cows behind and adopt new practices. In my experience, company culture is the most overwhelming factor in getting these practices instituted. The size of organizations, the number of geographic locations, the disparity in businesses and products, and the magnitude of legacy systems are all factors but secondary to cultural issues.

The Cultural Underpinnings of Digital Organizations

If you ask any executive whether he wants to be an agile organization, then the answer is going to be yes. Who wants to be slow and rigid? Ask the same executive whether he would rather see a stable technology architecture that can be used to drive winning customer experiences and share data ubiquitously. No doubt.

Do you want to build new products that grow revenue? Of course! Do you want a process to track investments and enable the organization to share their best ideas? Of course, you do. Do you want products that delight customers and grow market share?

When you ask questions like this, you're going to get a lot of head nodding and support. These are simple expectations that any executive wants and expects for the organization to grow. For organizations that want to compete in a digital world, this all comes down to two simple attributes that organizations need to target.

Digital organizations need to be both smarter and faster.

Do You Want to be Smarter and Faster?

You see successful startups that might have a natural edge going faster but must work really hard to be smarter in order to outfox larger competitors and to bring on early customers. You see some enterprises that have all the data and practices to be smarter but may not have the culture, leadership, communications, or practices to move faster and pivot to beat out new competitors. Being digital requires organizations large and small, old and new, in entrenched markets or defining new ones in order to be smarter and faster.

You can also see that being smart but not fast doesn't work and that being fast but not smart also has its limitations. That's one reason being digital is so hard for many organizations as it requires a balanced approach to becoming smarter and faster in mutually beneficial ways.

You can build products really fast but target the wrong customer segment and deliver a poor-quality experience. You can be overly methodical and scientific and therefore slow and miss a market opportunity. You can be extraordinarily smart finding insights in your ERP and CRM data but have no practices to action them fast enough.

Other attributes companies pursue are by-products of smarter and faster. Companies that are more automated and efficient are both smarter and faster. Higher quality, better user experiences, and higher levels of security are smarter ways to engage and service customers. Innovative companies that attract top talent and have modernized workplace technologies and policies can be both smarter and faster.

Becoming smarter and faster is what truly differentiates digital organizations from their peers. They empower employees with data to make smarter and faster decisions. They invest in platforms so that they can bring new capabilities to bear faster. They leverage agile to be smarter and faster in reacting to customer feedback and market conditions. They experiment bringing minimally viable products to market faster and then are smarter to react to prospect and customer needs. These leaders also recognize that bringing new competitive digital capabilities to market is required to ward off competition, to grow, and to become more profitable.

Figure 7-1 shows this at a more detailed level. How do you explain to the organization why agile practices, technology practices, portfolio management, data practices and product management enable the organization to be smarter and faster?

Building a Digitally Driven Team

Now that you understand the basics of digital, one of your primary objectives is to find other leaders that will align with you on becoming smarter and faster. You can't take on this transformational challenge alone, and eventually you'll need to get the whole organization on board. In my experience, change starts by finding the early adopters—the ones that "get it" right away and who are willing to partner with you on approaches and practices.

Driving Digital Practice Area	Smarter	Faster
Agile practices	• Self-organizing multidisciplinary teams are motivated to deliver quality solutions. • Transparency enables teams to make balanced decisions, prioritizing new capabilities and operational improvements.	• Frequent review of priorities based on customer feedback brings optimal competitive capabilities to market faster. • Teams can get started working with minimal upfront planning.
Technology practices	• Enable developers to focus on driving innovation while operational needs can be addressed in parallel. • Enable ubiquitous access to data to deliver new products and drive smarter decision making.	• Invested expertise in fewer platforms enables reapplying technical expertise to bring new capabilities and innovations to market faster. • Collaborative technology teams enable employees to focus on delivering high-quality results.
Portfolio practices	• Enable capturing and reviewing a large number of ideas and making balanced decisions on where to invest. • Transparent financial tracking enables realignment of resources and spending on the initiatives that show the most promise.	• Define minimal and focused criteria on what project founder's planning steps and deliverables are so that execution can start sooner. • Lightweight and frequent communication methods enable leaders to address bottlenecks, provide assistance, or pivot initiatives.
Data-driven organization	• Empowers managers and individuals to make data-driven decisions and be responsive to customer and operational needs. • Leveraging new Big Data technologies and self-service data practices enables the organization to be smarter compared to competitors.	• Looking at both internal and external data enables organizations to respond to customer needs and market conditions faster. • Data-driven organizations become more competitive by leveraging predictive analytics and artificial intelligence to deliver more convenience and insights to customers faster than competitive offerings.
Product management	• Defined practices to capture market opportunities and needs of existing customers ensure that product investments are optimized. • Evolving go-to market plans enables marketing and selling digital products when customers have many options.	• Pursuing MVPs enables bringing products to market faster, with less investment while capturing customer-driven enhancements. • Aligning teams on big picture vision, short-term priorities, and defined acceptance criteria enables teams to execute efficiently.

Figure 7-1. How driving digital practices enable a smarter-faster organization

You will certainly need at least a couple of supporters from the executive leadership team and ideally the CEO or business GM as an active sponsor. However, you will also need to identify early adopters that will be strong participants or leaders within the transformation program. It helps to get technologists on board with agile, sales operators involved in your citizen's data science program, and financial analysts participating in your portfolio management programs.

When you think about bringing early adopters on board, you should think about their personal goals and mission. Let's break this into three categories of whom you will be pitching and how you will have to position the transformation program to them.

- **Board and CEO**—What's the vision, and how will these practices help transform the business? Where and when will new revenue and cost efficiencies materialize? Who will be new target customer segments, who are competitors in these spaces, and how is the corporation going to develop a winning program?
- **Executive team**—How does the transformational program enable me to achieve my goals and objectives?
- **Managers and employees**—How can I get my job done faster, smarter, and with less stress? What skills will I pick up along the way, and what incentives are there for my accomplishments?

I know, it's a lot to swallow. In addition to just getting the mechanics of the processes instituted, you now need a strategy on how to communicate and sell this program across the organization. Individuals have different motivating factors and constraints, so you're not going to be able to do this with a one-size-fits-all approach.

How do you identify potential early adopters? They have to be willing to participate with little considerations for how it will personally benefit them. They need to have good listening skills and be willing to learn but also know how and when it is time to lead, contribute, and question. Ideally they should be good communicators and educators so that they can help sell your practices and bring others on board. They should show a willingness to take some risk and work harder. They should be somewhat dissatisfied with the status quo and show a yearning to do more, smarter, and faster.

In the early days of transformation, you must be very strategic about whom you bring on, what practices you focus on, and what you lay out as both a vision and short-term goals. In my experience, this can be different depending on business needs, company culture, skills available, barriers to becoming digital, competitive threats, and alignment or conflicts with existing practices. If the organization already practices agile, then maybe all it needs is an upgrade in specific practices. If the greatest threat to the organization is new products from startups, then maybe the organization needs a product management practice and nimble technologies to test some competitive offerings. If the organization is entrenched in legacy practices and has limited funds to invest, then becoming more data driven and enabling portfolio management practices may help find efficiencies.

So let's look at an example. Let's say you're instituting agile practices to help bring new digital products to market. Who are your early adopters, and how can you use the smarter-faster framework to get them on board?

Agile is democratic process, and it's most important to get the team on board. Sell them on both smarter and faster as they will less likely be distracted and have better short-term requirements when business users are asked to prioritize and define acceptance criteria every sprint. You're going to need the product owner on board with a process that enables adjusting priorities and delivering an MVP to market sooner. If sales is the primary stakeholder, I would pick out some key salespeople who have valuable input on the product and sell them on the same vision. To the CEO and Board, I would sell them on a process that can be driven by customer needs, that will become more predictable as the team matures the practice, and that ultimately will help execute on a roadmap of growing products.

How Fast Must Organizations Change?

Driving digital requires you to make some concrete, focused decisions about people and practices that you target and demonstrate a strong alignment to business priority. Take on too many people too quickly or attempt to impact too many practices, and you increase the likelihood of burning out participants or failing completely. Investing in practices too far ahead or outside of business needs, and you're likely to lose strategic support if short-term business priorities are compromised or if participants push back when they fail to see the alignment.

Going too slow can also be very detrimental. It can lead to business failure and disruptions to entire industries. To see this, let's look at what happened to the newspaper industry.

The internet started to go mainstream in 1995.[1] Some newspapers responded early to this "new media," as it was called then, by finding ways to develop websites and push their content online. I know this because AdOne, the startup I joined in 1996 offered newspapers an SaaS solution for hosting and searching classified ads. By 1999, 11 newspaper companies had invested in AdOne,[2] and we had a majority of their newspapers participating in at least one of our products.

But just enabling newspaper readers to search ads online was not sufficient once digital disruptors emerged. By 1997, eBay had hosted 2 million auctions.[3] In May 1999, Monster.com[4] was serving 42,000 clients, listing 204,000 jobs, holding more than 1.3 million active resumes, and recording 7.6 million "hits" per month. By 2001, Craigslist[5] was in at least 10 major U.S. markets. So, while newspaper revenue increased in the booming late 1990s, they came to a crashing halt 2001–2009 once the Internet bubble burst in 2001 and digital disruptors changed the business model to low-cost digital listings that enabled buyer and seller marketplaces. The Newspaper Association of America shows the impact to newspaper advertising revenue[6] falling by approximately 70% over the last ten years.

As I see it, newspapers had a three- to five-year window to enable digital transformation. By 2001, they needed to be willing to cannibalize their print revenue and move aggressively into digital businesses with competitive pricing and winning user experiences.

If other industries follow the path that newspapers did, then they have this three- to five-year period to execute their digital transformations. This implies that maturing many of the practices I outlined in this book should occur over the first one or two years. Now that may sound like a long time, but people and organizations move slow when making foundational changes to practices, values, missions, and goals. So, while you should adjust to the pace of the organization, your job as digital leader is to drive them smarter and faster because you may not have the luxury of time.

Cultural Barriers to Smarter-Faster

Many but not all your leaders will want to be smarter and faster. Some executives still try to keep decision making at the top and would rather see an organization of followers. They prefer to use their instincts and gut to make decisions and are overwhelmed when too much data is presented to them. Some are comfortable with the pace of today's operations and are not overly interested in the challenges to make things faster or more efficient. Some are conservative business decision makers and risk averse, so practice changes, product development, and the need to transform are not things they will easily embrace. Some expect to leave the organization or retire before transformations materialize and have no interest in rocking the boat, learning, or taking any personal risks. Some will just not have the skills to perform in a digital world and will make it difficult to transition from existing practices and tools.

The other barrier worth calling out is that the company's incentive plans will need adjustments to gain the support of middle and later adopters. This is especially the case when compensation has a significant variable component that is performance based and likely aligned to the legacy business model and operations. An advertisement salesperson commissioned 10% for $100,000 print display ads isn't going to be on board selling $5,000 digital banner ads at the same percentage if the effort involved in closing the sale is equivalent.

It's important to recognize who and why individuals are resistant to change, but in my experience, their actions are what you will witness first. You'll need to be able to recognize the patterns of these actions and have approaches to deal with them.

Some will listen, agree to the principles and practices that you are instituting, but elect not to get involved. They go back to doing things the old way and don't challenge themselves to do things differently or pave the way for others to follow them. If their intentions are honest, then these people may be too busy to participate or are overly driven by goals or incentives aligned to the legacy business.

The best thing to do for these people, especially if they are critical to the success of the transformation, is to spell out exactly what you need them to do in small chunks. Hopefully by spelling things out, they'll challenge you on any adjustments needed to make the plan successful and will find a way to execute it. If not, then they probably weren't on board in the first place.

In the second type of reaction is the passive-aggressive group that listens, nods their heads, claims that they are on board, but has no intention of taking an active role. You can tell that they are passive-aggressive if you confront them and spell things out but then get a bunch of excuses from them. Some will avoid meeting you, skip group meetings, and find other reasons for not following through on commitments. The good news about passive-aggressive individuals is that they are unlikely to be confrontational and won't battle your mission or goals openly. The bad news is when they hold positions of authority and their staff is not led by example or driven to participate in the transformation.

Your best option to bring along passive-aggressive leaders is to recruit others with positions of influence to play a role in getting the desired behaviors and actions. This may be someone on their staff, a peer that they trust, their boss, or a leader higher up in the organization. People on their staff should demonstrate where the transformation is bringing success. Use peers to expose where they may have dependencies and to provide some pressure to get involved. Use superiors when you need help getting a carrot and a stick to drive change.

Others still go beyond passive-aggressive behaviors and force you down paths that suck time and energy away from your important priorities. They'll ask you to repeat things that you sold them on months ago. They'll demand more explicit training for their staff but won't dedicate the time required for them to learn new skills. Some will have you chase unnecessary details or force you to respond to a trickling stream of questions. They may ask for reports or metrics before you're ready to measure or communicate them.

These behaviors can go from an annoyance to being confrontational very quickly. If the individual or group begins setting unrealistic expectations or ups the bar when you demonstrate some success, then they are, with or without realizing it, undermining the transformation.

This is a difficult situation, but I can offer a couple of suggestions. First, dramatically minimize your needs and expectations from these individuals. Be very specific on what's needed from them, and keep the scope as confined as possible. When you do need them, make sure you have the request documented and detailed. Make these persons look good where possible. Most importantly—and this is contrary to many of the principles outlined in this book—you need to be careful on the level of information and details you share with them. Arming them with more information feeds the beast, and their response will likely be to ask more question, demand more details, and send you farther down a path of little return.

But the most difficult barrier is when someone buys into the vision but is antagonistic to the methodologies and practices you are driving. They may like the concepts of agile but want to run initiatives using waterfall plans. They want to build up digital talent but are driving for different sourcing strategies. They drive MVPs that are orders of magnitude greater than what's necessary or feasible. They are perfectionists and elect to pick out flaws more often than compliment the team on the benefits of their deliverables. They hoard information and share it only in forums that challenge your authority.

These people are likely to be your colleagues and senior people in the organization. They may be on your steering committees or are key stakeholders in some of the initiatives. You can't dismiss or ignore them.

Every transformation program that I've led or participated in has one or more people exhibiting these behaviors from time to time. Leaders like yourself, entrusted to drive an organization through transformation, wield great power and authority, so it's natural that other leaders will be envious and want a piece of the action. Your colleagues have had success leading and managing change, driving initiatives, developing KPIs, or developing products and want influence and some control of business methodologies and future practices. They want to own a bigger piece of the program.

You might have a few things working against you. You might have been hired to run the transformation program and have to work with colleagues who mistrust outsiders. You might be a CIO, CTO, or technology leader working with leaders who prefer the "old" IT that were stewards to the business need and not entrusted to lead the business. You might be a woman working on a male-dominated leadership team, or you might be a decade or more younger that your colleagues. These are all potential areas for your colleagues to either distrust, challenge, or exploit you to get more power and control.

This is why it's all too important that the CEO participate in enterprise-wide transformational initiatives and that General Managers or Presidents oversee individual business transformations. One of the primary roles these leaders need to own is setting roles and responsibilities and resolving leadership conflicts. These challenges can't be sorted out up front as new issues will emerge and flare up as leaders get involved, feel challenged, or possibly feel threatened by the transformation. The CEO, President, or GM needs to either recognize the conflicts, or you must take steps to expose them and get their involvement.

Make sure that not only the issue at hand is resolved but that some structure is identified and documented to provide clarity and used to avoid future confrontations. Sometimes that's clarity on roles, sometimes it may be who or how specific decisions are made, and sometimes it's to reshape vision or scope. The point is that you can't allow key organizational decisions to linger, and you can't afford the time to revisit them.

Driving Digital—The Lens of Smarter-Faster

We started this journey with the transformation imperative and why virtually all business need to reimagine their digital businesses. The practices laid out regarding agile, technology architecture, portfolio management, data science, and product management are all there to help you lead an organization and drive digital results smarter and faster.

As you move smarter and faster, you'll start to see the world differently and through what I call the digital lens, shown in Figure 7-2.[7] You'll have the product management practices to better connect with customers and prospects on ways to make your products and services more convenient. You'll be developing mature interfaces like web and mobile but also considering emerging interfaces like voice, wearables, and virtual reality in the upcoming years.

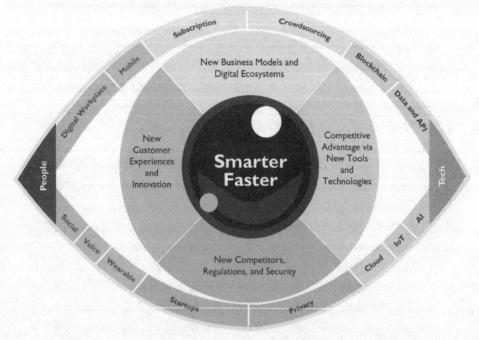

Figure 7-2. How smarter-faster organizations see the world through a digital lens

When the underlying capabilities of the organization require an upgrade, then you'll no longer consider new technologies as large, risky, disruptive investments. You have portfolio practices to help sort out which investments and upgrades to prioritize and agile practices to bring new capabilities from pilot to production. You'll be investing in your data architecture, so leveraging your data with the new frontier of data services like AI, blockchain, or IoT will no longer feel unattainable. You'll also be able to see where your business's assets can be used to provide your own data services or APIs to either provide benefits to your customers, enable new sales channels, or expand reach into new markets.

Once you are smarter and faster, the threats of new digitally native competitors and startups may feel less intimidating. You should be able to size up their strengths and weaknesses and find ways to either compete, cooperate, or partner with them.

Similarly, when new regulations emerge, a new security threat requires remediation, or you elect to provide customers more privacy options, the steps required should no longer feel insurmountable. You'll have a more practical way to set a vision on what needs to be done and have more efficient ways to implement.

Finally, stronger practices and more reliable execution will enable business leaders to contemplate new business opportunities and models. Maybe there's an opportunity to transition a group of services into a subscription with recurring revenue? Maybe crowdsourcing a process will enable you to collect new data that will be valuable to customers? Maybe you'll have more time to explore partnerships?

Competitive threats, new opportunities, impacts of maturing technologies, and the need to provide increasing value to customers require leaders that can leverage the digital lens. They need confidence in the organization's capabilities to go smarter and faster, which enables them to see the world through a lens of digital opportunities.

That is the meaning of driving digital.

ABOUT ISAAC SACOLICK

Isaac Sacolick is a successful CIO who has led digital transformation, innovation, agile, and data science programs in multiple organizations. He has transformed underperforming businesses by delivering new digital products, investing in strategic technologies, enabling agile practices, outsourcing commodity services, and establishing performance metrics. Isaac has twenty years of experience as CTO in startups and CIO in enterprises. He has expertise in the financial services, data/analytics services, media, internet, construction, travel, and biomedical industries.

Isaac has been recognized as an industry leading, agile, innovative CIO. In 2015, he was interviewed by Forbes on "5 Things to Do When You Lead a Digital Transformation," was listed on their Top 20 Social CIOs, and was recognized as a Top 100 CIO in STEM. In 2013, he received TechTarget's CIO award for Technology Advancement. In 2016, 2015, and 2014, he was listed on Huffington Post's Top Social CIOs. He is an industry speaker on many business-enabling topics including innovation, enterprise agile, and Big Data analytics. Isaac has been writing a blog, Social Agile and Transformation for over ten years with 300+ posts covering topics on CIO leadership, digital transformation, agile execution, big data, innovation, and digital marketing.

Isaac is an entrepreneur and specialist in agile management, product development, Big Data, citizen developer programs, data science, data warehousing, NoSQL XML search technologies, artificial intelligence, CMS, media and publishing technologies, social networking, CRM, digital marketing solutions, web analytics, digital advertising, and enterprise collaboration practices.

NOTES

INTRODUCTION

1 Isaac, Sacolick, *Social, Agile, and Transformation*, http://blogs
.starcio.com

CHAPTER ONE

1 "A visual summary of VC activity in 2015," PitchBook, January 11,
2016, http://pitchbook.com/news/articles/a-visual-summary-of-vc-
activity-in-2015-datagraphic

2 "Bringing Big Data to the Enterprise," IBM, http://www-01.ibm.com/
software/data/bigdata/what-is-big-data.html

3 Andrew Perrin, "Social Media Usage: 2005–2015," *Pew Research Center
Internet, Science & Tech*, October 8, 2015, http://www.pewinternet.org/
2015/10/08/social-networking-usage-2005-2015/

4 Andrew Perrin, "One-Fifth of Americans Report Going Online
'Almost Constantly'," *Pew Research Center Fact Tank—Our Lives in
Numbers*, December 8, 2015, http://www.pewresearch.org/fact-tank/
2015/12/08/one-fifth-of-americans-report-going-online-almost-
constantly/

5 Scott Brinker, "Marketing Technology Landscape Supergraphic (2015),"
ChiefMarTec.com, January 12, 2015, http://chiefmartec.com/2015/01/
marketing-technology-landscape-supergraphic-2015/

6 Scott Brinker, "Marketing Technology Landscape Supergraphic (2016),"
ChiefMarTec.com, March 21, 2016, http://chiefmartec.com/2016/03/
marketing-technology-landscape-supergraphic-2016/

7 Cooper Smith, "How Beacons— Small, Low-Cost Gadgets—Will
Influence Billions in US Retail Sales," *Business Insider*, February 9, 2015,
http://www.businessinsider.com/beacons-impact-billions-in-reail-
sales-2015-2

8   "Worldwide Wearables Market Forecast to Grow 173.3% in 2015 with
     72.1 Million Units to be Shipped, According to IDC," *IDC*, June 18,
     2015, http://www.idc.com/getdoc.jsp?containerId=prUS25696715

9   Daniel Van Dyke, "Mobile Banking Outpaces Branch Banking for First
     Time in 2015," *Javelin*, January 12, 2016, https://www.javelinstrategy.
     com/press-release/mobile-banking-outpaces-branch-banking-first-
     time-2015

10   Arjun Kharpal, "Why Bitcoin's Tech Could 'Change Everything' for
     Banks," *CNBC Tech Transformers*, December 31, 2015, http://www.cnbc
     .com/2015/12/31/blockchain-what-the-big-banks-say-about-the-
     tech.html

11   "Bring Your Own Device," *The White House Digital Government*, August 23,
     2012, https://www.whitehouse.gov/digitalgov/bring-your-own-device

12   Julie Weed, "Airbnb Grows to a *Million* Rooms, and Hotel Rivals Are
     Quiet, for Now," *The New York Times*, May 11, 2015, http://www
     .nytimes.com/2015/05/12/business/airbnb-grows-to-a-million-rooms-
     and-hotel-rivals-are-quiet-for-now.html

13   Jason Clampet, "Measuring Airbnb's Real Threat to U.S. Hotels Using
     Industry Metrics," *Skift*, February 3, 2016, https://skift.com/2016/02/
     03/measuring-airbnbs-real-threat-to-u-s-hotels-using-industry-metrics/

14   Andre J. Hawkins, "Uber Just Completed Its Billionth Trip," *The Verge*,
     December 30, 2015 http://www.theverge.com/2015/12/30/10690854/
     uber-billionth-trip-london-2015

15   "Driving Hard," *The Economist*, June 13, 2015 http://www.economist.
     com/news/business/21654068-taxi-hailing-company-likely-disrupt-deli
     very-business-driving-hard.

16   James Hickman, "Uber, Lyft Continue Growth Among Business
     Travelers; Taxis, Rental Cars See Share Decline," *The Street*, January 21,
     2016, https://www.thestreet.com/story/13430707/1/uber-lyft-continue-
     growth-among-business-travelers-taxis-rental-cars-see-share-
     decline.html

17   Matt Turner, "Here Is the Letter the World's Largest Investor,
     BlackRock CEO Larry Fink, Just Sent to CEOs Everywhere," *Business
     Insider*, February 2, 2016, http://www.businessinsider.com/blackrock-
     ceo-larry-fink-letter-to-sp-500-ceos-2016-2

18   Mark J. Perry, "Fortune 500 Firms in 1955 vs. 2014; 88% Are Gone,
     and We're All Better Off Because of That Dynamic 'Creative
     Destruction'," *AEIdeas*, August 18, 2014, http://www.aei.org/
     publication/fortune-500-firms-in-1955-vs-2014-89-are-gone-and-
     were-all-better-off-because-of-that-dynamic-creative-destruction/

19 Isaac Sacolick, "Gartner Focuses on Algorithms as the Foundation to Digital Business," *Social, Agile, and Transformation*, October 11, 2015, http://blogs.starcio.com/2015/10/Gartner-Algorithms-Digital-Business.html

20 David Wagner, "CIOs Need to Welcome Age of the Algorithm, Gartner Says," *InformationWeek*, October 5, 2015, http://www.informationweek.com/strategic-cio/cios-need-to-welcome-age-of-the-algorithm-gartner-says/d/d-id/1322492

21 "Gartner Says It's Not Just About Big Data; It's What You Do with It: Welcome to the Algorithmic Economy," *Gartner Newsroom*, October 5, 2015, http://www.gartner.com/newsroom/id/3142917

22 "Gartner Says Digital Businesses Will Spot Opportunities in a Matter of Seconds," *Gartner Newsroom*, April 10, 2014, http://www.gartner.com/newsroom/id/2705317

23 Nigel Fenwick, "The Future of Business Is Digital," *Forrester Nigel Fenwick's Blog*, March 20, 2014, http://blogs.forrester.com/nigel_fenwick/14-03-20-the_future_of_business_is_digital

24 Karel Dörner and David Edelman, "What 'Digital' Really Means," *McKinsey Insights*, July 2015, http://www.mckinsey.com/industries/high-tech/our-insights/what-digital-really-means

25 Gil Press, "5 Things to Do When You Lead a Digital Transformation," *Forbes Tech*, March 9, 2015, http://www.forbes.com/sites/gilpress/2015/03/09/5-things-to-do-when-you-lead-a-digital-transformation/

CHAPTER TWO

1 Don Wetherby, "Retail Construction Goes Agile," *Construction Today*, February 16, 2016, http://www.construction-today.com/sections/columns/2579-retail-construction-goes-agile

2 "Manifesto for Agile Software Development," http://agilemanifesto.org/

3 Isaac Sacolick, "10 Best Practices in Configuring Your Agile Project Management Tools," *Social, Agile, and Transformation*, March 15, 2016, http://blogs.starcio.com/2016/03/best-practices-configuring-agile-project-management-tools.html

4 Design by Amir Khan, Clipart by Web Icon/Shutterstock.com.

CHAPTER THREE

1 "Subreddit", https://www.reddit.com/wiki/faq#wiki_what_are_subreddits.3F.

2 Scott Brinker, "Marketing Technology Landscape Supergraphic (2016)," *ChiefMarTec.com*, March 21, 2016, http://chiefmartec.com/2016/03/marketing-technology-landscape-supergraphic-2016/

3   Matt Turck, "Big Data Landscape 2016 v18 FINAL," *Matt Turck*, March
     28, 2016, http://mattturck.com/big-data-landscape-2016-v18-final/
4   Ibid.
5   Checklist Configuration Item (CI) Record, IT Process Maps, http://
     wiki.en.it-processmaps.com/index.php/Checklist_Configuration_
     Item_(CI)_Record
6   Design by Amir Khan, Clipart by Bloomicon/Shutterstock.com,
     nexusby/Shutterstock.com, Macrovector/Shutterstock.com.

CHAPTER FOUR

1   Charles Arthur, "What is the 1% rule?", The Guardian, July 20, 2006,
     https://www.theguardian.com/technology/2006/jul/20/
     guardianweeklytechnologysection2.
2   Design by Amir Khan, Clipart by nexusby/Shutterstock.com, Line–
     design/Shutterstock.com, Alexandr III/Shutterstock, chuckchee/
     Shutterstock.com.

CHAPTER FIVE

1   Isaac Sacolick, "Dear Spreadsheet Jockey, Welcome to Big Data," *Social,
     Agile, and Transformation*, March 30, 2012, http://blogs.starcio.com/
     2012/03/dear-spreadsheet-jockey-welcome-to-big.html
2   "EuSpRIG Horror Stories," *EuSpRIG European Spreadsheet Risk Interest
     Group*, http://www.eusprig.org/horror-stories.htm
3   Thomas Wailgum, "Eight of the Worst Spreadsheet Blunders," *CIO*,
     August 17, 2007, http://www.cio.com/article/2438188/enterprise-
     software/eight-of-the-worst-spreadsheet-blunders.html
4   Linette Lopez, "How the London Whale Debacle Is Partly the Result
     of an Error Using Excel," *Business Insider*, February 12, 2013, http://
     www.businessinsider.com/excel-partly-to-blame-for-trading-loss-2013-2
5   Peter Coy, "FAQ: Reinhart, Rogoff, and the Excel Error That Changed
     History," *Bloomberg Businessweek*, April 18, 2013, http://www
     .bloomberg.com/news/articles/2013-04-18/faq-reinhart-rogoff-and-the-
     excel-error-that-changed-history
6   Heather Havenstein, "Excel Error Leaves Barclays with More Lehman
     Assets Than It Bargained for," *Computerworld*, October 14, 2008, http://
     www.computerworld.com/article/2533631/desktop-apps/excel-error-
     leaves-barclays-with-more-lehman-assets-than-it-bargained-for.html
7   Christopher Ingraham, "An Alarming Number of Scientific Papers
     Contain Excel Errors," *The Washington Post*, August 26, 2016, https://
     www.washingtonpost.com/news/wonk/wp/2016/08/26/an-alarming-
     number-of-scientific-papers-contain-excel-errors/

8   Felienne Hermans, "A Modern day Pompeii: Spreadsheets at Enron,"
    Félienne, October 29, 2014, http://www.felienne.com/archives/3634

9   Felienne Hermans and Emerson Murphy-Hill, "Enron's Spreadsheets
    and Related Emails: A Dataset and Analysis," *FigShare*, January 19,
    2015, https://figshare.com/articles/Enron_s_Spreadsheets_and_
    Related_Emails_A_Dataset_and_Analysis/1222882

10 Rebecca Burn-Callander, "Stupid Errors in Spreadsheets Could Lead to
    Britain's Next Corporate Disaster," *The Telegraph*, April 7, 2015, http://
    www.telegraph.co.uk/finance/newsbysector/banksandfinance/11518242/
    Stupid-errors-in-spreadsheets-could-lead-to-Britains-next-corporate-
    disaster.html

11 Larry Alton, "Spreadsheets Are Destroying Your Business. Here's How,"
    Inc., April 21, 2016, http://www.inc.com/larry-alton/spreadsheets-are-
    destroying-your-business-heres-how.html

12 Katrina Bishop, "Spreadsheet Blunders Costing Business Billions,"
    CNBC, July 30, 2013, http://www.cnbc.com/id/100923538

13 Isaac Sacolick, "Please, Stop Creating Microsoft Access Databases!,"
    Social, Agile, and Transformation, April 1, 2013, http://blogs.starcio.com/
    2013/04/please-stop-creating-microsoft-access.html

14 Thomas H. Davenport and D. J. Patil, "Data Scientist: The Sexiest Job
    of the 21st Century," *Harvard Business Review*, October 2012, https://
    hbr.org/2012/10/data-scientist-the-sexiest-job-of-the-21st-century

15 Steve Lohr, "For Big-Data Scientists, 'Janitor Work' Is Key Hurdle to
    Insights," *The New York Times*, August 17, 2014, http://www.nytimes
    .com/2014/08/18/technology/for-big-data-scientists-hurdle-to-insights-
    is-janitor-work.html

16 Lukas Biewald, "The Data Science Ecosystem", Crowdflower Blog ,
    May 1, 2015, https://www.crowdflower.com/
    the-data-science-ecosystem/.

17 Arthur Lapinsch, "Bedrock Data Scoop $3.1m Series A for Data
    Integration Platform That Cuts Out the Coding," *Dataconomy*, http://
    dataconomy.com/bedrock-data-scoop-3-1m-series-a-for-data-
    integration-platform-that-cuts-out-the-coding/

18 Byron Connolly, "Overcoming the Cloud Integration Challenge," *CIO*,
    April 10, 2015, http://www.cio.com.au/article/572365/overcoming-cloud-
    integration-challenge/

19 Frank Burkitt, "Six Ways to Define Your Internet of Things Strategy,"
    Forbes, December 5, 2014, http://www.forbes.com/sites/strategyand/
    2014/12/05/six-ways-to-define-your-internet-of-things-strategy/

20 Isaac Sacolick, "Dark Data—A Business Definition," *Social, Agile, and Transformation*, April 10, 2013, http://blogs.starcio.com/2013/04/dark-data-business-definition.html

21 Jeanne G. Harris, Nathan Shetterley, Allan E. Alter, and Krista Schnell, "The Team Solution to the Data Scientist Shortage," *Accenture*, 2013, https://www.accenture.com/us-en/_acnmedia/Accenture/Conversion-Assets/DotCom/Documents/Global/PDF/Dualpub_22/Accenture-Team-Solution-Data-Scientist-Shortage

22 James Manyika, Michael Chui, Brad Brown, Jacques Bughin, Richard Dobbs, Charles Roxburgh, and Angela Hung Byers, "Big Data: The Next Frontier for Innovation, Competition, and Productivity," McKinsey Global Institute, May 2011, http://www.mckinsey.com/business-functions/digital-mckinsey/our-insights/big-data-the-next-frontier-for-innovation

23 John Leonard, "Computing Big Data Review 2016," *Computing*, March 17, 2016, http://www.computing.co.uk/ctg/news/2451345/computing-big-data-review-2016

24 Ibid.

25 Matt Turck, "Big Data Landscape 2016 v18 FINAL," *Matt Turck*, March 28, 2016, http://mattturck.com/big-data-landscape-2016-v18-final/

26 Design by Amir Khan.

27 Design by Amir Khan.

28 Design by Amir Khan, Clipart by Kapralcev/Shutterstock.com, Who What When Where Why Wector/Shutterstock.com.

29 Design by Amir Khan.

30 Chris McShea, Dan Oakley, and Chris Mazzei, "The Reason So Many Analytics Efforts Fall Short," *Harvard Business Review*, August 29, 2016, https://hbr.org/2016/08/the-reason-so-many-analytics-efforts-fall-short

31 Chris McShea, Dan Oakley, and Chris Mazzei, "How CEOs Can Keep Their Analytics Programs from Being a Waste of Time," *Harvard Business Review*, July 21, 2016, https://hbr.org/2016/07/how-ceos-can-keep-their-analytics-programs-from-being-a-waste-of-time

CHAPTER SEVEN

1   Matt Novak, "Fun Places on the Internet (in 1995)", Smithsonian.com, Dec 14, 2012, http://www.smithsonianmag.com/history/fun-places-on-the-internet-in-1995-161757121/.

2   Carl Sullivan, "AdOne Gets Six New Owners," *Editor & Publisher*, July 17, 1999, http://www.editorandpublisher.com/news/adone-gets-six-new-owners/

3   "The history of eBay", April 15, 2011, http://www.telegraph.co.uk/
    finance/personalfinance/8451898/The-history-of-eBay.html.

4   "TMP Worldwide Inc.—Company Profile, Information, Business
    Description, History, Background Information on TMP Worldwide
    Inc.," *Reference for Business*, http://www.referenceforbusiness.com/
    history2/66/TMP-Worldwide-Inc.html

5   "Craigslist.com," *Internet Archive WayBackMachine*, http://web.archive
    .org/web/20001204124400/http:/craigslist.com/

6   Henry Blodget, "Newspapers Are Losing $13 of Print Revenue for
    Every $1 Of Digital Revenue," *Business Insider*, December 3, 2012,
    http://www.businessinsider.com/newspapers-are-losing-13-of-print-
    revenue-for-every-1-of-digital-revenue-2012-12

7   Design by Amir Khan.

INDEX

actionable insights, 170
AdOne, 257
agile architecture, 88–114
    Big Data platforms in, 102–110
    necessary platforms in, 95–102
    and platform selection challenges,
      89–91
    platforms for, 91–94
    reference architecture in, 110–114
    terminology and capabilities in,
      94–95
agile data organizations, 199–205
agile development (stage), 61–63
agile estimation, 39–45, 248–249
agile operations, 73–88
    development team in, 75–77
    and DevOps practices, 78–85
    operations team in, 77–78
    transformation to, 85–88
agile planning practices, 33–50
    and agile execution, 36–37
    and architecture, 48–50
    at *Businessweek*, 47–48
    and estimation, 35–36, 39–45
    evolution of, 33–39
    implementation of, 45–47
agile portfolio management,
    123–154
    capabilities of, 142–146
    for financial planning, 147–154
    implementing, 131–146
    importance of, 123–131
    platforms for, 101

scaling up, 154
    at startups, 132–134
agile practices, 17–70, 254
    classic approach vs., 18–20
    in digital transformation, 20–21
    improvements from, 69–70
    instituting, 256
    management and collaboration
      tools for, 29–32
    over release lifecycle, 60–69
    of product owners, 236–239
    roles and responsibilities in, 21–29
    and SoDL practices, 50–60
agile teams, 21–32
    data, 200–204
    distributed, 26–28
    large, 25–26
    management/collaboration tools
      for, 30–32
    multiple, 28–29
    product owner's work with,
      241–242
    single, 22–25
    stakeholders and, 36–37
Airbnb, 7, 8, 11, 12
Amazon, 12, 93
analytics planning process, 178–181,
    202
Angie's List, 12
antagonizing behaviors, 260
APIs, 99, 164–165
Apple, 7, 93, 126, 173
application development, 96–97
approvals, 234–235

architectural review session, 46–47
architecture
    agile, *see* agile architecture
    and agile planning practices, 48–50
    messiness of, 160–161
    nimbleness of, 167–168
artificial intelligence, 8, 10, 99–100
auditing, by platforms, 98
automation, 54, 100, 162
Autotrader, 12

backlog, 46, 235, 236
beacons, IOT, 7
beta testing, 141
Big Data organizations
    analytics planning process for,
        178–181
    citizen scientists at, 184–186,
        188–189
    democratization of analytics at,
        181–182
    developing, 174–176
    mindset at, 184–186
    operational reviews at, 176–178
    roles and responsibilities at, 182–184
    self-service BI technologies at,
        186–188
    technical services for, 188–189
Big Data technologies
    and agile platforms, 92
    definition of, 155–156, 165
    digital platforms for, 102–110
    history of, 103–106
    selecting, 106–110
blame, 118
blockchain services, 100
BMW, 173
Board, 255
bottom-up approach, *xvii–xviii*, 172
Box, 190
branding, 245
browser support, 95
budgets, 147, 148, 151–152, 237–238
bundling, product, 245
business analysts (BAs), 23, 26–27,
    32, 62, 64
business intelligence (BI)
        technologies, 152, 181–182,
        186–188

business leaders
    in agile planning, 34–35, 38
    in analytics planning process,
        180–181
    data integration for, 163
    data quality issues for, 198
    operational reviews by, 176–178
    platform selection by, 89
    portfolio management support
        from, 128
    presenting DevOps to, 87–88
    technology leaders and, *xv–xvi*
    as tight competitors, 174
business model, 227
business platforms, 100–101
Business Process Management
        (BPM) tools, 140
business products and tools, 96, 118
business team, 35, 36, 130–131
Businessweek magazine, 3, 4, 35–36,
    47–48, 72

caching, 98
Cars.com, 12
centers of excellence, 197
CEOs, 124–126, 141, 255, 261
CFOs, 128–129
change, pace of, 256–257
change management, 82, 192–194,
    205, 209
change resistance, 116, 132, 258–261
charters, *xiv–xv*, 54, 179, 224, 225
Chase Bank, 173
Chef, 82, 84
CIOs, 85–88, 115–117, 128, 129
Citigroup, 173
citizen data scientists, 184–186,
    188–190, 204
citizen development, 102, 140
cloud environments, 83–84
coaches, agile, 35
code deployment tools, 81
code repositories, 51, 52
collaboration
    in agile operations, 75
    for data services, 190–192
    with IT team, 120, 171, 200–203
    on product development, 236,
        242–243

on project management tools,
144–145
collaboration platforms, 102
collaboration tools, 29–32
commitment, 48, 232–234, 236–237
communication, 120, 240–241
competence, 88, 163
competitive advantage, *xiii*, 156, 224,
227
complexity, data, 107
compliance requirements, 193, 244,
247
Computing Big Data Review, 171
configuration management tools, 81
consensus building, 221–222
consistency, product, 229
consumers, collaboration with,
191–192
context-based convenience, 229
continuous delivery, 68–69
continuous integration, 68–69
control, version, 50–52, 97
cost(s), 37–38, 55–56, 86, 149
Craigslist, 11, 12, 257
credibility, 247
crowdsourcing, 102
culture
for agile planning, 36
and Big Data, 109, 156, 157
of data-driven organizations,
208–210
of DevOps, 78, 80, 86
of digital businesses, 252–261
IT, 114–121
leaders as drivers of, 120–121
customer-driven product strategies,
213–215
customer experience, 131, 228–229,
232
customer relationship management
(CRM) systems, 100, 169–170,
233, 246
customer service, 230–231

dark data, 6, 165–167
dashboards, financial, 152
data analytics
and avoiding data landfills,
160–162

and current data architecture,
167–168
dark data in, 165–167
data integration in, 162–165
democratization of, 181–182
legacy of, 157–168
spreadsheets and databases in,
158–160
database administrators (DBAs),
159–160, 162
databases
documentation for, 194–195
in history of Big Data, 104
monitoring performance of,
197–198
quality issues for, 167–168
selecting, 102–103, 106
siloed, 159–160
data collection, 134–137, 231
data-driven decision making, 121,
249
data-driven organizations, 155–210,
254
agile, 199–205
agile estimation for, 39
Big Data use at, 173–189
challenges with becoming,
168–173
cultures of, 209–210
data governance for, 206–209
and data legacy/culture, 157–168
data services by IT teams at,
189–199
and definition of Big Data,
155–156
practices of, 176–182
data flows, 194–195
data governance, 175, 206–209
data integration
for agile portfolio management,
138–139
definition of, 161
modifying, 162–165
monitoring performance of,
197–198
platforms for, 98–100
providing, 196–197
data integrity testing, 57
data landfills, 160–162

data management, 183–184,
   199–200
data management platforms, 98–100
data preparation technology, 99
data programs, 182–184
data quality, 93–94, 177, 198–199
data science, 102, 160–162, 168–173,
   200–203
data scientists
   citizen, 184–186, 188–189
   collaboration of IT and, 171,
      200–203
   documentation from, 195
   roles and responsibilities of,
      182–184
data services
   change management for, 192–194
   collaboration tools for, 190–192
   at data-driven organizations,
      189–199
   data integration in, 196–198
   data quality measurements in,
      198–199
   data warehouses in, 196–197
   documentation by, 194–195
   monitoring in, 197–198
   platforms for, 98–100
data stewards, 182–184, 187, 199, 204
data stream processing tools, 99
data visualization tools, 99
data warehouses, 167, 196–197
debt, technical, 58–60, 244
defined stage (product development),
   223, 224
delivery, 61–63, 68–69, 202–203
delivery and operational (DevOps)
   teams, 50
   in agile operations, 83–85
   continuous integration/delivery by,
      68–69
   evolution of practices for, 79–80
   implementation by, 81–83
   practices of, 78–85
   transformation to, 85–88
delivery leaders, 44
delivery managers, 29, 60, 62, 63
demos, product, 242
developer pools, 97
development personnel, 24, 93

development stage (product
   development), 223, 235–249
   agile practices in, 236–239
   approvals for, 234–235
   collaboration in, 191
   go-to market plans in, 245–247
   product management in, 247–249
   product owners in, 239–245
development teams
   in agile operations, 74–77
   DevOps practices for, 79–80, 82
   estimation by, 37, 38, 40
   in platform selection, 90–91
   and quality assurance testing,
      53–55
   tasks of operational vs., 71–73
   testing by, 55–56
diagnostic information, 92, 98
dictionaries, data, 195
digital business(es), 251–263
   attributes of, 12–13
   culture of, 252–261
   as data-driven organizations, 210
   definition of, 10–15
   digitized businesses vs., 7
   industry conditions favoring, 5–8
   mindset of, 261–263
   product strategies of, 216
   transformation to, 9–10
digital ecosystem, 94, 231, 244–245
digital innovations, 8–9
digital product extensions, 212–215
digital revenue products, 211–250
   development of, 235–249
   in digital transformation, 217–222
   enabling product management for,
      250
   product planning for, 223–235
   strategic planning for, 211–217
digital strategy, 14–15, 215–217,
   219–222
digital transformation, 1–15
   agile practices in, 20–21
   assessing readiness for, 1–3
   beginning, 5–10
   and data-driven organizations, 210
   definition of, 13–14
   and digital businesses, 10–15
   digital strategy in, 215–217

financial planning for, 150–154
need for, *xiii–xvi*
portfolio management for, 130–131
product strategy in, 215–222
succeeding with, *xvi–xviii*
timing of, 256–257
digitized businesses, 7
disaster recovery, 98
discounting, product, 245
discovery process, 201–202
distracting behaviors, 259–260
distributed teams, 26–28
distribution, 246
Docker, 82, 84
documentation, 194–195, 222
Dropbox, 190

early adopters, 255
eBay, 11, 257
e-commerce sites, 104–105
email sharing, 190–191
employees
    adoption of portfolio management tools by, 133–134
    on digitally-driven teams, 255
    portfolio management ideas of, 126–127, 144–145
    prioritizing future work by, 125–126
    product use and promotion by, 231
    tracking current work by, 123–125
    see also specific types and teams
encryption, 97
enterprise applications, 92
enterprise resource planning (ERP) systems, 100–101, 128–129, 147–149, 169–170
epic backlog review, 46
epics, estimation of, 42, 44
estimation
    agile, 39–45, 248–249
    and execution, 34–35
    in product development, 237
    with story points vs. hours, 37–39
ETL platforms, 99
Etsy, 12
evangelists, product, 243–244
execution, 34–37, 65

executives
    change-resistant behaviors of, 258–260
    consensus building with, 222
    and digitally-driven teams, 255
    portfolio management support from, 128, 141
    product development approval from, 234–235
    and product management, 250
    readiness of, 2
    underinvestment in quality assurance by, 55–58
expenditures, tracking, 148–149, 151–152
exporting, 98
extensibility, 91–92, 97, 188
extensions, product, 212–215
extract, transform, and load (ETL) procedures, 99, 161, 162

Facebook, 93, 132, 133, 171
failure, 120, 128–129
feasibility, product, 224
features, 42
feedback, 5, 61–63, 67–68, 180
Fenwick, Nigel, on digital businesses, 10–11
financial considerations, with products, 247
financial modeling, 153–154
financial planning, 147–154
financial platforms, 100–101
Fink, Larry, on impact of digital innovations, 8–9
Ford, 173
Fortune 500 companies, 9
founders, 224–228, 235
front office, platforms for, 95–98
functional testing, 53, 54, 57
funding, 179
FutureAdvisor, 7

Garmin, 12, 212
Gartner, 150
GE, 171
General Managers, 261
Gilt, 12
GM, 125–126, 173

Google, 7, 93, 100, 105, 126, 132, 159, 171, 173, 177, 190
go-to market plans, 227, 245–247
governance, 32, 132, 175, 206–209
growth, financial practices during, 148–150

Hadoop technology, 105
Hermans, Felienne, 158
Hilton, 8
HomeAdvisor, 12
HomeAway, 11
Honeywell, 126, 173
hours, estimates in, 37–39
HR systems, 101

IBM, 100, 171
ideation stage (product development), 223–225
incentive plans, 258
incomplete information, 41
inflection points, 134
information hoarding, 119
initiatives, 118, 135, 138
innovations, digital, 8–9
insights, actionable, 170
Internet of Things (IoT), 6–7, 12, 99
interoperability, 230
IT culture, 114–121
IT team(s), 71–121
    agile architecture for, 88–114
    at agile data organizations, 200–203
    in agile operations, 73–88
    collaborations with, 171, 200–203
    current conditions for, 2
    at data-driven organizations, 189–199
    in digital transformation, 15
    operational and development tasks for, 71–73
    portfolio management for, 130–131

JP Morgan, 171, 173

large agile teams, 25–26
lead generation, 234
lead qualification, 233

legal considerations, for products, 247
Lehman Brothers, 158
LendingTree.com, 7
LinkedIn, 12, 132, 133
load balancing, by platforms, 98
load testing, 54
logging information, 98
Lopez, Jorge, on digital businesses, 10
low-code platforms, 140, 151–152

machine learning services, 99–100
management tools, 29–32
managers, of digitally-driven teams, 255
MapReduce, 105
marketing, product, 218
marketing automation systems, 100
marketing plans, 245
marketing team, 35, 232–234
Marriott, 8, 126
master data management tools, 99
Maytag, 173
McGraw-Hill Companies, 72
McGraw-Hill Construction, 3, 4, 67
McGraw-Hill Information and Media, 3
Microsoft, 100, 103
Microsoft Access, 159
Microsoft Excel, 158–159
Microsoft Office, 177
Microsoft Office 365, 159, 190
Microsoft PowerPoint, 143, 192, 193
minimally viable product (MVP), 227, 228, 239
minimal viable implementation, 39–40
minimal viable practice (MVP), 51–52
mobile-specific product capabilities, 230
model-view-controller (MVC), 96
monitoring and feedback (stage), 61–63
monitoring systems, 82
Monster.com, 12, 257
multidevice support, 95
MySQL, 103

Netflix, 215
newspaper industry, 257
New York Times, 215
Nexus of Forces, 9–10
nondisruptive digital products,
    215–216

operational platforms, 101–102
operational tasks, reviews of, 176–178
operational teams (operations)
    in agile operations, 74, 77–78
    in agile planning, 35
    DevOps practices for, 79–81,
        83–85
    digital platforms for, 97–98
    portfolio management ideas of,
        127
    story points vs. hours for, 39
    tasks of development vs., 71–73
Oracle, 103
outsourcing, 26–27

partnerships, 220, 240, 244–246
passive-aggressive behaviors, 259
payment options, 230
performance testing, 54, 57
personalization, product, 228–229
personas, 226, 228, 249
Philips, 173
pilot teams, 33–34
pipeline management, 224–225, 246
planning stage (product
        development), 223–235
    approvals in, 234–235
    and development, 235–236
    for digital products, 228–232
    founders in, 225–228
    and pipeline management,
        224–225
    sales and marketing in, 232–234
platform as service (PaaS) platforms,
    164
platforms
    agile, 91–94
    Big Data, 102–110
    capabilities of, 94–95
    for digital products, 231–232
    necessary, 95–102
    selecting, 89–91

portability, data, 93–94
portfolio management, 128–131, 254,
        see also agile portfolio
        management
portfolio tools, 138–140
PostgreSQL, 103
Presidents, company, 261
pricing, 230, 245
prioritization
    at agile data organizations,
        204–205
    in agile development, 237, 240
    in IT culture, 119
    of new epics, 46
    for operational teams, 75–77, 84
    in portfolio management, 125–127
    and release lifecycle, 67–68
    of technical debt, 60
privacy, 229
product charters, 224, 225
product definition, 218–221
product development, *see*
        development stage (product
        development)
production releases, 68
product leadership teams, 216,
        221–223, 225, 227, 234, 235
product management, 214–215, 254
    digital leaders' enabling of, 250
    in digital transformation, 216–222
    disciplines in, 217–218
    establishing, 247–249
product marketing, 218
product owners
    agile development practices of,
        236–239
    agile estimation by, 39–40, 45
    agile planning by, 34–36
    on agile teams, 23
    management/collaboration tools
        for, 31
    over release lifecycle, 62–64,
        66–67
    product management by, 217,
        248–249
    project development by, 239–245
    and technical debt, 59, 60
product planning, *see* planning stage
        (product development)

product roadmaps, 49–50, 205, 234
product strategy, 217–223
profiling, 97
program managers, 29
project managers, 25, 129, 236
project portfolio management (PPM)
    tools, 131–132
Prosper.com, 7
prototypes, 141
Puppet, 82, 84

Qlik, 191
quality
    data, 177, 198–199
    product, 237–238, 244
quality assurance (QA), 52–58, 74–75
quality assurance (QA) lead, 24, 28

R3, 7
ramp-up time, 91
recurring revenue, 231
reference architecture, 110–114
reference models, 94–95
regression testing, 53
release delivery, 61–63
release lifecycle, 60–69
release planning, 61–63
releases, 68, 193, 205
reliability, 77–78
repackaging products, 245
reporting, 139, 177, 179
research partners, 109
resource management tools, 146
responsiveness, 119–120
reusable platforms, 88
revenue potential, product, 224
rigidity, of operations teams, 77
roadmaps, product, 49–50, 205, 234
Rogue IT, 89
rollout plans, 141–142

sales-driven product strategies,
    213–215
Salesforce, 93
sales opportunities, qualifying, 233
sales process, 246
sales team, 127, 232–234
Samsung, 7
scalability, 92, 154, 170, 231

scenario planning, 153–154
scenarios, 42, 49
scope, product, 237–239
scoring, 201, 227
scrum, 22
scrum masters, 25
search, in project management tools,
    139
search engine technologies, 103–104
security
    data, 195, 207
    and DevOps practices, 84
    of digital products, 229
    of platforms, 92, 97–98
security testing, 53, 54, 57
self-documentation, 96–97
self-organizing teams, 21
self-service BI technologies, 181–182,
    186–189
self-service platforms, 92–93
serial starters, 220
server loads, 84
service desks, 196–197
service-oriented architectures, 99
service providers, 26–27, 32
sign-on interfaces, 97
silos, 127, 159–160
Social, Agile, and Transformation
    (blog), xviii
social networking sites, 6, 104–105,
    132–133, 231
social responsibility, 232
software as service (SaaS) platforms,
    92, 164
software development lifecycle
    (SoDL) practices, 50–60
solution review, 46
speed, of data changes, 107
spikes, story, 42–44
spreadsheets, 158–159, 190–191
stability, in agile operations, 77–78
stakeholders, 36–37, 46, 207–209,
    215
standards, 91, 143
Starbucks, 12
startups, 4, 6, 7, 108, 132–134, 174
Status Updates, 143–144
steering group, 145
stories, estimation of, 41–45

story points, 37–39
strategic customers, 215
strategic planning, 14–15, 131, 211–217
StubHub, 12
stubs, story, 41–44
support, from IT teams, 72–73, 76
support costs, 37–38
system administration, 97–98

Tableau, 191
target customers and markets, 220, 224, 226
TaskRabbit, 12
TD Bank, 173
team leaders, 46
team(s)
    at agile data organizations, 203–204
    data program development by, 182–184
    over release lifecycle, 62–64
    see also specific types
technical debt, 58–60, 244
technical leads (TLs)
    agile estimation by, 39–40, 42, 44
    on agile teams, 23–24
    on distributed teams, 26–27
    management/collaboration tools for, 31–32
    over release lifecycle, 62–64, 66
    in product development, 240
    and technical debt, 60
technical services, 188–189
technology, 2–3, 9–10, 254
technology leaders, *xv–xvi*
technology plans, 227
technology roadmaps, 112–113
Tesla, 173
testing, 82, 97, 193, 220
testing charter, 54
third-party platforms, 97
Tibco, 158

timeline, as product constraint, 237–238
time reporting systems, 124
top-down strategies, 126–127
training, in data analytics, 177
transformation, 148–150, *see also* digital transformation
transformational leaders, 120–121, 206, 208
troubleshooting, 92
trust building, 230, 247
Turck, Matt, 172
turnaround periods, financial practices in, 148–150
Twitter, 93, 132

Uber, 7, 8, 11, 12
unbundling products, 245
underinvestment, in quality assurance, 55–58
upgrades, 212, 213
user acceptance testing (UAT), 56–57
user experience, 91, 139, 226
user experience testing, 53, 54, 57
user personas, 226, 228

value proposition, 224
version control, 50–52, 97
vision, 13–14, 67–68, 224–226, 248
voting, 45, 227

Wall Street Journal, 215
Waze, 12
Wealthfront.com, 7
wearable devices, 7
web service platforms, 99
workforce, digital, 7–8

XML, searches in, 104
XQuery, 104

Yahoo, 105, 132

Zillow, 12